Royal
Horticultural
Society

Sharing the best in Gardening

*The*
# Garden
ANTHOLOGY

# The Garden
## ANTHOLOGY

Celebrating
the best garden
writing from the
Royal Horticultural
Society

Edited by
Ursula Buchan

Illustrated by
Jenny Bowers

F

FRANCES LINCOLN LIMITED
PUBLISHERS

Frances Lincoln Limited
74–77 White Lion Street
London N1 9PF
www.franceslincoln.com

Designed by Arianna Osti

978-0-7112-3485-7

Printed and bound in China

1 2 3 4 5 6 7 8 9

# CONTENTS

# FOREWORD

For many years, and from an office in Peterborough, the editorial team of *The Garden* – the magazine for the Royal Horticultural Society – has put together one of the leading international publications about plants, gardens and gardening. It is a tall order and one that I, and the team, relish.

The role of working on *The Garden* is divided into two. The first is the professional task of ensuring our vision for an article is realised 'on page' and that it meets the needs of the members (gardeners). Is it correct? Does it read well? How does it look? Reading the thousands of words each month can be challenging, but the demand for accurate and timely information never leaves our minds. The second, more personal view, is the joy that revelling in your passion can bring. For many of those who work, and have worked, on *The Garden*, gardening is a genuine interest. Many of us have been lucky enough to marry our hobby with our day job.

But of course it is a collective contribution that informs our work. Whether the latest findings in the wider horticultural world, or feedback from RHS members and committees, we are never short on topics. So too the ongoing – and ever-expanding – work of the Society. Colleagues across the charity help our work – from advisory services at RHS Garden Wisley to the shows team; from the curatorial staff to scientific findings; from the membership teams to our advertising and production colleagues.

As you may expect, it is for the 400,000-plus RHS members that all this is done. They represent a broad range of interests in gardening, horticulture and garden creation; a vocal, passionate group of people who tell us if they disagree, and praise us when we have done well. I am always grateful for this constant and attentive audience.

Ultimately, *The Garden* is a magazine to be enjoyed, learned from and sometimes, challenged by; but it should always help readers connect with their gardening interests. Created by a dedicated team, working with superb photographers, illustrators, and some of the world's leading writers, it is ultimately about sharing the enjoyable art of gardening with members. This splendid book, beautifully edited by Ursula Buchan, helps celebrate not only the written word – but the very breadth of that art.

CHRIS YOUNG, Editor, *The Garden* magazine

# INTRODUCTION

The Royal Horticultural Society was founded in 1804 (as the Horticultural Society of London) by a group of wealthy and horticulturally-inclined gentlemen, including John Wedgwood and Sir Joseph Banks. Its aims were '...to collect every information respecting the culture and treatment of all plants and trees', both culinary and ornamental, and one of its intentions was to disseminate this information to its members, known in those days as Fellows.

Initially, until 1830, this information was to be found in *The Transactions of the Horticultural Society of London*. Between 1846 and 1854 it was called *The Journal*, after which there was something of a hiatus, due to money troubles, until 1866, by which time the Society had received a new charter and become the Royal Horticultural Society. The volumes of *The Journal*, which began again at Volume 1 at this point, were then erratically published until the end of the century, the 25th being issued in 1901. In the 20th century, timings became regular, and indeed *The Journal* continued to be published during both world wars, although paper and ink restrictions reduced its size. It became monthly in 1934.

In 1975, *The Journal* underwent a drastic revamp: its name was changed to *The Garden*, colour pictures were integrated with the text, contributors began to be paid for their efforts, and the result was a more accessible, less scholarly but probably more suitable vehicle for a Society that was beginning to expand its membership beyond the core of well-heeled and knowledgeable Fellows based in the Southeast of England.

In 1979, a quarterly, *The Plantsman*, was founded, which was aimed at satisfying the most erudite members, leaving *The Garden* to appeal to the majority. Although there has always been editorial direction, the themes pursued in the publication are as much chosen by the members as by the Society. It is their preoccupations and interests, successes and failures that appear on many of the pages. As a house magazine, this is very right and proper.

In 1992, the format of *The Garden* was altered once more: the magazine increased in size, and the quality of paper and photographic images improved with it. Since then there have been some further changes to layout and content, prompted by the changing demographic of the membership, and also the fact that there are now RHS regional gardens

in Yorkshire, Devon and Essex, as well as Surrey. Whenever there has been a revamp, there have been disgruntled members; so much is inevitable. But the nature of a house magazine is that it has to please most of the people most of the time, and those people may not be the most vocal or influential.

Over the years, *The Garden* has played an important role in the history of horticulture. It was the first to unveil important scientific results relating to gardening – such as the Reverend Miles Joseph Berkeley's discovery of the pathogen, *Phytophthora infestans*, causing potato blight, and Gregor Mendel's experiments on genetics – as well as entering contentious debates on, for example, the use of peat in growing media, and climate change as it affects professional and amateur gardeners.

I became a member of the Royal Horticultural Society in 1975, the year I spent training as a gardener at Wisley, and have read, and profited in knowledge from the monthly copies of *The Garden* ever since. My first essay into journalism was an article in *The Garden* on the royal glasshouses at Laeken in Belgium in 1976, and I have continued to contribute to the magazine over the years, even writing a regular column, 'Garden Talk', from 2007 to 2010.

None of that, however, prepared me for the task of reading millions of words in order to put together this anthology. (The Greek origin of the word 'anthology' is, most appropriately, 'flower-gathering'.) It was a Herculean task and it would be wrong of me to say that I have read everything published since 1866. How could I? However, I have read a great deal and have learned much, which I hope will help me become a wiser, more thoughtful gardener. I am humbled by, and hugely admiring of, the accumulated knowledge to be found in those pages.

Almost all the luminaries who have made an impact in some way in the horticultural world – as garden designers, garden makers, entomologists, plant pathologists, meteorologists, plantsmen and women – have either been profiled in the journal or have written for it. Moreover, the best writers have also found a niche here, in particular E A Bowles, Anna Pavord, Roy Lancaster, Hugh Johnson and Ken Thompson, to name just a few. Hugh Johnson mainly appears in his guise as Tradescant or 'Trad', which he took on in 1975; in these highly personal monthly diaries, which appeared at the front of the magazine until 2008, he wrote about his garden at Saling in Essex as well as one in France. (Biographies of most of the selected authors appear at the end of the book – see page 311.)

The articles that I have chosen for the anthology are included for a number of diverse reasons: because they represent the first expression of an important change in horticultural attitudes, which had lasting repercussions; the first exposition of new research, or a new technique; aspects of horticulture that have enduring appeal and interest to gardeners; or examples of very good writing, regardless of the subject. Of course, I have usually consulted my own interests and inclinations, so this is naturally a very personal compilation.

Although there are extracts from articles that have appeared early in the journal's life, the balance is inevitably tipped towards those published in the last 30 years, that will (I hope) strike chords with a modern audience. Apart from anything else, I suspect that most modern readers are impatient of the leisurely progress of any scientific article written in the 19th century, however interesting the subject matter. Fashions come and go, but it is true to say that since 1975 'think pieces' have been more frequently published, under titles such as 'Viewpoint' or 'Garden Talk'. These 'think pieces' are well represented in this anthology, alongside striking news stories and interesting letters from readers.

The articles are arranged in chapters according to the subject matter: for example, 'Garden Design', 'People', 'Science and Innovation',

'The Environment', and so on, although many articles cover topics that bridge chapters. While putting them in categories is simply a device to make some sense of the enormous amount of suitable material, it is also a way of helping the reader who may have a particularly strong interest in one area. The articles mostly appear as they were originally printed, although some have been abridged where necessary.

*The Garden* is probably the only British special-interest magazine that concentrates so much space on individual plants and genera, and is punctilious about up-to-date naming (as you would expect from an organisation that also publishes the *RHS Plant Finder*). For this reason, if for no other, it is required reading for a wide spectrum of horticulturists – from plant scientists to first-time gardeners.

Another strong area of RHS interest is the international scene, testament to the fascination felt by British gardeners with plant hunting in the past as well as the close ties that now exist between gardeners across the world.

The magazine is published each month, come rain or shine, which inevitably means that certain subjects reappear from time to time, especially in the winter issues – snowdrops being a keen favourite because of their willingness to flower in the shorter days. It would be intriguing to know whether this fact is the reason why there are now so many galanthophiles in this country, or whether it is galanthophiles who are all too happy to write about their darlings. Certainly, the decline in interest in shrubs and trees since the 1980s, and the corresponding rise of flowering bulbs and perennials, is reflected in the magazine, but then so are the social changes – in particular, the shrinking size of most gardens – which underpin such a change of emphasis.

Today *The Garden* has photographs on every page. This book contains none, but is imaginatively and most attractively illustrated by Jenny Bowers. That difference alone has influenced my choice of article, for I have wished to include those (and there are many of them) that can stand without photographs. This is an instructive lesson, but not one that photographers will necessarily appreciate, particularly as they have developed their skills to such a high level of quality in recent years.

I very much hope that, like me, the reader will come away from this anthology with a strong consciousness of the extraordinary range and quality of the work achieved by the RHS, as well as professional and amateur gardeners in Britain, and with a deep sense of both the possibilities and the challenges which face us in the 21st century.

# SEASONS &
# THE WEATHER

*Note from the editor*

Two of the deepest preoccupations of thoughtful gardeners are the weather and the passage of the seasons. These two natural occurrences govern almost everything we do, yet we cannot control either of them.

Shrewd gardeners therefore find ways of mitigating the worst, and harnessing the best, of the weather. They also take account of the seasons as they unfold, not as dates to be ticked off a calendar.

Geoffrey Dutton's 'Marginal Garden' series in the 1990s introduced us to a poet, writer and retired scientist who gardened in the wilds of Perthshire, on ground that most people would not have considered could be gardened at all.

His perceptive, lively and reflective articles were always the first to which I turned.

As we can see from Matthew Pottage's most illuminating article on frost, successful gardeners need to understand what weather does to the garden; but so variable and unpredictable can be its progress that there is always the joy, or sorrow, of the unexpected, as I have found out in the past. As a trained gardener, cultivating a large garden, I have necessarily been attuned to the variability of the weather, season by season, and have often been moved to write about it.

And due to the change in climate in recent decades, which directly affects both weather and seasons, we are often now in uncharted territory. The RHS' concern with climate change is well known, so it is interesting to see reproduced here the first article on the subject published in *The Garden* – as long ago as 1992.

**URSULA BUCHAN**, editor

# Spring in the Scottish Highlands

GEOFFREY DUTTON, APRIL 1992

W e feel the first hint of spring here some day in early March: the delicious scent of warm dry grass in melting snow, or the tang of birch buds on a damp evening. The best birch (almost as aromatic as the balsam poplars a month later) is that Highland subspecies of *Betula pubescens* once called ssp. *odorata* and now sometimes ssp. *tortuosa*, both names appropriate for this low twisted canny kind of tree with its tight filigree of purplish twigs against the sky.

"Foliage is a major pleasure here, and the spring leafing of many trees rivals the kaleidoscopic understorey of wild flowers"

Spring generally arrives, well wrapped up, at the end of March, to stay until mid June. Then, in April sun, pine needles creak underfoot, pine bark is creamed with resin and cracked with heat, and pine-buds sharpen to gold as they swell, a sure sign of rising life. A south-facing slope among pines is a good place to welcome spring; or any turfy bank when the temperature touches 10°C (50°F) and everything moves into growth, when sap drips sparkling from winter-broken birches, bronze flies stud the warm boulders and small awakened beetles run up and down the straws of last year's grass. There are many good places to sit and I should have erected benches on them, out of our surplus logs; but I find the earthy medieval equivalent, scooped out of banks or built up from turves, excellent alongside our steep paths, easily made and maintenance-free. Cold? Damp? You simply carry a featherweight piece of plastic foam (as from a camper's bedroll); this transforms turf seats, boulders, tree-stumps or any inviting piece of ground into two square feet of warm dry luxury.

Our first 'spring' flower (before even *Leucojum vernum*) is *Pulmonaria rubra*, poking brick-red out of melting snow in a mild February, retreating, blue-nosed, as winter resumes. Later, in real spring, you can gaze across the Gorge to the north-facing blue gloom, where *P. rubra* is triumphantly re-emerging through the last, or almost last, snow – which may dog it for weeks yet.

The pool, spring-fed, never freezes solid and, when an April sun melts the surface, pondskaters venture out to warm themselves on exposed stones; then they scuttle across the ice to the first patch of water in search of equally enterprising flies. Frogs also queue up, and sometimes splash amorously among miniature ice-floes. I often mistake their burbling love song for the drumming of snipe, who conduct their courtship at a somewhat higher level about this time.

## Tender new shoots

Wind governs our spring festivities. A north wind brings night frost that nips fresh growth of baby oaks in exposed places throughout June (tree-shelters afford little protection), but under our hard-won tree-canopy we are free by the third week. When prized rhododendrons were small I covered them on clear nights with various materials, finding plastic curtain netting the least likely to exacerbate damage by freezing-on; the danger is not to blossom or shoots, which come again, but to flushing branches. Bark-split can kill whole boughs and small plants, and I used to tape the injuries to keep out desiccating winds; one veteran *Rhododendron wardii* (only the late-flushing Ludlow, Sherriff and Taylor strains survive here) still bears pieces of bandage in its many scars. Nowadays, both they and I are too old for that sort of thing and my only concessions are a golf umbrella above *R.* 'Elisabeth Hobbie' and a howdah of pine slash built about the lower trusses of a huge *R. rex* known as The Elephant.

Foliage is a major pleasure here, and the spring leafing of many trees rivals the kaleidoscopic understorey of wild flowers. Red oak (*Quercus rubra*) remains sulphur-yellow until mid July, remarkable against blue sky or above battalions of lupins; and aspen foliage ripples an unexpected suede-soft white, more eye-catching than any of the *Sorbus* blossoms nearby. This brilliance of deciduous leaf (especially from young fountaining birch) is wonderfully set off by the blue-black spires of common juniper, so lovingly described by Miss Jekyll.

Spring builds, of course, a paradise for birds. Let me finish by recalling a glimpse of a young woodcock family (miraculously preserved from our unselectively policing cats) scrambling away from me among blueberry stems, while the mother flapped with an uncharacteristically heavy beat across the Gorge, clearly (to my eyes) bearing beneath her a fluffy bundle from which dangled two tiny matchstick chick-legs.

# Air Frost in May

URSULA BUCHAN, AUGUST 2010

In the general run of things, I look forward to August. I stay at home specifically to enjoy – indeed, revel in – the sweet juiciness of sun-warmed greengages and the fecundity of plums and damsons, to be made into jams or frozen to provide puddings in winter. Not this year, however: a string of air frosts in May blighted the fertilised blossom before it could properly 'set'. Here and there I can see a fruit maturing nicely, where it was obviously protected by a sheltering leaf; but, between five trees (two greengage, two plum and one damson), I can count no more than a score of ripening fruits.

> "Much of the pleasure of caring for a garden is anticipation"

Much of the pleasure of caring for a garden is anticipation – this year's fruit, next month's flowering, maturity in the years to come – that, when it is dashed, that care can seem a dreary thing. My hopes have been blasted along with the fruit.

# A Change in the Weather

RICHARD HUTSON, NOVEMBER 1992

Samuel Johnson observed that when two Englishmen meet their first talk is of the weather. In a country where the weather is so changeable there has always been plenty of talk about, but only very recently have the British people begun to comment on the climate. This may be defined as the average weather conditions experienced in a given area over a long period of time and it varies little from one year to another.

What matters to gardeners are the extremes of weather. We have vivid memories of hard winters, long, hot summers and damagingly cold springs and the longer our memories grow the more we enjoy relating these experiences, but always we speak of extremes. Climatologists, however, deal with averages; they are masters of the generalisation. But who, other than such specialists, can find anything interesting to say about an average season? Climate is rarely a topic of conversation at our dinner tables.

That was true until recently when, suddenly, we became aware of global warming. Our planet, we discovered was sick and the prognosis alarming. We were poisoning our atmosphere and driving holes through the ozone layer to let through the unfiltered rays of the sun to threaten our health. As a result of pollution we were encouraging the temperature of the atmosphere to rise at a dangerous rate.

Climatologists have warned us that should the temperature continue to rise it will have disastrous effects upon vegetation, with serious consequences for agriculture and horticulture. Sea levels will rise and storms in the atmosphere will become more violent. The most recent studies suggest that these forecasts have not been exaggerated, although their development will be slower than was at first believed.

> "Sea levels will rise and storms in the atmosphere will become more violent"

## Taking the long view

Britain has undergone many changes of climate in geological time, most notably as a result of continental drift. This is a term used to describe the manner in which the land masses, floating like scum on the surface of the globe, were able to drift into higher or lower latitudes and so experience a range of climates.

Evidence for this can be found in the rocks which were formed under climatic conditions very different from those we know today. When we garden on the red soils of Devonshire for example, our spades are turning ancient desert sand, and when we cultivate a limestone soil in eastern England we are gardening among the residues of shells and corals where once a shallow sea shimmered under a tropical sun.

Such changes resulted from a shift in our geographical position relative to the sun and not from a change in the climate itself. For the most recent change in climate we need to go back through 10,000 years to the time when the last glaciation melted away to leave the remnants of that frozen world, still visible today, in the form of polar icecaps and high mountain glaciers.

During the last 500 years there have been no dramatic changes in the British climate but many fluctuations of hot or cold, wet or dry seasons. From 1500 through to 1700 cool, unsettled weather was characteristic but was followed in the 18th century by colder and drier conditions with warm summers and cold winters. In the winter of 1740, for example, Londoners were able to cross the frozen Thames on foot. The century ended with several very cold winters and much hardship. During the 19th century cold and wet conditions were frequent. The Thames froze again in 1874 and 1895, but owing to the construction of embankments the speed of flow was increased and a narrow channel remained open.

Well within living memory several very severe winters, notably in 1940, 1942 and 1947, led some observers to forecast an increasingly cold climate later this century, but in fact only the very hard weather of 1962 has since reminded us of a forecast which seems now to have been greatly mistaken. During the last 30 years [to 1992] there have been no hard winters comparable to the four weeks which bridged the years 1962 and 1963. Such was the intensity of the frost at that time that ice floes drifted along the coast of the Irish Sea and marine life suffered as dreadfully as the birds and mammals.

"Today's climate crisis is wholly due to man's neglect of the earth on which he lives"

Today's climate crisis is wholly due to man's neglect of the earth on which he lives. Like a child with a box of chocolates who has gobbled the lot he has exploited the earth's resources regardless of all other considerations and, not unlike the greedy child who is left with a torn and empty container, man is now repentant, faced with the implications of his thoughtless pillage. It has been estimated, for example, that by the year 2020 at the present rate of plunder all the hardwood forests will have been felled. The simple truth which gardeners have always understood, that trees turn carbon dioxide into health-giving oxygen, goes unheeded: the carbon dioxide continues to rise and the earth gets warmer.

The greenhouse effect, so called because carbon dioxide and other industrial emissions blanket the earth and raise its temperature, has increased over the last 100 years as fossil fuels have become more widely used. It has been aggravated by felling of forests, which would have been able, by transpiration from their leaves, to increase the water vapour in the atmosphere, i.e. more rain. So one man's forest clearing becomes another man's desert.

Drought in parts of Britain has not yet created desert conditions nor is it likely to do so but in London and the south-east of England, together with much of the south-west, the serious water shortage is causing anxiety. It is not possible to relate these dry conditions to global warming. However, a combination of low rainfall and dry summers, if they continue, will make it difficult to meet the unprecedented demands on the water supply.

Scientific methods of recording the changing climate in past years include the study of pollen, the advance and retreat of glaciers, variations in the tree line on mountainsides and evidence of changing types of vegetation as average temperatures rose or fell. To forecast future change in climate is a much more formidable problem.

So complicated are the structures of atmosphere and ocean, so complex are the interrelationships between the two and so great our ignorance that even if we had computers powerful enough to deal with the problem we should not know what information to feed them.

Climatologists have asked for another decade of observations before they will forecast global warming with complete confidence. To go further and explain how each particular place on the earth's surface will be affected by rising sea levels, storms of increasing severity or altered vegetation may never be possible. What we do know with certainty is that we are poisoning the planet and that it is imperative that we stop before it is too late. To be unable to prophesy the death from terminal illness is no excuse for delay in treating the patient.

Among the benefits which current concern about climate has encouraged is a growth of philosophical debate about the nature of the earth and its atmosphere. Some are asking if all the manifestations of nature are interdependent. Is Earth, like a well-managed garden, greater than the sum of its constituent parts? Does it have a life of its own, can it be killed or, given half a chance, could it heal itself?

If left in peace, no doubt the earth could restore its forests, purify its waters and cool its atmosphere. In short, it could change its climate. But are we mature enough to allow it to do so?

# Bridal Bouquet

URSULA BUCHAN, MARCH 2010

The moment has come, which fills me both with delight and apprehension: my daughter has announced that she is engaged and would like the reception after the wedding to be held in our garden. After the initial intense relief that the wedding was not to take place on a beach in Bali, there was the sudden sharp anxiety about whether 'the garden would be looking its best'. Thank goodness our daughter accepted the marriage proposal on Christmas Eve, so a summer wedding is in prospect, for no gardener wants their daughter to marry in December, however much fun the festive party afterwards might be for the guests.

Early July. I breathed a sigh of relief because, with luck, the roses would still be flowering madly and I still had time to order masses of summer bulbs, especially lilies, to cram into borders and plant in tall pots, perhaps even using them to act as a leitmotif in church, garden and marquee. What is more, lilies come in so many colours that even the most particular bride should be able to find cultivars to suit her colour scheme.

> "...a summer wedding is in prospect, for no gardener wants their daughter to marry in December"

At this point in my post-Christmas reverie, I was feeling pretty chipper, even smug. Then a thought hit me like a book thrown at the back of my head. Last Christmas, the night-time temperatures were regularly well below zero, sometimes as much as -9°C (16°F). After such a warm autumn, I had failed to remember to protect my *Myrtus communis* subsp. *tarentina* which grows in a south-facing wall border. Now it might well be too late. I had planted this myrtle years before, for the express purpose of providing sprigs to put in my daughter's bridal bouquet; now it was in danger of dying before the wedding took place.

I had read that the myrtle in Princess Anne's wedding bouquet in 1973 had been taken from a shrub struck from a cutting from Queen Victoria's posy in 1840, and such a pleasing tradition seemed just right for my girl. I don't yet know whether the myrtle has come through unscathed. It is now blanketed in horticultural fleece; I fervently hope that the fleece won't turn out to be its shroud. [It did not.]

# Summer in the Scottish Highlands

GEOFFREY DUTTON, JULY 1992

Summer I take as our longest frost-free period protected by tree-canopy. It stretches (sometimes with considerable effort) from mid June to late August. In summer, vegetation engulfs our breezy, bony prospects of rock, brae, branch and tree-bole. The small wind-sheltered 'rooms' of the design become stuffed with flowers and curtained by foliage; they hide away. Yet the overall structure of such a topographically diverse garden must remain evident: otherwise, in summer, rather than inviting surprise it merely bewilders with an apparently disorganised profusion. ('Where the devil are we now?')

To restore calm to the visitor, other reassurances, other clear verticals and horizontals, must replace the now-obscured tree trunks and distant perspectives. Our summer horizontals are, in fact, the welcome flat (or fairly flat) grassy areas; the vertical points of reference are cleanly-contrasting bushes in strategic places. Mowing and trimming, respectively, ensure they continue to provide this sense of order. Flowers and romantically-inclined shrubs can then fire away happily and set up their own echoes within the defined scheme.

> "...late summer relaxes into an upholstery of foliage"

For example, our summer roses (native and exotic species) romp freely above their herbaceous attendants, and so they should, for a clipped wild rose is a pinioned bird. But they brandish their flowers about a dark vertical framework of juniper, mountain pine, holly and beech bushes, and are separated into the positions of their dance by alleys of well-shaven turf, the horizontal component of the plan.

Mowing, as well as satisfying the eye, diverts flies. On certain sticky summer days they dance and sing in clouds about your head. Everywhere you bear this swirling chitinous halo. Nothing will dislodge it. You may decant some, skilfully, on your companion; but he will return them gladly, as you incautiously pause to admire the next *Philadelphus* x *lemoinei*. When you mow paths, however, flies immediately abandon your eyes and hair to drink the fresh green cuttings – and you leave them behind as you push on. Bliss. You do not, of course, return that way.

I only barber a very small proportion of trees and bushes, to let the others, especially tall trees, show off their wonderful variety of colour, shape and movement, unobstructed and without distraction. The result is peaceful and satisfying; late summer relaxes into an upholstery of foliage. However, two points should be remembered when a garden depends on high trees for structure. If the scale, as here, is intimate, the upper leaves must be small and lively. Otherwise you will suffocate. Those of birch, silvering in wind, rippling along every ridge, lit by a million points of light, are ideal. They are given basal solidity by a lower storey of large coarse hazel leaves. Again one or two species only should dominate in any area, to avoid fuss. Here, birch and hazel frame the others year-round, and in late summer preside above a myriad paths and glades where flowers are going out one by one. With their leaves slowly yellowing and conifers reappearing beyond, they prepare you for the grand parade of autumn. It will come soon. Already red squirrels are window-shopping impatiently along the nut alleys. They scold your aesthetics!

# Understanding Frost

MATTHEW POTTAGE, DECEMBER 2012

When the first frost of autumn dusts itself over our gardens, we have no choice but to accept winter is arriving. Frost is frozen water that forms when temperatures fall below 0°C (32°F). Clear skies and still conditions will turn moisture such as dew into ice crystals. A light frost can be as little as -1°C (30°F) whereas a severe frost can send temperatures plunging to -12°C (10°F) or lower.

> "The frost that sends many of us running for our cameras is hoar (or radiation) frost"

The first frosts are typically encountered from September to November, depending on locality and local geography. Coastal districts experience milder winter temperatures due to the warming effect of the sea. Inland areas often encounter earlier frosts and experience more severe winter weather. Many New Zealand plants such as *Olearia* or *Cordyline* are suited to British coastal climates, but tend to struggle in colder, inland areas. By contrast, the last frosts of winter can be as early as April in milder districts, or as late as June inland.

Frost manifests itself in several forms, all having similar effects on our garden plants. Air frosts are typical in autumn when the ground retains heat, but the air above ground level freezes. Foliage may be damaged but plants are not always killed outright. In contrast, ground frosts occur when the ground level freezes. Frosts are common during periods of high pressure when skies are clear with sunny days but cold nights.

The frost that sends many of us running for our cameras is hoar (or radiation) frost, with its white, often needle-shaped crystals typically formed when the air is humid. While this may look to have damaging weight implications, it is usually short lived and recedes in the morning sun.

Plants are damaged by frost as the water inside the plant cells freezes, rupturing cell walls. Some hardy plants react to cold weather by lowering

the freezing point of their cell contents, whereas others, such as birches, simply drain much of the moisture from their cells during winter months, rehydrating in spring.

Try not to cause hardy plants any physical stress when frosted. Walking on frozen grass is a fine example of this; defrosted lawns show blackened footprints, which is the result of damaged cells.

Autumn is an essential time for plants to shut down, allowing wood to ripen after growth ceases in late summer. A sudden severe frost can damage poorly ripened wood (which can still be soft and sappy) even on hardy plants, often resulting in stem dieback. A warm autumn may produce a late flush of growth on plants such as *Eucalyptus*, which is more prone to damage if followed by a sudden cold snap, as experienced in 2010. In cool coastal, areas, there may be insufficient summer heat for wood to fully ripen, and repetitive dieback can occur each winter, making plants such as *Magnolia grandiflora* difficult to grow. Planting against a warm south wall will help to remedy this.

Plants starting to wake up for the season ahead can be affected by late spring frosts, typically to breaking buds, young leaves and flowers. Magnolia flowers are readily spoiled by frost, turning brown and limp – though petals emerging from frosted buds are usually unaffected. A severe spring frost can kill some plants outright: *Prunus mume* is a prime example, though damage to emerging hydrangea shoots, apple blossom or vegetable seedlings is more often seen.

Vulnerable material should be covered with a double layer of horticultural fleece where possible. Hardy plants might display a delay in leaf production, an abortion of fruit or stem-tip dieback. Young foliage can show yellowing, virus-like mottling or blackened margins as a result of early cold damage, though hardy plants will grow through this healthily as temperatures improve.

The coldest period of the day is often just after dawn; frozen plant material can be damaged by rapid warming as the sun rises, not allowing the plants to adapt to the changing conditions. Use fleece to protect the flowers of shrubs such as *Camellia* from early morning sun, or site plants in the shelter of other trees and shrubs, or against a wall that faces in any direction other than east.

Prolonged periods of frost prove more damaging than short spells of subzero conditions, and given most plants are in an inactive state due to the low light levels and temperatures, they are ill equipped to recover from this stress. The survival of a plant in a half-dead state by late January/early February can often depend on the early onset of spring bringing much needed warmth. A plant which has not shown signs of recovery or produced leaves by midsummer should be presumed dead.

# MONITORING TEMPERATURES TO PREDICT FROST

BY IAN CURRIE, DEC 2012

Air temperatures are measured at the standard height of 1.25m (4ft). A thermometer placed over short mown grass will often show lower temperatures than at the standard height on a clear, calm night. Hence if the weather forecast predicts a minimum air temperature of, say, 3°C (37°F) this could well be down to -1°C (30°F) at plant level close to or on the soil surface: so called 'ground' or 'grass frost'. On a breezy or cloudy night there is much less of a difference.

The nature of the soil is another factor influencing the frequency and severity of a frost, with sandy soils losing heat to the air more rapidly and hence reaching colder surface temperatures than a clay soil. All soils will lose less heat if they are moist and so reduce the severity of the frost.

In cool, stable air with the air pressure rising and the likelihood of a clear, still night to follow, you can predict whether a frost is possible. Mount an outside thermometer in the shade, preferably facing north-east, and set at 1.25m (4ft) above the ground. Note the temperature around 2pm and again around 7pm. Double the temperature at 7pm then subtract the 2pm reading. For example, if you measured 14°C (57°F) at 2pm and 8°C (46°F) in the evening, twice the later value is 16 (92) so the predicted dawn reading would be 16–14 (92–57) = 2°C (35°F) and a ground frost may be quite likely.

Expressed as an equation:

**Predicted dawn temperature =** $2y-x$

Where x is temperature at 2pm, and y is temperature at 7pm.

These values are for the air temperature, and you will need to take off several degrees to forecast the minimum ground temperature.

# Groping Towards the Light

URSULA BUCHAN, JANUARY 2010

It goes without saying that everyone who reads this article will be a gardener and, very likely, a keen one at that. But, if you do not garden for a living, you probably don't get a chance to enjoy fully one of life's minor pleasures, namely, the gradual lifting of the gloom in January. When I was a full-time gardener, I knew that, at the turn of the year, I would be able to finish work in the light, instead of having to clean and put away tools in a dreary murk. 12th January was the tipping point, when the days perceptibly lengthened and my spirits lifted. Whatever the weather gods threw at me after that, at least I knew I would endure it in daylight.

> "…the pleasure to be had in a fully unfurled Algerian iris flower is surprisingly intense"

There are other, as persuasive, reasons for being outside in the garden in January. It is very far from being a dead place, and the pleasure to be had in a fully unfurled Algerian iris flower is surprisingly intense. What is more, since most of us lead such hermetically-sealed, sedentary lives (unless we choose to climb Ben Nevis in the winter, of course) we too easily lose our sense of awe at really bad weather. If that seems bizarrely masochistic, I don't mean it to be; but I cannot deny that my pleasure in a warm, balmy April day is measurably heightened by having had my hands frozen picking curly kale or pruning apple trees in January. In the words of the hymn: 'Not for ever in green pastures, do we ask our way to be' – or not if we *really* want to appreciate being in the garden in spring.

# Autumn in the Scottish Highlands

GEOFFREY DUTTON, OCTOBER 1992

Summer packed its blossom and foliage so tightly into two and a half busy months, that September (the beginning of our autumn) introduced a leisurely note, with the fuss largely over and leaves beginning to thin and make space. Even the days shortened and ripened.

Now they carry a chill, refreshing edge. Their light blue skies are travelled by pale cirrus and washed with showers of cold rain. To the north, beyond our 30 years of shelter, the clouds pile up black and purple; from early October, hills are dusted white against them.

> "...our own incendiary hues burn against grey boulders and the smouldering tones of surrounding hillsides"

Autumn can be our brightest season. From deep in the Gorge up to morning-frosted slopes of turf and heather, everything – stem, leaf, berry and bud – wakes to a carnival of colour. You realise then the insufficiency of green. And flowers become superfluous, not just to a restful garden, but to a brilliant one.

Flowers, anyway, are relics now. September buds of roses like 'Nevada' or 'Schneezwerg' flinch to brown as they open. Beneath them – well, willow gentian may peer hopefully through yellow tatters of Solomon's seal and astilbes cling to dignity, but the herbaceous community is generally sad enough now, like a last chapter in Proust. Trees and shrubs resume command.

Although we lack the wonderful autumnal variety of Wakehurst or Westonbirt, our own incendiary hues burn against grey boulders and the smouldering tones of surrounding hillsides. They share a single harmony, from acid-yellow moss through russet bracken to the high crimson of red oaks; everyone joins in this feast of leaf and berry.

Late autumn, before the snow-load, calls for those marginal forestry tasks needed on a few exposed acres like these, especially felling and planting. We fell on days too cold or dry for planting. To preserve scale and shelter, trees grown too tall *must* be removed: understorey is then not shaded out and their successors have room to rise. Failure to fell selected dominant trees (from lack of foresight – or more commonly, courage!) condemns you to draughty corridors and to eventual clear-felling in desperation or through the inevitable storm. A range of heights – deciduous and evergreen – must be maintained, and in the right places.

We have four tree understoreys beneath the dominant trees: suppressed, aspirant, small shade-bearing, young transplanted. Suppressed trees will probably never recover even if local dominants are felled; still useful shelter while remaining unbroken, they must eventually make way for the elite aspirants. Small deciduous shade-bearers such as *Amelanchier lamarckii*, bird cherry or *Acer pensylvanicum* are cherished, but room is made among them for young transplants, aspirants in their turn. Not easy. Like maintaining a herbaceous border on a longer and less forgiving time-scale. But rewarding.

Following our usual spring and summer drought late autumn is often wet, and the burn rises fasts. Heard from the house, its rumble breaks to a bellow when you open the door. Beside it, you feel the thud and grind of boulders trundling down and smell the tang of racing water. No rock, pool or cascade is visible, just a great white rope writhing down the Gorge. At the garden bridge it is 10.6m (35ft) across, pier to pier, its walloping fringe snuffling among *Luzula* or meadowsweet, blowing Guinness froth about your feet. When really high the water makes less noise – a swift, alarming *shoosh* – so much is then above boulders and bankside rocks. In fact, it is convex – higher in the middle. No wonder drowned-out dippers complain bitterly along the edges.

After such a spate the scenery of the burn is quite altered. This kind of aquatic marginal gardening is irresistibly dynamic. I used to climb its course then and note the changes, some predictable – a fragile waterfall abolished, others surprising – cliffs dissolved overnight into rapids. The lip of the big waterfall, 12m (40ft) high, has retired upstream some 3m (10ft) in 33 years, and an 18m (60ft) tower beside it is wearing back at the same rate: summit hazels straddle with bare roots and a Sitka sprucelet I pushed into its flat blueberry top all those years ago is now a tall tree whose time has come, only a foot from the plunging slab.

In quieter periods, autumn leaves pile up among stones in the burn and I collect them in a bucket for mulch. One day the bucket rattles with ice. Cold air from the hill brushes past, stirring the grass beside you; the grass has not rustled on a calm evening since early June. Leaves are all down, and the pool surface is starred with pondskaters feeding on drowned bees.

Signs like these ensure last-minute husbandry: bracken is strewn over nurseries and packed about sensitive limbs; crutches are stuffed under invalid junipers, snow-shovels and snow-poles lined up. Thick socks, jerseys and scarves are looked out. We all get ready to welcome winter again.

# GARDENS

*Note from the editor*

The descriptions of thousands of gardens have
found their way into *The Garden*. This is inevitable,
considering that Britain has such a rich and
established variety of gardens, some 5,000 of
which open at some point in the year to paying
visitors. Most keen gardeners think of the making
of gardens as an act of difficult and exacting
creativity and are mystified when the outside
world can often be so sniffy about that creativity.
In this chapter, Lucinda Lambton, an art historian,
argues for garden making being one of, if not
*the*, highest art form.

The urge to create gardens is hard to quell,
even in very difficult circumstances, and the RHS
encouraged the making of them in internment
and prisoner-of-war camps in both world wars
by sending seeds, books and even, during the
Second World War, RHS examination papers.
Brent Elliott describes the remarkable horticultural
activities that took place in Ruhleben internment
camp in Germany in the First World War.

Mostly, however, *The Garden* has chronicled the high points of the development of gardens, made rather more easily, but all the same underlining Stephen Lacey's view (see page 284) that Britain is still – for the moment – viewed as the leading nation of garden makers. Certainly anyone like me, who writes about gardens and gardening, has a powerful sense of the enormous variety of gardens made in the United Kingdom.

However, too many descriptions of gardens in magazines follow the 'turn left at the fishpond' style and, although a straight description is plainly necessary, the best writers add something more by conjuring up in words what it is like to be in the garden – its atmosphere – as well as telling the story of its creation, and the people who have made it. That is why I have chosen, for example, Ambra Edwards writing about Moor Wood, Hugh Johnson on Hergest Croft, Jean Vernon on Osborne House, Roy Lancaster on Highdown and Chris Young on Plaz Metaxu. All these gardens are different, as exemplified by the fact that the creators of both Plaz Metaxu and Orpheus at Boughton have been inspired by the ancient Greeks, but there the similarity ends.

**URSULA BUCHAN**, editor

# Are Gardens Art?

LUCINDA LAMBTON, MAY 1996

Where do gardeners and gardens stand in relation to the so-called high arts – music, painting, sculpture, architecture and poetry? Rather than trying to tackle the question directly, let me borrow the very first paragraph of the great art historian Ernest Gombrich's slim classic *The Story of Art*: 'There is really no such thing as art', he begins. 'There are only artists.'

> "Gardens are always in flux; continually travelling, hopefully, to perfection"

With that assurance from such an authoritative source, I will plunge into the issue on a different route. Why on earth, I wonder, are not the great gardeners and the great gardens more often recognised as great artists and works of art? Here I think, the answer is sweetly simple. It is because gardens are always changing, not only when the gardener wants them to but of their own obstinate accord.

Gardens, in short, have minds of their own: or rather natures of their own. I can think of no other works of art of which this is true. A great painting does not have a life or will of its own. True, its colours may fade, but over centuries and not, like flowers, overnight. Musical masterpieces, once completed, are not forever sprouting new symphonies, or great cathedrals new spires, or great sculptures new arms and legs all without so much as a by your leave to their respective creators. If they were, the critics would have a terrible time, forever revising their judgements.

As it is, the great works of art are static. The Tintoretto painting, which Ruskin saw in the 19th century is essentially the same work of art which Lord Clark of *Civilisation* saw in the 20th century. The beauty of a garden, however, is so much more ephemeral and transient; here today and possibly gone tomorrow, or, if not gone, subtly altered, its perfection ruined perhaps by frost, lack of rain or, just as likely, enhanced by wondrous weather.

In a great garden more than in any other great work of art, nature plays a crucial role. Some would credit the Almighty. No wonder the art critics and boffins galore give even the greatest gardens a wide berth. Difficult as it is often to be dogmatic about who wrote a particular play (Shakespeare or Bacon) or painted a particular picture (master or pupil), these difficulties are compounded when it comes to gardens where the hidden hand could well be that of the Creator!

So it would seem to be that the reasons why gardens rank lower in the hierarchy of the arts than the so-called high Arts are not so much aesthetics as practical. A garden, unlike most other works of art, cannot be placed in a museum or library. A gardener can never lay down his spade and trowel and say his work of art is finished.

Gardens are always in flux; continually travelling, hopefully, to perfection rather than arriving. It is not surprising, therefore, that the scholars and arbiters of taste prefer to write their treatises about paintings, sculpture et cetera – the arts which they can dragoon into some kind of order. Their pontifications, though, should not be the final word. A more important question has to be asked. Which of the arts affects the souls of mankind most deeply, can be relied upon best to soothe the troubled brow, send the sunken spirits soaring and soften a jaggedly broken heart? Here surely gardeners can proudly proclaim that they triumph in equal measure with the highest art forms.

'Come into the garden, Maud', wrote Tennyson; not 'the room where I write my poems, Maud'. From Shakespeare to Kipling, all the great poets have celebrated gardens as the nearest thing on earth to heaven itself. Where did Adam and Eve dwell before the Fall but in the Garden of Eden?

Another purpose of art, of course, is to improve us morally, and here I would claim that gardens actually have the edge over all the other arts, as you see when visiting most garden centres throughout the country. Suddenly the world is a more pleasant place with incomparably gentler, politer and more civilised people wherever you go. *Gardeners' Question Time* also tells the same story. By no other programme on radio or television is your heart so warmed. The people who both ask the questions and answer them, gardeners all, sound so thoroughly delightful and decent. The elevating effects of the so-called high Arts are much less certain.

More eloquent than the art of poets or musicians are the actions of millions of ordinary mortals who immerse themselves more and more in their gardens for the only peace they know. Only in their gardens are they taken out of themselves, beyond themselves, above themselves, in their earthly paradise.

# Rambling Roses at Moor Wood

AMBRA EDWARDS, JUNE 2011

Henry Robinson shows a certain amount of alarm at appearing in the pages of this magazine. 'I don't think we qualify,' he says, with a fetching show of modesty. 'You couldn't really call this a garden.' True, there is not a border in sight, let alone a firmly staked perennial or neatly cut edge. And Henry feels honour-bound to point out unruly patches of ground elder and the holes badgers have dug in the lawns. But you might as well say Glendurgan is not a garden, or Ninfa. And while rural Gloucestershire is hardly the Roman Campagna, and Moor Wood extends to a scant two acres (8,000sq m), in many ways the comparison is not so far-fetched. There is that same poetic profusion, with roses clambering into trees and tumbling over walls, scrambling down banks and burrowing into hedges. They scale the house and romp through the orchard; they threaten to engulf the seldom-used tennis court, cascading from the roof of an old pavilion that groans under their weight.

> "We think of it as a landscape rather than a garden. It was a garden once, but we've been steadily ungardening it for more than 20 years"

'We think of it as a landscape rather than a garden,' says Henry's wife, Susie. 'It was a garden once, but we've been steadily ungardening it for more than 20 years.'

Henry's grandparents arrived at Moor Wood in 1911. They found a slender valley, tucked beneath a high beech-clad bank to the east and sheltered by woods to the west. A modest farmhouse, which had gained in dignity with elegant Georgian additions, was then shaded by a mighty cedar of Lebanon. They gardened in high Edwardian style, with a staff of four maintaining grand herbaceous borders and a prodigious vegetable garden. When Henry's mother took over the task, she soldiered on with two gardeners, then one.

By the time Henry and Susie took up the reins in 1984, the garden was in a poor state: 'For 10 years, things had just gently ebbed away.' 'We couldn't possibly garden in the way Henry's parents did,' says Susie, who was busy with their three young children. So she set out to simplify the garden, sweeping away labour-intensive borders and island beds. The kitchen garden became an orchard, planted with an old Gloucestershire apple,

'Ashmead's Kernel', while alpines in the rock garden gave way to sturdy Mediterranean shrubs.

Just the bones of the old Edwardian garden remained in its fat yew hedges and handsome walls of Cotswold stone. In front of the house, Susie made a quiet green garden, bounded to the east by a row of golden Irish yews (*Taxus baccata* Fastigiata Aurea Group), so bent and sculpted by winter snowfalls that they resemble tongues of golden flame. Behind rises a bank planted with *Rosa* 'Polyantha Grandiflora', and *R.* 'Paul's Himalayan Musk' swings up into a tree. 'That,' says Henry, at once admiring and apprehensive, 'is a properly rambling rambler. It's the devil's own job to keep it out of the yew.'

> "...roses grow among grass and wild flowers, twine over seats and spill over the walls"

## An informal collection

It was a friend who suggested rambling roses. 'We were told they required no care whatsoever,' says Henry in the tones of a man who has been the victim of a hoax. Perhaps the friend meant only one or two – but Henry decided to establish a National Plant Collection. Today there are 150 ramblers and almost 100 other roses, loosely grouped by colour: pinks and whites in the old rock garden, peach and yellow tones in the orchard; scarlets and crimsons round the old stone cottage where Henry was born. Each is labelled and catalogued – yet they are grown in an informal, naturalistic way and left largely to their own devices. 'It is a family garden first and a National Plant Collection second,' says Henry firmly. 'A certain amount of romantic disorder fits the bill.'

This style of growing is superbly displayed in the orchard, where roses grow among grass and wild flowers, twine over seats and spill over the walls. They do not, however, grow up the trees, which are still too young to bear the roses' weight. Henry points out various flowery mounds in the lawns where ailing trees have proved unequal hosts for the ramblers and keeled over. Roses and apple trees do make good companions, but Henry advises choosing less rampant selections, such as *Rosa* 'Goldfinch' or 'Madame Alice Garnier' that will not swallow up the tree. Beautiful bullies such as 'Wedding Day' are only suitable for forest trees or large buildings.

At Moor Wood, the most vigorous roses – *Rosa* 'Apple Blossom', 'Janet B. Wood' and 'Brenda Colvin' – are trained up the house, while *R.* 'American Pillar' (an Edwardian survivor) gallops along the drive. Bidding to take over the old rock garden, where the core of the collection is concentrated, is pink and white *R.* 'Francis E. Lester'. 'I spend a lot of time trying to get roses to the top of walls so that they will clothe both sides,' says Henry. So *R.* 'Blush Rambler' and 'Sander's White Rambler', for example, are planted the far side of a wall so they cascade over in a gorgeous scented waterfall of bloom: 'I think of them as outside Eden, trying to break in.' Within this enclosure jostle many choice selections: historic *Rosa* 'Princesse Louise' and 'Adélaïde d'Orléans'; frilly, pale pink 'Laure Davoust' and rare 'Mrs F.W. Flight', her chirpy rock-pink colouring now quite out of fashion.

But who could fail to adore her virginal neighbour 'White Mrs Flight', with long, golden stamens and each snowy petal exquisitely scalloped? Then there are oddities such as *R.* Dentelle de Malines ('Lenfiro') which, although a rambler, grows as a handsome 2m (6ft) shrub, or *R.* 'Alida Lovett', with huge, blowsy blooms of soft shell-pink: 'quite stiff and formal – not at all what you expect from a rambler,' says Henry. But it is a modern rose that really has stolen his heart: *R.* 'Wickwar' – a chance cross of *Rosa soulieana* that was named for the nearby Gloucestershire village in which it was found in 1960. This gorgeous monster, now sprawling 12m (40ft) across, has grown from a single, treasured cutting from the original plant, given to Henry in 1984. With its papery, reflexed blooms and pale grey foliage, *Rosa* 'Wickwar' has all the natural grace of its parent – and is a perfect plant for this romantic setting, where it has all the space it deserves.

'Our basic philosophy is to try and get the amount of work and the amount of help available into some sort of balance,' says Henry. 'Susie does all the twiddly bits. I do roses and destruction. We try to walk the thin dividing line between romantic disorder and complete chaos. We don't water or spray anything: ramblers are hard to kill, and most disease is cosmetic. Visitors ask us how we deadhead. The answer is we don't – there aren't enough hours in the day. Every plant gets a dollop of manure in spring, and pruning to keep it within bounds.' Susie sighs. At Moor Wood, as elsewhere, pruning of ramblers is a matter of debate. While Henry favours an all-out hack, removing most of the flowered wood every few years, Susie is mindful that 'growth follows the knife', and intervenes more lightly 'and more artistically'. Then, 'some never get pruned at all, just left to get on with it'. The Robinsons call it a regime of 'benign neglect' – but it clearly suits both garden and gardeners to perfection.

# Fit for a Queen

JEAN VERNON, AUGUST 2010

Surprisingly few British gardens with strong royal connections open their gates to the public but, among them, those at Osborne House on the Isle of Wight are some of the finest. One of the highlights for visitors to what was the summer home and much-loved rural retreat of Queen Victoria (1819–1901) is the recently redesigned Walled Garden. Many similar gardens in recent years have been renovated to their former magnificence as kitchen gardens for the landed gentry; the garden at Osborne after restoration and replanting now reflects its noble ancestry.

> "Osborne House became a royal residence in 1845, eight years after Victoria's accession and five years after her marriage to Prince Albert"

Osborne House became a royal residence in 1845, eight years after Victoria's accession and five years after her marriage to Prince Albert [who granted the RHS its Royal Charter in 1861]; the Queen and the Prince had been searching for a home away from the stresses of London, and the setting of Osborne Manor appealed to them. The original house was demolished in 1848 as their grand, new palace by the sea, designed largely in the Italianate style by Prince Albert himself, took shape. The 4,000sq m (1 acre) walled garden was a rainy-day destination for the Queen during her stays at Osborne House, which she continued to visit after the death of Prince Albert at Windsor in 1861.

Originally the garden would have provided fruit and cut flowers for the royal household; it was also the site of several display glasshouses, which Queen Victoria used to visit during inclement weather to view hothouse flowers and plants.

After the Queen's death at Osborne House in 1901, King Edward VII presented the house, gardens and estate to the nation. Today it is managed by English Heritage and is open to the public. During the First World War and until 2000, secondary wings were used as an officers' convalescent home and over the years the Walled Garden fell into disrepair. 'It still had pathwork original to the garden from the late 1770s,' says Jen McIntosh, Senior Gardener in charge of the Walled Garden and nursery. None of the original plants have survived, although many existing trees on the estate were grown within its walls and then planted out by the Royal Family.

'There is a sequoia on the lawn that was planted by Prince Albert, and we think he placed most of the trees, too,' says Jen. 'He used to stand on one of the towers and use semaphore to get them to move the trees left and right.'

At the end of the 20th century it was decided to give the Walled Garden a new lease of life as part of the English Heritage Contemporary Heritage Garden initiative. It needed to be contemporary but still recognise its origins and rich atmosphere. Prospective designers were chosen by open competition to complete designs for various English Heritage properties – Rupert Golby was chosen for the redesign of the Osborne House Walled Garden, which opened in July 2000. 'It didn't alter too much of the atmosphere of the place,' says Jen. 'Rupert's design was the most sympathetic. It is a summer garden with a Victorian feel; we try and grow what would have been grown when she was here. So we have the cut flowers and we also have fruit for the house, and have a free rein on the annual beds. The flowers in them change every year; this keeps it interesting for our return visitors, as well as fresh for the gardeners.'

## Regal rhubarb

'Fresh' and 'interesting' do not do it justice. The first glimpse through the wooden doors into the Walled Garden reveals a scene of wonder. In late summer soft blue agapanthus, pale pink Japanese anemones and low hedges of lavender line formal avenues and paths that dissect this tranquil space. It is a scene reminiscent of a spectacular, romantic wedding but, as with all good gardens, there is more here than first meets the eye.

It is a practical, productive cutting garden. Where once before this walled garden grew flowers fit for a queen, it now fulfils English Heritage's aims to inform and inspire children and adults alike. Plants have been selected either to be representative of the Victorian era, or to have a link to the garden's royal roots. In the perennial canal borders, for example, every other row is punctuated with a clump of established rhubarb. There are two cultivars: short, squat 'Victoria' and taller, slimmer 'Prince Albert'. You cannot help but wonder who named these plants so aptly.

Each canal border also supports three types of flowers for cutting to provide a continuous supply of summer flowers for the house, such as peonies (including *Paeonia lactiflora* cultivars 'Albert Crousse' and 'Duchesse de Nemours'), dahlias (*D.* 'White Aster' is a favourite) and agapanthus. It is a fascinating insight into the flowers of the day and includes surprises: asparagus was grown for its feathery foliage; here it jostles for position with *Achillea* and poppies.

Along the elaborate galvanised arches and walkways, espaliered culinary apples 'Queen' and 'Lane's Prince Albert' as well as dessert pear 'Louise Bonne of Jersey' bear flower-laden branches followed by masses of fruit. Shrubby roses such as *Rosa* 'Reine Victoria', *R.* 'Prince Camille de Rohan', *R.* 'Reine des Violettes' and *R.* 'Baronne Edmond de Rothschild' ('Meigriso') are planted between arches; the roses are chosen for their charm and use as cut flowers.

> "In the quiet of the garden you can hear the boats passing by..."

The garden is so full of colour and depth that it is hard to believe that a huge part of this vibrant tapestry is made up of annual flowers grown from seeds. Within almost half of the garden, swathes of flowers for cutting create banks of colour alive with the sound and activity of bees. 'We grow things that would be typical for flower arrangers, such as clarkia, dahlias and sunflowers,' says Jen. 'But we also grow things people don't normally consider to be cut flowers, but we know were used, such as cornflowers; they don't particularly stand out, but they are nice as fillers. We've got things with smaller flowers such as felicia: the Victorians would have liked posies – it wasn't all just big flowers. We try to keep to Victorian cultivars as much as possible.'

The red-brick walls facing the four points of the compass protect the garden from the sea-borne, salt-la den winds. In the quiet of the garden you can hear the boats passing by, just two miles or so from this peaceful, coastal garden. On the north-facing wall, fan-trained morello cherries are interspersed with pillars of climbing ivies, and beneath, in the cool shade, fine-leaved *Athyrium filix-femina* 'Victoriae' (lady fern) is planted with other shade-lovers. The sunny, south-facing wall supports peaches and figs, but records from the 1870s show that there was an orange trained here at that time. In fact, since 2002, an orange tree has been growing here, though as yet no fruit has been produced. On the east-facing wall, plums – of course including quintessential 'Victoria' – as well as gages nestle between pillars of pears, while on the west-facing wall, apricots and pears greet visitors as they enter through the portico doorway that forms the entrance to the garden. This grand structure was rescued from the original house by Prince Albert.

Just as it was in the days of Queen Victoria, this garden is hugely labour intensive. Back then there would have been a dozen or more gardeners. 'They would have had a head gardener, lots of under gardeners and a boy to stoke the fire. They lived in the nearby bothy buildings, as, especially in winter, the fires had to be kept burning through the night to heat the greenhouses,' says Jen. By contrast, today the garden has tractors, powered cultivators and just one full-time member of staff, although Jen is assisted by an army of 30 or so volunteers. 'Some just come for a morning or afternoon once a week, some for a full day. I wouldn't be able to do it without them'.

Some plants grown within the Walled Garden are said to have been personal favourites of the Royal Family. Prince Albert was fond of *Zantesdeschia aethiopica*, while Queen Victoria loved violets. Today the garden has a small *Viola* collection in her honour, which includes aptly named *V.* 'Princesse de Galles', *V.* 'The Czar', *V.* 'Prince Henry' and *V.* 'Prince John'.

The Walled Garden, however, is more than a collection of plants that charmed a queen. Now, after years of neglect, it is both beautiful and informative, transporting visitors back to a time when flowers and fruit for 'the big house', grown on site in a dedicated walled garden, were – for some – everyday commodities.

One may dismiss these gardens as trappings of wealth and power, but the horticultural achievements made by Victorian gardeners who worked within the walls have yet to be surpassed.

# Manor Magic

URSULA BUCHAN, JUNE 2009

For generations of young children, the name 'Green Knowe' has meant a magical, time-shifting world, involving a delightful, curious, small boy called Tolly and his remarkable great-grandmother, Mrs Oldknow, the occupier of an ancient house, Green Knowe. What those readers will not know is that the moated house, and lovely, mysterious garden, with its enormous trees, eccentric topiary and river flowing at the far end of it, all exist and can be visited at any time of year.

Green Knowe was the fictional name Lucy M Boston gave to The Manor, Hemingford Grey in Cambridgeshire, where she lived from 1939 until her death, aged 97, in 1990. It is a remarkable Norman hall house (with 18th-century additions), which has been in continuous occupation since the 1130s, and can claim to be the oldest domestic building in the country.

Lucy Boston saw it first in 1915, while on a visit to her brothers at the University of Cambridge. She glimpsed the house from the River

Great Ouse, and thought that it looked tranquil but unloved in its field by the river.

In the late 1930s, while living in lodgings in Cambridge, she was told that a house in Hemingford Grey was for sale. She set off immediately, knocked on the door of The Manor, and astonished the owners by offering to buy it, since they had only talked of selling the house that morning at breakfast.

Lucy wrote and sewed exquisite patchwork quilts in winter, and gardened all summer. She made a country garden out of the field by the river, with rectilinear borders running north-south, divided by lawn, ditch or gravel path, and filled it with summer flowers. These included tall bearded irises and an impressive collection of Old Roses, at a time when these were not at all fashionable; she even imported clay soil to make her light river gravel heavier and more suitable for them. Her guide and mentor in this was the great rosarian, Graham Stuart Thomas, then working at Sunningdale Nurseries, who sought out unusual cultivars for her. In all, she amassed some 200 selections, including rare Hybrid Perpetual *Rosa* 'Paul Ricault'; *R.* 'Botzaris', a Damask Rose much like 'Madame Hardy', but rather more compact; and another sweetly scented, deep pink Damask, *R.* 'La Ville de Bruxelles'. The labels accompanying them contain not only their names, but also the dates of introduction, which shows admirable seriousness of purpose.

> "The most striking feature, at first sight, is the double row of large, dumpy, topiary shapes, composed of crowns and orbs that run down the lawn to the river"

Diana Boston, Lucy's daughter-in-law, lives at The Manor now, having first stayed there, part-time, with her architect husband Peter (who illustrated the Green Knowe books), after Lucy's death. Sadly, he died suddenly in 1999, at which point Diana made the decision to move to the house permanently. She became guardian of Lucy M Boston's memory, publisher of a number of the books, and guide to visitors who come each year to see Green Knowe and wander in the tranquil garden which complements so well the fascinating atmosphere of the house.

Diana began gardening as a child, under the tutelage of her own mother, so it was the garden, as well as the house, which appealed to her. 'You do have to be slightly eccentric to live here,' she says, refraining from mentioning the resident poltergeist. I was too polite to mention it, either.

Bringing the garden back to its former quality was difficult, of course, as it so often is when the creator has grown too infirm to maintain it. 'The bindweed is still appalling,' she says ruefully. 'There was a lot of restoration to do.' At the start, she had no help in the garden, though now she has three excellent part-time gardeners.

The irises were nearly dug up after the first year but, as Diana says, it was a good thing she didn't get round to it as 'they flowered their socks off' the following year. They earned a lasting reprieve. Many – for example *Iris* 'Benton Argent', 'Benton Susan' and 'Benton Sheila' – also came from Sunningdale Nurseries via Graham Stuart Thomas. They were bred after the Second World War by plantsman Sir Cedric Morris, of Benton End, Suffolk, who selected for intriguing colours and was the first to breed a true pink iris.

## Enclosed by a moat

This is a romantic, generously-planted country garden, which surrounds the house and is governed in structure by the barns, walls and moat. There are 1.8ha (4½ acres) altogether, of which 0.4ha (1 acre), the area beyond the moat, is 'jungle', according to Diana. Inside the moat the garden is intensively cultivated. The most striking feature, at first sight, is the double row of large, dumpy, topiary shapes, composed of crowns and orbs that run down the lawn to the river. (Lucy was brought up near Levens Hall in Cumbria, so had a taste for such conceits, and the confidence to know that small yew saplings could become strong visual elements in her lifetime.)

Chickens strut freely, a cockerel crows, and the wind soughs in tall trees. Most remarkable is a Huntingdon elm (*Ulmus* x *vegeta*) growing in the southwest corner, close to the river. It is one of the finest in the country, important for historical and aesthetic reasons and because of its partial resistance to Dutch elm disease. Elsewhere, a felled mature purple beech, a victim of honey fungus, has been left prone, to be colonised by insects and beetles.

The far end of the garden floods every year. 'I am surprised the irises do so well, as they do get flooded from time to time,' says Diana. In 900 years, however, the water is thought never to have entered the house; in 1947 it came close, up to the top step, and Lucy was trapped inside for a week – no wonder floodwaters feature in her books.

The best time for the garden, according to Diana, is late May and early June, principally because of the irises and Old Roses, but the inclusion of many herbaceous perennials – asters, grasses and *Verbena bonariensis* in particular – means that all summer and autumn there is much to see. Diana has tried to preserve the atmosphere of the Green Knowe garden, retaining the layout, while adding many plants that she likes. She has introduced modern, repeat-flowering English roses, such as *R.* The Dark

Lady ('Ausbloom') while tall white foxgloves and blue delphiniums now augment rose plantings, providing important vertical accents.

An example of this development is the replacement of flowering cherries (which deteriorate after some 50 years) with handsome *Crataegus persimilis* 'Prunifolia' (cockspur thorn), which has cherry-shaped leaves, but a longer life span, and interest in both spring and autumn.

Altogether, this is a garden that over the years has survived the change in ownership and moved on – through hard work rather than magic, it must be said. Thanks to Diana's respect for the intentions of its creator, the garden of Green Knowe continues to charm all those who visit it.

# Behind Barbed Wire

BRENT ELLIOTT, NOVEMBER 1988

Local horticultural societies have sought to become affiliated with the Royal Horticultural Society for over a century, but seldom can a society have grown up in conditions as extraordinary as one which requested affiliation in September 1916. The letter bore the printed heading 'Englanderlager Ruhleben' – the internment camp for British civilians in Germany. Civilians caught in the enemy country at the outbreak of the First World War were little affected at first. But after rumours began to be heard that German civilians were being interned in England, the German government retaliated, and on 6 November issued an order for the arrest of all British males aged between 17 and 55. The 4-ha (10-acre) Ruhleben racecourse, on the outskirts of Berlin, was turned into an internment camp.

"In the early days of Ruhleben Camp, many of the gardens were confined within the walls of biscuit tins"

Into this racecourse were herded 4,000 men – the number was eventually to reach 5,500. They were accommodated in the Tea House and 11 stables, now renamed barracks, with ten men occupying a horse-box. The sports field and its enclosing racetracks were to provide a drill ground and games facilities for the prisoners.

The story of the camp has been told by one of its inmates, the Canadian psychologist J. Davidson Ketchum. 'In the early days of Ruhleben Camp, horticulture was limited to a few enthusiasts and many of their gardens were confined within the walls of biscuit tins. These primitive efforts were followed by an era of barrack garden enterprise, somewhat sporadic in its outbursts, but nevertheless, in many cases, achieving remarkably good results, results which indicated possibilities of gardening in the camp on a much grander scale.'

A gift of seeds from the Crown Princess of Sweden served as the spark to ignite the gardening passion. A horticultural society was formed, with Mr L P Warner, President and Chairman, and Mr Thomas Howat, Secretary. One of Mr Howat's first tasks was to write to the Royal Horticultural Society.

'We desire to become affiliated to the Royal Horticultural Society. Under the circumstances in which we are presently situated we are unable of course to remit the usual fee but trust this will be no hindrance to our enjoying the privileges of affiliation.' (At this point, the Society's Secretary, William Wilks, scrawled on the letter, 'certainly not'.) 'As the work we have in view is a large one we should be very grateful for gifts of bulbs and seeds.'

Wilks replied with the announcement that affiliation had been approved. Six cases and one parcel of seeds and bulbs were sent off, accompanied by six pamphlets on gardening; a further 11 cases of seeds and bulbs were despatched by the end of November. By 20 December, Howat could write that a syllabus of lectures on gardening had begun 'with great success'. From 50 members at the inaugural meeting, the Ruhleben Horticultural Society grew until by the time of the first annual report, in September 1917, it had 943 members.

A nursery was set up behind the wash-house in a plot of approximately 600 square yards. 'This plot was cleared, trenched, treated with drain refuse and tea leaves (manure not being available)', and, as funds allowed, equipped with frames. At this stage most of the funds came from members' subscriptions at 1 mark each, but the first autumn's work resulted in a successful harvest of dahlias and chrysanthemums, which were sent to England for sale and raised 300 marks. This was the beginning of economic success for the Society.

On 29 January, 1917, Howat wrote to London again, saying: 'You will be pleased to know that permission has been given us to cultivate a Vegetable Garden in the Camp, so we are now in a position to make use of the seeds which you so kindly sent us in your first consignment of bulbs. In order to utilise the ground at our disposal we require a further supply of seeds and we would esteem it a great favour if you could let us have the quantity of seeds shown on enclosed list.' The seeds were duly sent, the firms of Sutton,

Carter, Cutbush, and Barr among those contributing.

The vegetable garden was inaugurated at the end of March, 1917; it was divided into 30 plots, devoted to a wide variety of crops. Thirty loads of 'very poor quality pig manure' were obtained from the *Wacht Kommando* and augmented with slag and bone meal. The late start meant that only two crops were obtained by the autumn of 1917, and those had suffered from wireworm and other pests, but the workers had reason to congratulate themselves on their achievement, for by selling their produce to the canteen they raised over 6,000 marks, and ended with a profit of nearly 800 marks after expenses.

During the course of 1917, the Ruhleben Horticultural Society extended its work into the competitive sphere. Two flower showers were held and prizes awarded for vegetables, sweet peas, cut flowers, table decorations, buttonholes, window boxes, and gardens. A greenhouse was built in the nursery ground, and a rock garden laid out near the washhouse using seeds from the RHS. Promenade beds were planted competitively alongside the barbed wire fences, and each barrack was furnished with a garden. Photographs of several of these barrack gardens were sent to the RHS, and show the efforts of the inmates to recreate the English gardens of the Edwardian period within the confines of their prison camp.

The Armistice brought an end to the Ruhleben Horticultural Society. By 24 November the last prisoners had left the camp, which returned to its former role as a racecourse until it was demolished in 1958 to accommodate a new sewage plant.

# The Virtues of a Valley

CHRIS YOUNG, OCTOBER 2010

Sitting on the lawn at the front of Coombe House, Alasdair Forbes' intensely private garden in Devon, can be a disconcerting experience. This is a semi-circular space, suggesting an 'offering' to a 'tamed' Artemis, Greek goddess of hunting, forests and hills. From landform and symbols referencing mythological figures to physical relationships between garden and landscape (such as the use of a ha-ha), there is meaning at almost every turn. Topography, too, can throw the visitor, with views across the steep-sided valley, up and down, in and out. However, it is best to accept this constantly changing view of the garden. Whatever you take from this creation, it cannot be denied that this is a place full of spirit and atmosphere.

> "...where do you begin to unravel a design as complex as Plaz Metaxu?"

In its simplest form, the garden at Coombe House, called 'Plaz Metaxu' (translated from Greek, meaning 'the place that is in-between'), is a series of spaces linked together by meaning, metaphor and modulation. Extending to 13ha (32 acres) in total, half is gardened, the other half is farmed with flocks of sheep, interspersed with woodland. It is a garden of a whole, as well as parts; and, as its name suggests, it is a place that makes the visitor stop and think about the spaces he or she walks through. Making reference to stories and people from literature and myth, Alasdair has created a garden of large proportions, both physically and emotionally; a space that has its own identity, using planted material, sculpture and the landscape itself to tell a medley of stories. But where do you begin to unravel a design as complex as Plaz Metaxu?

It is perhaps easiest by starting with its creator. Alasdair, a quiet and deeply private man, bought this house and landscape as a reaction from life in London. Having been an art historian at the Courtauld Institute of Art, he was well aware of the romantic nature of landscape, and began 'to realise that gardens could be as moving as the paintings I was studying'. With this in mind, he began to travel, as he says, 'to educate myself in understanding gardens, natural rhythms and the issues involved in maintaining a large garden'. In 1992, he bought Coombe House, an old whitewashed farmhouse sitting at the base of an east-west valley; and, since then, his desire to redeem academic understanding has led him to create this one-off of outdoor spaces.

For Alasdair, there is a clear sense of catharsis in his creation. He chose Coombe House because of his desire to make a garden – 'I really wanted to conceive a garden as a way of working things out' is how he describes it. However he did not want to stick to strict design rules. Instead, he has balanced the inspiration from his studies with the valley's topography and site, letting the landscape offer design ideas. A good example of this is the Avenue of the Hours – a long walk running up a slope in a field dedicated to the goddess of order, law and custom, Themis. Her aides (the 'hours') are represented here by nine pairs of different trees, some with seasonal interest, such as the splendid summer foliage of lime, *Tilia* x *europaea* 'Wratislaviensis', or the deep green-grey of evergreen oak, *Quercus ilex*.

"... and from the underworld, Hades swirls round in a dark, circular yew room nearby"

You can almost sense relief in his voice as he describes such areas, of why one seemingly innocent element can have such substantial implications on another; this is healing in motion. 'You can often get taken by surprise,' he says, 'as nature always intervenes in mysterious ways. As a result, I am constantly modifying or refining elements in the garden.'

It is almost impossible to describe the feeling you get when walking round, except to say that there is constantly a great sense of atmosphere. Near the lake, the spirit of hero Narcissus is clearly referenced when looking down onto the water; further into the lake a stainless steel 'alarm sail' rises, being both a figure of soulful Psyche and a visual link to the mount of Eros; and from the underworld, Hades swirls round in a dark, circular yew room nearby. For many, these have incomprehensible meanings that require a description to aid their understanding; but the reality is that as a garden experience, it still 'works'. The ground may be heavy in meaning, but you do not have to speak the language to appreciate it.

The perhaps surprising aspect of Plaz Metaxu is that Alasdair is a passionate plant enthusiast. Near the house, in what was the old garden, fine examples of *Rosa* 'Constance Spry', *Schizophragma integrifolium* and *Paeonia delavayi* grow plentifully; the planting combinations here are domestic and soft. In the courtyards, *Phillyrea latifolia* has been clipped into buttress shapes; *Stauntonia hexaphylla* commands attention; and *Magnolia grandiflora* 'Exmouth' looks substantial against the walls. Further from the house, an old orchard welcomes a range of trees that Alasdair has planted – *Abies pinsapo* 'Kelleriis' gives strong, grey-blue colour in winter, and *Larix kaempferi* 'Diana', a corkscrew larch, adds visual interest. Further from the house, plantings of *Taxodium distichum* var. *imbricarium* 'Nutans', *Cornus*

'Eddie's White Wonder' and *Acer campestre* 'Pulverulentum' give protection to more intimate areas of planting. The result is a garden of imaginatively planted, quite dense areas, all set within the wider rolling landscape.

At the heart of Plaz Metaxu, it is this conflict that is most enthralling – personal and public, horticultural and agricultural, domesticated and wild. At certain times it can be a lonely garden, making the visitor feel on his or her own, walking through a space that has no sense of direction. But then, in just a few steps, it can be a landscape of hope. These may sound strong emotions to be gained from a garden, but so great is the strength of place that such feelings do emerge. The main body of the garden, nearest the house and lake, does have a more domestic feeling, but surrounding it on three sides sits the ever-present agricultural landscape: sheep roam the pasture, visually reminding you that this is farmland.

This close connection also hints at a garden in tension, the gardener keeping the spaces near the house in control while allowing more natural-looking areas space to breathe. At times in Alasdair's garden this constant argument between 'the domestic' and 'the agricultural' can be quite intense, but at other times it is as natural as walking around a Picturesque landscape.

And what of the name, Plaz Metaxu? It is easy to forget its meaning, so it is well worth considering why Alasdair named it such – 'the place that is in-between'. This can be interpreted on many levels: physically, for instance, in the path between hedges; or imaginatively, in the play between the literal and figurative. However you read it, by remembering the name you start to consider the 'empty spaces'.

In most gardens, if planting is used to direct a view, the normal approach is for a focal point to be installed – maybe an urn or statue – yet Alasdair leaves the space empty. At other times, the path through the garden forces you to enter narrow spaces, acting as chambers taking you from one space to another – their role essential to the journey. However you view this garden, there is no denying its beauty and drama. It is a solitary garden, best experienced on your own, and with an open mind. Whether you understand the meanings superficially or intimately, ultimately it is still a garden of substance – acknowledging Alasdair's beliefs only helps to improve the experience. The garden may well be called 'the place that is in-between', but what has been created is a confident, soulful garden that is now nowhere in between – rather is a place of itself, by itself, created by its valley virtues, and its owner's vision. For that he should feel great pride.

# Hergest Croft

HUGH JOHNSON, APRIL 1980

A t the RHS Autumn Show in 1960 there was a competition for freshly-gathered cones, to see who could produce the best collection. The Queen, drawing on her resources at Windsor Great Park, came first. A short head behind came Dick Banks. All his cones came from his own conifers at Hergest Croft. He had gathered them himself, often having to climb to the top of tall trees to reach them. I hope he will forgive me for mentioning it, but he was nearly sixty at the time.

"To any visitor who loves trees and feels the magic of woodlands it must be one of the three or four most inspiring gardens in England'

The Banks family have lived at Hergest Croft (the name is pronounced Harguest) or nearby in the little town of Kington near the Welsh border, for 170 years. For the past 90, three generations have been gardening their ancestral ground with fervour amounting to passion. To the visitor with a sense of the history of plants as well as their beauty it is a place of outstanding interest. To any visitor who loves trees and feels the magic of woodlands it must be one of the three or four most inspiring gardens in England.

The special historical interest of Hergest Croft lies in the fact that it was planted during the climax of Chinese plant-hunting, when E H Wilson and others were sending back regular consignments of 'novelties' to Veitch's and other nurseries. Veitch's annual catalogues for the first decade and more of this century, still kept and referred to at Hergest Croft, could be called the cornerstone of the collection.

The excitement of such planting is unknown to us today. It is a very rare tree or shrub that we can't look up in 'Bean' and find a resume of its performance in cultivation. First-time planters have to go on guesswork, helped only by the explorer's account of the plant's natural habitat and associations.

The collection at Hergest Croft shows that the Bankses were good at guessing. A remarkable number of the original plants survive. Perhaps their commonest mistake, and a very human one, was not to allow enough room for their unknown quantities. The resulting overcrowding led to a recourse, in itself historically interesting; in the Thirties, the Bankses invited Bruce Jackson of Kew (but above all of 'Dallimore and Jackson', the standard conifer book) to review their trees and advise on priorities; which of a competing pair or group should be done away with.

Thus the present garden is a skilfully edited collection of everything that was most prized in the first quarter of this century, constantly revised and brought up to date, but still essentially a period piece. Just the right amount of time has now elapsed for us to see it at its peak. Specimens of many rare plants are so well-grown that it is difficult to realise that there are few or no others like them.

It is natural to speak of Hergest Croft as a collection first and foremost, but that is far from being the feeling of the place. Unlike the older arboretum of Westonbirt it seems to melt into the native woods and fields. It contains areas of typical Herefordshire parkland only as it were more elegant for their population of exotic trees, and woods which from without seem merely tall and thriving, but which within, below the high canopy of oak and larch, are (at least to me who has never been to China) like a dream of the eastern foothills of the Himalayas.

# New World Order

URSULA BUCHAN, FEBRUARY 2010

It is a fact of life that anyone who wishes to do something new and innovative in an historic landscape has a hard furrow to plough (if that is not a highly inappropriate metaphor). The constraints are enormous, the regulations fearsome. Of course, these exist to protect what is there already, but the unintended consequence of stern regulation can be to hobble contemporary imagination. So let us give three cheers for the tenacity and vision of the current Duke of Buccleuch and Queensberry, landscape designer Kim Wilkie and landscape manager Lance Goffort-Hall who, with the main contractors Miles Waterscapes, have ensured that a bold new landform, named Orpheus, now enhances the historic landscape surrounding Boughton House near Kettering, Northamptonshire.

The park at Boughton is, arguably, the finest of the few extant baroque (that is, influenced by the French and Dutch) formal landscapes in England.

> "...a bold new landform, named Orpheus, now enhances the historic landscape surrounding Boughton House..."

In the late 17th century, Ralph Montagu, later 1st Duke of Montagu, one-time ambassador to Louis XIV's court, employed a Dutch gardener, Leonard van der Meulan, to lay out a coherent and complex landscape in Boughton's late-medieval deer park, to complement his new, French-influenced house. The layout consisted of canals, a cascade, parterres and avenues, on a strongly axial geometry.

After 1709, the second Duke ('Planter John') expanded the formal gardens to more than 100 acres (40ha) and simplified many of the original parterres and basins; garden designer Charles Bridgeman (who, prior to 'Capability' Brown, also designed the gardens at Stowe, Buckinghamshire) was on the payroll between 1726 and 1731 and surely influenced the design. The main lake, the Broad Water, was enlarged, and an imposing square-based grassy pyramid, called the Mount, built; from the flat top, the Duke and his guests could view the whole.

After his death in 1749, the family lived mainly elsewhere and the estate went to sleep for 150 years, thus avoiding the wholesale changes imposed by the 'landskip improvers', such as Brown.

## An opportunity revealed

However, since 2003 the landscape at Boughton has been the subject of a sensitive and meticulous restoration by the present Duke, relying heavily on a bird's-eye view plan of 1729. Most of the canals have now been dredged, their sides reinforced with 2 miles of green oak boarding, and the masses of seedling trees removed from the Mount. The clean, crisp lines of the landscape have re-emerged, with only the square, grassy Grand Étang (pond) still waiting to be dug out and filled with water once more. [It is dug now – 2014.]

Close to the Mount, though divided by a canal, was an area of flat grassland, devoid of features on the 1729 map; what evidence there was of a one-time flower garden, if any, had been unwittingly disturbed when the nearby Broad Water was dredged in the 1970s.

As it turned out, that was good fortune, for it gave a rare opportunity to the present Duke to plan a new feature. He invited Kim Wilkie, the landscape designer – well known for his sculpted landforms at, *inter alia*, Heveningham Hall, Suffolk, Great Fosters, Surrey and Shawford Park, Hampshire – to suggest a design. This was an inspired choice in the circumstances: Kim studied history at Oxford before environmental design at University of California, Berkeley, and is most alive to symbolism and to what he calls the 'ghosts of occupation'.

Standing on the top of the Mount with the Duke, Kim commented that he thought it would be interesting 'to go down rather than up'. He proposed an inverted, truncated, square grass pyramid, the same size and shape as the Mount, 7m (23ft) deep and 60m (197ft) square. English Heritage was persuaded, once they knew that the view to the Mount would remain unimpeded.

"A grassy ramp runs down in a spiral, reminding me of Escher's infinite staircases"

The sensation of coming across this deep depression in the landscape is a novel and thrilling one, since Orpheus is not visible until you are almost upon it. The sides, made of puddled blue clay (a seam of which conveniently runs through the park), covered with a 25cm (10in) deep layer of topsoil, are at a 41-degree angle. A grassy ramp runs down in a spiral, reminding me of Escher's infinite staircases. (In case you are wondering, a special remote-control mower has been acquired to cut the grassy sides.) The spiral continues into the pool at the bottom, which is lined with synthetic turf, giving the illusion that the grass grows under the water. The pool is dark, and reflects the sky.

The Broad Water gradually disappears from view as you descend. Lance Goffort-Hall, the tireless project manager, explained to me that Orpheus is a 'reverse reservoir', keeping water out rather than letting it in. As you walk down the slope towards the pool in the bottom, the air becomes tranquil, and distant traffic noise is stilled. The acoustics are good, and provision has been made to erect a platform just above the pool to accommodate a small group of musicians.

On one side of the flat terrace that surrounds Orpheus, Kim has designed a curving, stone, narrow water-filled rill in the shape of a spiral; this winds tighter and tighter towards a small square pond in the middle, above which stands an open steel cube. The cube lines up with the elevated Lily Pond some way to the east and close to the house. The spiral, and the rectangles that its curves touch, obey the rules of the golden section. Even for those of us who are geometry duffers, these ground patterns seem orderly and congruous.

The Duke has described Wilkie's vision as 'one of power and intelligence, prompting awe-tinged surprise, which gives way to curiosity and then calm as the visitor descends into Orpheus... The creative Montagus,' says the Duke, 'would, I think, have been intrigued.' For sure.

Why 'Orpheus'? It refers to the Greek myth of Orpheus' love for his wife, Eurydice, who dies of a serpent bite and is taken down to the underworld. Orpheus goes to fetch her back to earth, and sings so beautifully that he is allowed to take her, provided that he does not look back as they leave. I confess a slight queasiness about the end of the story, but visitors need feel no such anxiety about their return from Boughton House's 'underworld'. Both in name and conception, Orpheus exhibits an admirably self-confident and expansive spirit, which seems to belong more to the 18th century than our own.

# Chalking up Success

ROY LANCASTER, JUNE 2010

Fifty years ago this year a book was published which, it might be argued, changed and enriched the lives of the many people who garden on alkaline soils. It was written by Sir Frederick Stern VMH (1884–1967) under the simple title *A Chalk Garden*, and described the making of his garden at Highdown on the slopes of Highdown Hill, 82m (269ft) above Worthing, on the West Sussex coast. Begun in 1910, the garden was regarded by Stern as 'an experiment to see what would grow on the chalk soil of the Downs'. The conditions were daunting: no part of the garden had a soil pH less than 8.0, and at best just 15cm (6in) of loam overlaid almost solid chalk.

Central to the experiment was a large chalk pit, then used to house pigs and chickens. Unsure initially as to what, if anything, might grow there, Stern sought advice from gardening friends, receiving both negative and positive responses. Encouraged by the latter and being of a determined, even adventurous nature, he went ahead with his plans and within a few years was sufficiently encouraged to throw himself whole-heartedly into his task. This coincided with his marriage, in 1919; his wife Sybil became a great supporter of his endeavours, which were many and varied.

Stern helped support many plant hunters of the early 20th century including Wilson, Forrest, Kingdon-Ward, Farrer, Rock, and Ludlow and Sherriff, which resulted in seed – and eventually plants. Some of the most notable of these can still be admired in the garden to this day. Stern was also an ardent supporter of the RHS, serving for many years on, in all, nine RHS plant committees. He was a Vice President of the Society and a member of RHS Council for, remarkably, 33 years in all. Stern did not deliberately set out to grow plants which were rumoured or known to have an aversion to lime, though he could not resist the occasional challenge. Rather, he sought plants which he knew or suspected to have at least a tolerance of alkaline soils and though he suffered his fair share of disappointments (not all soil-related), he enjoyed an even greater degree of success, which must have provided him with lasting pleasure.

He found planting in pockets made in the chalk often resulted in the plants failing, but if the chalk was broken up to around 75cm (30in) and organic matter such as old cow manure added, plant roots could spread out and establish. Planting small specimens generally proved more successful, too. Stern also mulched his plants with beech leaf mould or spent mushroom compost.

"Another of Stern's plantings here is South American tree *Maytenus boaria*, in excellent condition with multiple stems and a well-rounded crown..."

Inevitably, the garden expanded to accommodate the increasing collection, ending only with his death aged 83 in 1967, followed by that of his wife in 1972. In 1968, the 4ha (10 acre) garden was gifted to Worthing Borough Council, which has been responsible for its development and care to the present day.

My first visit to Highdown was in spring 1984. I was impressed with the many rare trees and shrubs, and colourful swathes of bulbous plants including anemones, daffodils, tulips, scilla and chionodoxas. The gardens were being cared for by Chris Beardsley who had been manager since 1976, and remembered visiting with a group of parks' apprentices in the 1960s when an elderly Stern waved to them from the house. Chris was full of energy and I left feeling that Stern, who was knighted for 'services to horticulture' in 1956, would have been pleased to have had Chris in charge.

It was with anticipation therefore, that I visited Highdown again in April. I was delighted to find Chris still in the post, though soon to retire. Following an all too brief meeting with his excellent staff, we set out on what was to be a trip down memory lane.

Close to the entrance, in an area known as The Orchard, I was thrilled by a collection of trees and shrubs including a fine, three-stemmed *Zelkova sinica* planted by Chris in 1979. Nearby was an equally impressive, though much older, original planting of *Acer davidii*, branching into several smooth stems from 1m (39in) high. Another of Stern's plantings here is South American tree *Maytenus boaria*, in excellent condition with multiple stems and a well-rounded crown of semi-pendent branches clothed with narrow, evergreen leaves.

Not far from here, I noted a huge *Buddleja colvilei*, producing in early summer panicles of large, reddish bell-shaped flowers, and red-barked *Arbutus andrachne* (Greek strawberry tree) to which Chris had added equally red-barked *Arbutus menziesii* (madrone) which, despite its reputed dislike of chalk soils, looked to be in good health. Just before leaving this area, I was surprised to see a huge *Viburnum betulifolium* with arching branches still carrying rich red (somewhat wrinkled) berry clusters from the previous autumn.

Our tour now led us to the old Chalk Pit, through shaded areas where the white-flowered crucifer, *Pachyphragma macrophyllum*, combined with narcissus, pulmonarias and forget-me-not-flowered *Brunnera macrophylla* to form a lush ground cover. There were large carpets of bulbs too: pale-blue *Scilla messeniaca* self-seeding in shade and rubble, and in full sun stoloniferous scarlet-flowered *Tulipa praecox*. The Chalk Pit had suffered at the hands of the recent winter with plants of Mediterranean origin damaged or killed. *Cistus*, *Choisya* and *Teucrium fruticans* were worst hit though survived elsewhere.

> "There were large carpets of bulbs too: pale-blue *Scilla messeniaca* self-seeding in shade and chalk rubble…"

## Challenging conditions

On the plus side, however, were fast emerging clumps of blue-flowered *Agapanthus praecox*, bright pink *Nerine bowdenii* and bold evergreen stands of *Euphorbia characias* subsp. *wulfenii*, its flowers brassy yellow against the white chalk walls. Pink *Tulipa saxatilis* Bakeri Group was also in good form, sharing its chalk rubble home with blue, red and pink blooms of *Anemone pavonina*, which Chris has grown from seed and planted in drifts. The same anemone together with *A. coronaria* forms drifts along a grass walk just as in Stern's day, while *A. apennina* has been planted in a patch at the base of amber-stemmed *Prunus maackii* (Manchurian bird cherry), forming a pool of blue and white flowers.

Two-tone yellow-flowered bulbous perennial *Iris bucharica* thrives in the Lower Garden and elsewhere, forming fine clumps popular with many visitors – though what they think of the huge clump of dark-purple flowered and evil-smelling *Dracunculus vulgaris* (dragon arum), I can only guess.

In the Middle Garden meanwhile (a large area of informal beds in grass) several of Stern's most interesting trees can be found, principal among them *Carpinus turczaninowii*, grown from seed collected on the Farrer-Purdom expedition to Gansu, China in 1913. It is a beautiful tree with a stout stem and broadly weeping crown of slender branches, clothed in summer with leaves that turn orange-brown in autumn. It is now recognised by the *Tree Register* as the Champion of its kind in Britain and Ireland.

In the same bed is a fine example of *Chionanthus retusus* (Chinese fringe tree), whose branches in summer are covered with white, narrow-petalled flower clusters. In his book, Stern commented on this being a good example of the Chinese species of a genus having no dislike of lime while the American species, *C. virginicus*, has an aversion to it. Other unusual trees here include May-flowering *Cercis racemosa* (Chinese Judas tree), differing from *C. siliquastrum* in its racemed not clustered flowers and a large, dense, bushy-crowned *Laurus azorica* (Canary Island bay), from the Atlantic Isles, whose hairy shoots and large leaves differentiate it from those of *L. nobilis* (common bay), though they have the same aroma when bruised.

Many of the acknowledged chalk-tolerant trees and shrubs are represented here especially Japanese cherries, lilacs, mahonias, crab apples, *Philadelphus*, buddlejas and *Chaenomeles*, so too less often seen *Abelia triflora* – the example here is a veteran of a plant, now split into three main stems. Stern enjoyed its sweet fragrance in June claiming that 'one of the charms of the garden is to have plants scattered around with pleasant scents, not too strong or heavy, but just right like the scent of this abelia'.

Stern authored two classic books on garden plants: *Snowdrops and Snowflakes* and *A Study of the Genus Paeonia*. Examples of both genera are well represented at Highdown, each, in their season, being sufficient reason alone to visit this garden which is open to the public throughout the year. For any gardener, especially a beginner, Highdown is a must visit, more so if you garden on an alkaline (especially chalk) soil for there is many a useful lesson to be learned.

As a major collection of trees, shrubs and perennials Highdown continues to delight, satisfy and surprise. We must sincerely hope that the pleasure it brings to so many people will continue without end.

# WILDLIFE & WILDFLOWERS

Attitudes to native wildlife and wild flowers in the garden have changed markedly over the last 150 years. Although the towering figure, William Robinson, was an enthusiastic advocate of 'wild gardening' from the 1870s onwards, His advice mainly fell upon deaf ears, since gardeners were seduced by the exotic riches of other countries and were often dismissive of their own flora. It was not until the 1980s that the grievous and inexorable loss of natural habitats, which has occurred since the Second World War, and the effect this has had on both native flora and fauna, were brought starkly home to us by ecologists, and the wildflower, wildlife-friendly garden began to be widely advocated. Before that time, it is hard to imagine a big garden being made largely with native plants, as is the case with Julie Wise's in Hertfordshire. And it was not until the 1990s that New Naturalism began to have such an impact on the thinking of ecologically minded professional gardeners like Keith Wiley.

The process was promoted by the sterling scientific research undertaken by zoologist Jennifer Owen, who minutely examined the inhabitants of her Leicester garden for 30 years, and greatly influenced a group of forward-thinking plant scientists and landscape technologists working at Sheffield University, in particular Ken Thompson, James Hitchmough and Nigel Dunnett. These men were responsible for helping to change common attitudes on wildlife gardening and sustainability by their work on pioneering urban meadows as well as green roofs. Articles by these scientists – also able writers – have been prominent in *The Garden*, which has always been keen to inform gardeners about the non-vegetable inhabitants of their gardens – beneficial and otherwise. The result has been that RHS members are now both more likely to include wild flowers and habitats in their gardens, and to understand better how wildlife, especially important insects like bees, operate. I have a personal interest here: my husband keeps honeybees, which has had a profound effect on my choice of plants, and we leave a large area of rough grass to suit the nesting habits of bumblebees.

But there is still a way to go. If Kevin McCloud is to be believed, we should really think in terms of tearing down the boundaries between our gardens to give wildlife the best chance. I cannot see it happening soon but you never know.

**URSULA BUCHAN**, editor

# Ecology Begins at Home (part 1)

KEN THOMPSON, JUNE 2010

t is a familiar scene. You are being shown round their garden, pausing occasionally to murmur your appreciation of this choice shrub or that artful piece of sculpture, when you come upon a corner that appears to consist largely of tall grass, nettles and brambles.

"Why is all this wildlife at home in an ordinary suburban garden?"

Your guide, with a light laugh, describes this as 'the wildlife garden', and you both quickly avert your eyes and move on to something less distressing. 'The wildlife garden' is a superficially appealing idea; after all, other parts of the garden have their specific uses (patio, veg plot, rockery and so on), so why not have a ghetto for wildlife?

And there probably is plenty of wildlife in there too – indeed the idea of 'wildlife garden as wilderness' has been a stock in trade of cartoonists for years. One of my favourites has two people looking at the uppermost extremities of a rhino projecting from some tall grass, one of them remarking, 'My, that's some wildlife garden'. The concept of 'wildlife garden as wilderness' also has the obvious attraction for many of requiring little actual gardening.

But does this mean there is little or no wildlife in the rest of the 'real' garden – the bit designed to look good and do what people want? It is worth considering ecologist Jennifer Owen's garden in Leicester, the only suburban domestic garden in Britain for which we have anything even approaching a complete wildlife inventory. For more than 15 years, Jennifer's garden was home, at least part of the time, to somewhere in excess of 8,000 species of insects. We do not know exactly how many because assembling a team of naturalists with the combined ability to identify everything living in the average garden would be almost impossible. But we do know, because she counted them, that her garden was host to around a third of Britain's large moths, butterflies, hoverflies, lacewings and ladybirds.

Jennifer's garden is really average. It is not unusually large (740sq m/ 7,970sq ft). It has a lawn, small pond, glasshouse, vegetable plot, fruit bushes, herbaceous borders, trees and shrubs. If it were lined up in an identity parade, along with my garden and another six randomly chosen suburban gardens, you would be hard put to pick it out as unusual. Perhaps its chief feature is that it is not particularly tidy. But I suspect – among Britain's 16 million gardens, many of whose owners are 'gardeners' by default rather than inclination – that makes it even more average.

So what is going on? Why is all this wildlife at home in an ordinary suburban garden? The fact is that gardens are just another habitat; wildlife does not care whether it lives in a 'garden', 'park' or other human-defined piece of land. In comparison with most natural landscapes, gardens are both intensively managed and hyper-fertile. This suits many animals, not least because there is usually plenty to eat, and a huge variety both of species and sizes of plants in a small space – far more than in any natural habitat.

On the other hand, undisturbed living space tends to be at a premium, which is why the chief feature of a garden good for wildlife is an abundance of permanent structure, both living and dead: trees, shrubs and hedges, compost heaps, fallen leaves and dead wood. In short, gardens, and the elements that go into them, are no better or worse for welcoming wildlife than any other space – they are just different. Consider this approach, and the designated 'wildlife area' soon seems counter-intuitive.

Thus wildlife gardening – or better still, gardening with wildlife in mind – is not about abdication of responsibility for part of your garden. It is not about trying to reproduce pale imitations of countryside habitats, first because this is almost impossible in an average garden, and second because the wildlife you are trying to please is very unlikely to notice anyway. Nor is it about sticking to a limited palette of native plants, not least because most native plants are not in cultivation, and you would not want to grow them if they were. But go ahead and grow natives if you want – some deserve to be more widely grown. Rather, it is about welcoming wildlife to your whole garden, not just a defined ghetto, whatever your gardening taste.

Many of the extraordinary number of species in Jennifer's garden were residents, but it is equally clear that many are part of a larger community that exploits a network of gardens and linked areas of other green space, such as parks, river banks, railway embankments and churchyards. All these parts of the jigsaw working together is what really generates the major benefits for wildlife, so one of the best things you can do is provide something otherwise lacking in your neighbourhood – a pond maybe. But just keep two thoughts in mind: don't be too tidy, and never forget that the wildlife in your garden is not there despite your gardening, but because of it.

# Ecology Begins at Home (part 2)

KEN THOMPSON, NOVEMBER 2010

Earlier this year, zoologist Jennifer Owen received two awards with little, at first sight, to connect them: the RHS Veitch Memorial Medal, and the British Ecological Society's Ecological Engagement Award. The former recognises Jennifer's unique contribution to gardening and the latter to the science of ecology. Both were for her long-term study of the wildlife inhabiting her modest suburban garden, and it is the garden's ordinariness, coupled with the length of the project – three decades – that makes her results so valuable.

"Few would contemplate assembling a complete inventory of the species in their garden for even one year; to persist for 30 years is an achievement that will probably never be equalled"

Jennifer graduated in zoology from the University of Oxford in 1958, then gained a PhD at the University of Michigan. In 1962 she moved first to the University College of Makerere (now Makerere University) in Uganda, then to Fourah Bay College, now the University of Sierra Leone. In Sierra Leone she first noticed that there seemed to be more wildlife in her garden than in the neighbouring forest. When she returned to a post at Leicester University in 1971, she wondered exactly what lived in her garden. Thus began the study that was to occupy the next 30 years.

Jennifer brought to this endeavour a thorough academic training in zoology, passions for natural history and gardening – and what turned out to be almost superhuman 'staying power'. Few would contemplate assembling a complete inventory of the species in their garden for even one year; to persist for 30 years is an achievement that will probably never be equalled. She recognised long before 'wildlife gardening' was fashionable (14 years before Chris Baines' first wildlife garden at the RHS Chelsea Flower Show), that gardens were an important, but unrecognised habitat for native wildlife. She saw that this did not depend upon creating 'fake countryside': her own Leicester garden is a neat, productive suburban garden for growing flowers and vegetables. Her only concessions have been to avoid pesticides and excessive tidiness.

From the start, Jennifer reported her findings in scientific journals, but she soon also began to communicate with a wider audience. Early results were published in a book, *Garden Life* (1983), and there were numerous articles in *The Garden, New Scientist* and the magazine *Organic Gardening*. In 1991 Cambridge University Press released an exhaustive summary of all her research in the book *The Ecology of a Garden: the First Fifteen Years*. This remains compulsory reading for anyone seriously interested in garden wildlife, and was at the time the most complete account of the wildlife of any garden anywhere in the world.

This month, the RHS publishes the complete story: *Wildlife of a Garden: a Thirty-year Study*. A third of a century is long enough to record many changes, the reasons for some obvious, others less so. For example, the effects of climate change are clearly shown by the arrival in the garden of gatekeeper and speckled wood butterflies, among the most abundant butterflies in the garden when surveying ended in 2001.

The study has demolished the belief that gardens are wildlife deserts – clearly the only reason anyone believed that was because no one had looked for wildlife there. Her meticulous records of herbivore host plants also led her to the insight that non-native, exotic garden plants can support a surprisingly high diversity of native herbivores. Jennifer has shown that any garden can be home to a range of wildlife. With recent well-documented declines in biodiversity in the agricultural landscape, this is a timely message – gardeners have never had such a responsibility for wildlife.

*The Ecology of a Garden* feels like a textbook, with long lists of Latin names. *Wildlife of a Garden*, though not a beginner's guide, is more accessible: anyone interested in garden wildlife will find it absorbing. You may think that does not include you, but this book could change your mind.

# Embellished by Nature

MATTHEW BIGGS, APRIL 2010

Natural history has been a passion for Julie Wise since childhood, when she would walk the Hertfordshire lanes identifying and picking wild flowers, her knowledge winning first prize for the most species in a posy at the local flower show. Rather than picking, Julie now plants. Over the past 15 years she has created a garden approximately 1.6ha (4 acres) in size – of which 1.4ha (3.5 acres) is wild flower meadow – at the cottage she shares with husband Tim, near Codicote, Hertfordshire; native plants blurring boundaries between countryside and garden. Hedges are shaped to echo the landscape, while wild flowers such as red campion and ox-eye daisies (blown into the garden or introduced by animals) are used as ornamentals, contrasting with garden plants such as grass, *Anemanthele lessoniana*, or peachy-pink poker, *Kniphofia* 'Timothy'. The garden is more than a hobby Julie enthuses, 'it was an antidote to my working life, as cabin crew, spending hours in an aircraft'.

*"...a giant laurel, with twisted stems and a crown raised by nibbling muntjac deer, provides an umbrella against winter wet..."*

Julie's early experiments with rampant roses and lavenders growing in clay were rapidly rejected. 'As I was away eight months of a year, my garden had to be self-managing; my whole philosophy had to be re-assessed,' she explains. The site is divided into several 'rooms', bounded by hornbeam and yew hedges radiating out from the cottage, creating a series of microclimates from shady borders to bogs and parched sunny areas.

Although Julie's job meant she was often unable to maintain the garden regularly, nature took up the task; self-seeded *Verbascum thapsis* (mullein) and patches of red campion soon appeared while she was not around to weed them out, and helped to shape her gardening ethos: 'I realised their beauty as garden ornamentals; where serendipity forms a pleasing combination, they are simply left to grow.' Wandering the meandering paths or from room to room, you find unexpected associations – bulbous buttercup with *Ligularia dentata* 'Desdemona'; cow parsley posing elegantly beside emerging foliage of *Crocosmia* 'Lucifer'; and the delicate features of common valerian highlighted by *Lysimachia ciliata* 'Firecracker'.

Yew hedges emanate from the lines of the cottage, creating a vista along double borders planted with robust, late-flowering herbaceous plants and grasses. One border is dry, the other wet. 'I wanted to use the colour and texture of emerging foliage as a feature, particularly in spring,' says Julie. A stellar blue haze of *Camassia leichtlinii* subsp. *suksdorfii* bursts above for a few weeks in May before foliage returns to the fore. There has been much experimentation and results are impossible to predict.

For example, *Digitalis ferruginea* was expected to cope in the dry border but failed, whereas October flowering *Aster lateriflorus* 'Lady in Black', with its purple-pink flowers and mildew-resistant dark foliage, has been a success. Julie takes advantage of the natural vigour of *Eupatorium purpureum*, growing it in the dry border, where conditions are not entirely to its liking; the location prevents it from becoming invasive, growing to only half its usual height, but it proves self-supporting and remains statuesque.

The double borders are weeded just once in the growing season (early April) and cut back in late January. Stems are shredded and material from the moist side is put onto the dry side, where the soil benefits from additional organic matter. Other areas are cut back earlier and debris thrown to the chickens who pick it over, adding their high nitrogen manure; composting is speeded up to about three weeks.

In the pretty kitchen garden where raised beds are filled with healthy looking vegetables, not all joints in the brick path are mortared. In some, pot marigolds, nasturtiums and *Chenopodium bonus-henricus* (good king Henry) self-seed to great effect. Elsewhere, below embracing boughs of a giant oak, an area that was constantly waterlogged proved to be the site of a woodland pond after it was found on an old map. The pond was re-dug and is now alive with newts, toads and frogs as well as the calls of young moorhens in spring. Around it, robust natives such as *Caltha palustris* (marsh marigold), *Iris pseudacorus* 'Variegata' (variegated flag iris) and *Osmunda regalis* (royal fern, thought extinct in the county as a wild plant) revel in moist shade. Nearby a giant laurel, with twisted stems and a crown raised by nibbling muntjac deer, provides an umbrella against winter wet. The area in its shadow has been topped with gravel to aid winter drainage, and is planted with dry-loving plants such as *Phlomis russeliana*, *Origanum laevigatum* 'Hopleys' and self-seeded *Agrostemma githago* (corncockle).

One surprising element to this garden is a formal-styled area, with a rectangular pond surrounded by lawn, yew cones and two tiers of clipped hornbeam hedges. It is a place of structured calm, whose green shades contrast with the billowing ebullience of the late summer garden. It has also become a valuable wildlife habitat. Frogs inhabit the pool and since the cutting height of the mower has been raised to 3in (7.5cm), *Prunella vulgaris* (self-heal) and daisies have colonised the lawn. Birds, including long-tailed tits, nest in the hedges.

'Throughout my career the garden was a saviour; it brought me back to reality, away from hotel rooms and airports to the wild flowers and countryside of my childhood. I'd often arrive home at dawn on a summer's day, exhausted from a long flight, put on my wellingtons and walk round the garden, still in my uniform – there's nothing more special than that,' Julie smiles.

# Wildlife and Rain-fed Ponds

RHS ADVICE, APRIL 2010

Some 50 percent of British native fresh-water plants and animals will thrive in non-permanent ponds, such as those fed by rainwater. Temporary ponds that may dry out completely are highly valuable habitats; the majority of aquatic animals live in shallow water only a few centimetres deep, so shallow ponds with gently sloping sides are best for wildlife.

Water levels in natural ponds usually drop 30–80cm (12–32in) between spring and autumn, so naturally-shallow ponds often dry out in summer. This is not a problem as such 'drawdown' leaves a valuable habitat of moist, muddy or sandy substrate around the edges colonised by a range of species, including many now highly endangered in Britain.

"Even newly-created wildlife ponds are quickly colonised"

Temporary ponds do not support fish, which are significant pond predators. Even newly-created wildlife ponds are quickly colonised. Try to resist the temptation to stock them with plants or animals – pond dwellers are adept colonisers by nature.

Among the invertebrates that will use non-permanent ponds are southern hawker dragonfly (*Aeshna cyanea*), which lay eggs in damp pond margins. Many aquatic insects, including the common great diving beetle (*Dytiscus marginalis*) and common backswimmer (*Notonecta glauca*) are good fliers, quick to colonise new ponds, and capable of leaving as they dry. Many caddis fly larvae also favour temporary ponds. A range of invertebrates can survive dry periods as eggs in the mud.

Amphibians such as frogs, toads and newts can all breed successfully in such ponds, providing they don't dry out until summer when their tadpoles have successfully metamorphosed into young adults. These in turn may attract predatory grass snakes.

Garden ponds may be visited by shrews, including the water shrew (*Neomys fodiens*). Our largest shrew, growing to 9.6cm (3¾in) and with a poisonous bite, hunts pond margins in the drawdown zone.

# In Praise of Bumblebees

URSULA BUCHAN, SEPTEMBER 2009

Have you ever watched a worker bumblebee suck nectar from a honeysuckle flower? What I find so fascinating about it is the way the bee balances on the protruding stamens of the flower to do so. 'Bumblebees are the best', my son used to say when he was small, and I couldn't find it in me to disagree. They are more interesting to a child than any other kind of bee, because the queens are so comparatively large, slow and clumsy, drone like Lancaster bombers and, if childish hands are very careful, can even be gently stroked on their backs without alarm (to them, that is, rather than the child).

To intrigue our children, we used to name bumblebees 'white bums', 'orange bums' and 'ginger bums', according to species. The use of the demotic appealed to them and so made these bees memorable. Its use also hid the fact that we grown-ups couldn't remember their Latin names, since bumblebees mostly don't have the common sort.

Quite a lot of what I do in my garden is aimed at fostering bumblebees, if only because they are excellent pollinators of fruit; indeed, they are as good as honeybees, although rarely given enough credit for it. Recently, when I opened the garden to visitors, I was asked why there were great swathes of thick and waving grassland, in what we call the 'paddock' beyond the garden proper. The grassland probably looked a little lank and dull to visitors, and was certainly an invitation to hay fever.

However, for me, it is a draw for butterflies, insects of many kinds, and a haven both for small mammals and bumblebees, which often nest in old mouse holes or in the basal tussocks of thick-growing grasses. Our policy of only mowing paths through the paddock, and leaving the rest to grow tall, has considerably increased the incidence of the commonest bumblebees – *Bombus hortorum, B. lucorum, B. terrestris, B. lapidarius* and *B. pascuorum* – in the garden. And, what's more, I now know their names.

# Get Extra Nectar Points in your Borders

NEWS, JANUARY 2014

Some garden favourites such as lavender and catmint have been recorded as being up to 100 times more attractive to pollinating insects than other equally ornamental plants.

A two-year study has revealed a surprising variation in how useful different garden plants are to bees and other pollinating insects. Researchers at the University of Sussex have been looking at the role flowering plants can play in helping to reverse declines in insect populations. Their report notes that by more judicious plant selection, gardens can be more bee- and insect-friendly at no extra cost, effort, or a loss of aesthetic attractiveness.

The results were striking. Of the 32 commonly grown summer-flowering garden plants assessed (including dahlias and borage), there was found to be a one-hundredfold variation in attractiveness to pollinators. *Agastache*, *Nepeta* and *Origanum* rated highly, as did lavender. However, the results demonstrated that not all lavenders are equally valuable. Cultivars of *Lavandula* x *intermedia* were much more attractive to pollinators than both English lavender (*L. angustifolia*) and French or butterfly lavender (*L. stoechas*).

Whether or not plants are native, a hybrid or a cultivar did not seem to affect its attractiveness to insects — openness of its flowers was far more important. Open-flowered *Dahlia* 'Bishop of Oxford' came 10th, whereas semi-cactus *D.* 'Tahiti Sunrise' was ranked 31st.

# Coffee 'Improves Bees' Memories'

NEWS, MAY 2013

Bees may enjoy a caffeine boost just as much as humans, suggest scientists at Newcastle University.

They found that bees that feed on nectar containing caffeine – present in the flowers of *Coffea* (coffee) and *Citrus* species such as grapefruit and oranges – are three times more likely to remember a flower's scent 24 hours later. Some bees remembered the scent for up to three days.

The team was studying caffeine as a defence compound, but found flowers seem also to use it to influence the behaviour of their pollinators, encouraging them to prefer their plant type as they are better able to remember it is a good nectar source.

# Stag Beetles

ANDREW HALSTEAD, JULY 2010

Stag beetles (*Lucanus cervus*) are Britain's biggest and heaviest beetles and should be encouraged by gardeners, as they help to break down dead wood and cause no damage to living plants. They can be relatively common in gardens in southeast Britain with light, sandy soils; small populations exist in a few other areas but elsewhere they are rare.

The male beetle gives this insect its common name – its pair of enlarged mandibles or jaws have a number of projecting spurs, like stags' antlers. Males vary considerably in size, being 35–75mm (1½–3in) long, including the mandibles, which they display to impress females and also use to push rival males aside. Despite their size and ungainly shape, male stag beetles are able to fly, doing so at dusk on warm evenings from May to August.

Female stag beetles have small mandibles without any spurs and range from 30mm to 50mm (1¾–2in) in length. Size probably relates to how well each insect was able to feed while it was in the larval stage. Grubs can be up to 110mm (4¼in) long, and curved like a letter C, with a plump, creamy white body and an orange-brown head. Larvae feed only on dead, rotting wood, so females seek out stumps and dead roots of deciduous trees, where they burrow into the soil to lay eggs.

The larval stage takes four to five years, sometimes longer, to complete before the grub is fully fed. It then encloses itself in an egg-shaped cocoon consisting of wood fragments and soil in which it will pupate. Adult beetles develop in autumn but remain in the pupal chamber until early summer of the following year.

Stag beetle larvae can be confused with cockchafer (*Melolontha melolontha*) grubs, but these feed on live roots and are unlikely to be associated with dead woody plants.

Numbers of stag beetles have declined in many parts of western Europe but distribution in Britain seems stable. The People's Trust for Endangered Species has organised several surveys since 1998 to help map UK distribution and to detect whether this may be changing. Stag beetles are most likely to be found south of a line from the Wash to the River Severn, especially the Home Counties, but there are scattered records in Wales, the Midlands and Yorkshire. Even within favoured parts of the country, stag beetles can be localised: they are uncommon in areas with chalky or clay soils.

Adult stag beetles are sometimes killed in large numbers by magpies and cats. In areas where stag beetles occur, they can be encouraged by leaving stumps of felled deciduous trees in the ground. Logs can be partially buried in the soil to provide feeding sites for larvae.

Stag beetles will also lay eggs in deep accumulations of wood chips, which provide moist conditions in which the larvae can develop.

# Natural Selection

KEITH WILEY, JULY 2000

A new style of gardening has been evolving in a relatively small number of gardens that has been loosely called 'new naturalism'. Its inspiration comes from natural landscapes and from the way plants grow in the wild. Around the world and independently of each other, some gardeners and a few designers are experimenting with a looser, freer form, each interpreting it in their own way. The style in my case differs from traditional planting primarily in the diversity and density of species occupying any given space. It appears as a flower-rich natural planting with certain species haphazardly recurring throughout the scheme. When wild flowers are part of the planting, these areas merge seamlessly with the broader natural landscape and, due to the greater number of species involved, the style lends itself perfectly to even the smallest of gardens. The relationship between new naturalism and traditional gardening is similar to that of the impressionist movement in art, in that I attempt to capture the impression of a natural planting rather than one of harmonised blocks, using colour in informal, blended drifts and dots instead.

"Many people return from overseas holidays or days out with postcards or small mementoes – but I come home with ideas, which may turn into another part of the garden"

When The Garden House, my garden in Devon, expanded into an adjoining field in 1993 I had room to give rein to this new style which had been slowly evolving in the older part of the garden. In this area, I have attempted to capture the essence of plantings that have caught my imagination in natural locations, not by slavishly copying them, but by using plants that I know will enjoy our exposed north-facing slope, high rainfall and acid loam soil. Many people return from overseas holidays or days out with postcards or small mementoes – but I come home with ideas, which may turn into another part of the garden. Touring the garden then becomes an exercise in revisiting all my favourite natural haunts – from Dartmoor in Devon to the South African Cape. New naturalism offers limitless possibilities to gardeners in that no two interpretations of the same landscape will be the same, but it may help to give a few guidelines that have produced a coherent style at The Garden House.

There are striking differences between communities of plants growing in the wild and in gardens. In nature it often appears that only a few species are dominating a given area. When I visited the south-western Cape of South Africa, one of the richest plant communities in the world, one specific area seemed dominated by the white, pink and blue of *Dimorphotheca, Senecio* and *Heliophila*. On closer inspection, the diversity became apparent, and I guessed that there could have been as many as 50 species in any square metre. Plants were growing at many heights like a miniature tropical forest, with various understoreys beneath the forest giants. The same colour combinations can be found in many West Country lanes in May with bluebells, pink campion and stitchwort – and other plants, notably ferns, primroses and buttercups – weaving almost unnoticed among these wonderful tapestries. This pattern is repeated time and again in nature. I interpret this in the garden by repeating a small number of species throughout the scheme as a framework, and allow other species to fill in the gaps.

Nature provides strong clues to the density of our planting. Gardeners traditionally plant at 'textbook' recommended spacings but these are more generous than usually occurs in the wild. For an example on a large scale, look into any natural woodland and notice the density and spacings of the trunks, or on a smaller scale how naturally occurring herbaceous plants find themselves only inches from their neighbours.

When making a new bed with herbaceous plants I do not deliberately plant close, in fact quite the reverse. The framework species are planted in informal groups with outlying singletons. Gaps are left before the next framework group and these spaces are filled with different species acting as dot plants or left unplanted to allow room for self-seeding. Quite deliberately, dot plants are often inveterate self-seeders, which are then able to colonise any space they can find. As I use home-made compost to make up many new beds, the surprise arrivals from self-seeding are usually most welcome. They are often seedlings of species growing elsewhere in the garden whose seedheads have been cut back and composted. *Verbena bonariensis* established itself initially by this unplanned route and is now determined (and invited) to colonise the garden.

Self-seeding in my informal naturalistic planting is one of the most important factors. However hard you try to plan informally, the finished result often looks as though it has been planted precisely. By allowing self-seeding you break up the 'planted' look and give the whole scheme a natural-looking diversity.

When making new beds it is more difficult to maintain a rich diversity of flora in a high-rainfall area and moisture-retentive soil unless the drainage is improved, as most of the best wild flowers occur on well-drained soils. I achieve this by raising the beds by 30cm (12in) or more into gently undulating mounds with whatever I can lay my hands on – often upturned turves buried 15cm (6in) deep, or spent potting compost and the soils from my own compost heaps.

This style of gardening may not suit everyone: there are no rules, no right or wrong way, and much is left to experimentation. But for those romantics flexible enough to enjoy the uncertainty of success, I guarantee a journey into an exciting new branch of gardening.

# Mini Meadows

NIGEL DUNNETT, JANUARY 2009

Interest in using wildflower meadows in gardens is still on the increase, but anyone who has tried to make a garden meadow from scratch will know that it is not as simple as it first appears, particularly if the meadow is in a small garden, or if it is intended to be attractive throughout the year.

When I began developing my own seed mixes for meadows it was with urban public space in mind, places such as housing areas and highways, where we desperately need to bring back nature, diversity and excitement into our everyday surroundings. Subsequently, however, the mixes have been used just as much at the small scale.

The term meadow is, in truth, something of a misnomer when applied to my mixes. Although they look like, and are managed as, meadows, these are not true wildflower meadows. They are a different concept: 'pictorial meadows', designed for visual impact and appeal, ease of maintenance, reliability, and non-stop flowering. True, I was partly inspired by beautiful displays of cornfield poppies in the countryside, but I soon realised that British native species on their own have a short flowering period, with little colour after mid-to-late July.

> "...I soon realised that British native species on their own have a short flowering period, with little colour after mid-to-late July"

I began to look further afield for species that come from similar habitats but which flower either earlier or later, or which give colours that are not available in the UK. For example, North American 'prairie annuals' such as *Rudbeckia hirta* (black-eyed Susan) or *Coreopsis tinctoria* (tickseed) do not flower until July and August, and will continue into the autumn. If I combined these exotics with British natives, could I develop a continuously flowering mixture?

Sixty hardy annuals were trialled at Sheffield Botanical Gardens. They were assessed for length of flowering, visual impact and ease of germination. The plants crucially received no irrigation or deadheading; only those that gave exceptional performance were considered further.

Colour-themed combinations of the best performers were then trialled for another year until we were confident enough to try the mixtures in large- and small-scale areas in public parks in Sheffield. Subsequently the mixes have been used in other locations, and then further refined according to practical experience and public reaction. The key to these mixes is that they have a long flowering season in the same piece of ground, with minimal input. We achieve this by using a successional approach to formulating mixes. Early-flowering species (usually flowering in about eight weeks from sowing) are short, and we use them in quite low numbers: they flower against a foil of the fresh green foliage of the later-flowering species.

We include a higher proportion of the later-flowering species in the mix – they are taller and grow up and hide the dying remains of the earlier species. After flowering, mixes can be left to stand over winter for their seedheads and skeletons, or can be cut back to ground level in autumn. They are annuals, so they do need to be re-sown each year, and grow best in good soil and full sun. In heavy shade or wet conditions they will not be successful.

The beauty of these mixtures is that they create big, impressionistic effects at the large scale, while at the same time they are highly effective used on a small scale, such as in a domestic back garden, or even, potentially, in a window box. Wherever the mixtures are used, the response is positive: they seem magnetic to children and adults alike. Looking forward, new and exciting colour blends, as well as mixtures for difficult or troublesome locations are in development, which will help broaden the appeal of these 'pictorial meadows' yet further.

# Leaps and Bounds

KEVIN MCCLOUD, SEPTEMBER 2010

We British are careful about delineating the edge of things. We love borders, fencing, trellis. Our lives are marked out by boundaries – the threshold of our home, the bodywork of cars, the office divider. Planning applications and deeds are marked with red boundary lines; garden edges are marked with red mist. And Leyland cypress.

I would argue that, right now, our attitude to the world outdoors is pretty dire. Garden design, thanks to the likes of Tom Stuart-Smith and Dan Pearson, may be attempting to reconnect to the rhythms and energies of the natural world but for most people nature is still the enemy. Gardening remains an introspective, artificial and chemically intensive activity. Every year in Britain (according to Georgina Downs' UK Pesticides Campaign) we tip 7,300 tonnes of pesticide, fungicide and herbicide onto non-agricultural land, comprising,

"...there are signs of more open and co-operative attitudes to gardening"

in a large part, gardens. A 2007 survey for the Pesticides Safety Directorate revealed that 45 percent of us that own a patch of land use lawn treatments, and 50 percent use weedkillers. Half of us also put unwanted pesticides in the dustbin ready to contaminate someone else's land. All together this makes gardening something of a selfish activity.

I say 'right now' when I really mean 'until recently' because there are signs of more open and co-operative attitudes to gardening. We are working more with nature: although no one knows just how many organic gardeners there are, organic clubs are available across Britain and the number of people applying to learn how to 'no-dig' garden, for example, with the luminary Charles Dowding and others, are increasing exponentially.

People are also co-operating more with each other. Guerrilla gardening – the practice of cultivating someone else's barren land without their permission, often on redundant building sites – has not taken off in these peaceable isles as it has on the streets of New York, but the blistering increase in allotment applications is testament to how we Brits like to redistribute the wealth of our land. As is the swelling interest in landshare, where growers are put in touch with landowners who hold fallow land; at least 50,000 people have subscribed so far.

But for some, this is not enough. Researchers from the University of Leeds, writing in February's *Trends in Ecology and Evolution* magazine, are calling for us to take down our boundary fences and smudge the red boundary line. Their paper says that if we act together we can create wildlife corridors through suburbia. If we collaborate with our neighbours we can form interlinking habitats, increase biodiversity and encourage more birds, mammals and insects. We need to start gardening ecologically and collectively.

I do not know if we are ready to break down the larchlap and merge our gardens, but I intend to find out. In Swindon, where my company, Hab, is building ecological housing, we are offering residents both small private gardens and larger shared spaces in collective ownership. We are letting people own fruit trees on the corner of the street and the polytunnel in the allotment. Let's hope our residents do not decide to buy up their share of those 7,300 tonnes of biocide.

## Pooling resources

Plans for future projects include private gardens shared between a dozen or so households (just look at how London squares have managed this idea so well for several centuries), shared sheds (think of the scale and the chance for bonding over the workbench) and shared power tools. The latter idea seems sacrilegious, but not when you consider that the average power tool only gets used for a total of four minutes, ever.

Sharing is the great secret weapon of sustainability, the principle of co-operation and coexistence that allows us to enjoy choice, as well as better relationships with each other and the natural environment. And gardening should be part of that natural environment. So let me suggest that although we would find it difficult to knock a row of houses into one and share our private dwellings, I think we would find it refreshing and rewarding – and so, it seems, would the wildlife – if we gardened with biodiversity in mind. Even a little. I'll be the first to visit a suburban street where the residents demolish half their fencing and co-garden a shared strip of biodiverse, organic land running behind their houses. I might even buy them a shed.

# THE ENVIRONMENT

*Note from the editor*

The words 'environment', 'biodiversity', 'sustainability', and 'conservation' were either not known to our Victorian forebears, or they meant something rather different. But they have become part of our everyday vocabulary now, as we learn more and more about what difficulties our planet and its inhabitants face. Gardeners, natural nurturers of course, have shown themselves extremely interested and affected by these difficulties, doing what they can to promote wild flowers and wildlife (as we saw in the previous chapter), as well as trying to garden sustainably and with a light carbon footprint. Nigel Dunnett – a pioneer in this field – writes about a green roof in London, while Lynne Maxwell sees the value of matching plant to situation, especially in a challenging environment like the seaside, and Susie Holmes ponders about a life after peat.

The RHS has lately been in the forefront of the debate as these complex issues affect both the amateur and professional gardener. There are not always easy answers nor does everyone agree with each other as to the nature of the problem – or solution (as can be gleaned from Helen Yemm's article on trying to be an almost organic gardener). For example, the claim, counterclaim and claim again, on whether alien plants are a real problem, shows that the Society's publications can be a source of lively, if very well-behaved, debate.

Conservation does not just mean shielding native plants from possibly thuggish aliens, or hanging on to heritage fruit and vegetable varieties to preserve a diverse gene pool (something which the garden historian, Toby Musgrave, emphasises). The word should embrace gardens as well as plants, although it does not do so enough. John Sales ponders the particularly fraught problem of how to save small gardens, while Tradescant (the nom de plume taken by Hugh Johnson for his diary column) reminds us that the environment has an aesthetic, as well as a scientific, meaning which should not be forgotten, if our gardens are to give others as much pleasure as they give us.

**URSULA BUCHAN**, editor

# Peaceful Enjoyment

HUGH JOHNSON (WRITING AS TRADESCANT), AUGUST 2005

I fear there is no landscape equivalent to the right to peaceful enjoyment. You are permitted to feel aggrieved (even if you have little redress) when someone insists on playing loud music in the open air. When they plant bright-yellow conifers in a green landscape you just have to look the other way.

It is a tricky subject, and I may well provoke the sort of letters I received when I wrote about garden-visitors' clothes. Scarlet anoraks, I said, did little for other visitors' appreciation of a colour scheme not including scarlet. I bring it up again now because we have just been in North Wales, in a valley where forestry trees jostle with ancient woodland in all-green harmony, which brings on the cliché of a tapestry faster than I can stop it. Tapestry or symphony, it is soothing, intricate and, during the growing season, when bright young beech, warm oak, soft hemlock and almost lurid shoots of Douglas fir are like the dabs of an Impressionist's brush, quietly beautiful.

Thick-walled cottages of dark slatey stone emerge from the vegetation like rocks in a shallow sea. They look less integrated, though, when their owners go down to the garden centre and buy a clutch of deviant cypresses and the rhododendron currently in flower: the red one. The effect is like flotsam (or possibly jetsam) – at any rate the sea polluted with foreign objects: a yellow oilskin, perhaps, and a red lifebuoy. Your instinct is to scoop them up and dispose of them, to restore the picture. Not so easy, though, if they have been chosen, paid for, and planted.

Loud colours are not called that by chance. And they seem loudest when they are isolated: a single rhododendron stirs you to pluck it out, while a whole hillside of them is almost soothing – except to foresters.

One can see the householder's point of view – from his window yellow foliage may give him a faint suggestion of the not-always-shining sun. And plants contrasting with the surroundings proclaim territory: this is my patch, they say, and I'll plant what I like. I am not suggesting that these pleasures are illicit (any more than a red anorak), only that they affect others more than you might think.

# Three Perspectives on Alien Plants

## THE 'ALIEN INVASION' MYTH

### DAVID PEARMAN, DECEMBER 2011

Gardeners are in danger of becoming scapegoats for the perceived threat of alien plants spreading in the countryside. The picture is hopelessly confused by unsubstantiated myths: that alien plants are deemed to be one of the great threats to biodiversity, and that it is gardeners who are responsible (and if we only planted from an 'approved list' all would be well).

> "...the gardener's contribution to the spread of aliens is the smallest of beers in the wider picture"

The truth is that nobody knows. For the last 20 years I have co-ordinated our Society's largest network of botanical recorders (from the Botanical Society of the British Isles): together we have accumulated about 18 million records, covering the entire area and 4,000 species. In simple terms, the data shows that most aliens are rare; that they occur overwhelmingly in and around towns and transport networks; and they are generally uncommon in the semi-natural habitats that we mostly want to preserve. The recording of alien plants is, broadly, a recent phenomenon, and all extrapolations should be taken with a large pinch of salt.

The trouble is that scare stories attract headlines, funding and a large industry – from the Government's Non-Native Species Secretariat to the 'invasive species officers' of conservation charities. There has been scientific research to show that Himalayan balsam (*Impatiens glandulifera*) largely only displaces other aliens or thuggish natives; that native bluebells (*Hyacinthoides non-scripta*) are under only a minute and local threat from garden outcasts; and even Japanese knotweed (*Fallopia japonica*) harbours both a spring flora and late pollen for bees.

But the real, inescapable line is that our countryside and flora is changing like never before, mainly from abandonment of traditional management practices and pollution. It is largely 'native' plants that are to blame – look at the chalk downlands of southern England (choked with gorse on the dip slopes) or our rivers (a vast increase in reeds, due to higher nutrients).

Yes, some gardeners are irresponsible, and yes, many ponds and some rivers have been harmed by garden plants dumped in the wild. But even taking those into account, the gardener's contribution to the spread of aliens is the smallest of beers in the wider picture.

## THE GB NON-NATIVE SPECIES SECRETARIAT STRIKES BACK

### NIALL MOORE, MARCH 2012

Non-native species (plants and animals) are vital for agriculture and our economy – only a minority of them become invasive. In Britain about 18 percent of established non-native species have known negative impacts, but more than 40 percent of established aquatic plants cause problems. Many terrestrial plants such as Japanese knotweed (*Fallopia japonica*), that seemed harmless a century ago, now cause serious problems. This is not just a problem in urban areas, with *Gunnera* taking over fields in Ireland, American skunk cabbage (*Lysichiton americanus*) threatening wet woodlands, and rhododendron invading oak woods.

"...invasive aliens (both plants and animals) are the second biggest threat to global diversity"

The Government recognises that there are many ways by which non-native species get into the wild, and we are working with many sectors to minimise introduction – prevention is far better than cure.

Addressing David Pearman's three 'myths':

Under the global Convention on Biological Diversity, invasive aliens (both plants and animals) are the second biggest threat to global diversity.

A 2010 report from international scientific organisation CABI estimated the cost of all invasive non-native species to the British economy at £1.7 billion per year, but this is likely to be an underestimate. Much of the cost is due to impacts on agriculture and horticulture, but extends to devaluation of properties. Japanese knotweed alone costs £166 million each year.

Involvement is far-ranging – the Invasive Non-Native Species Framework Strategy is a partnership between three administrations, their agencies, a range of non-governmental partners and community projects. But the administrative focus is the GB Non-Native Species Secretariat, with two staff members.

## IN SUPPORT OF ALIENS

NEWS, FEBRUARY 2014

A leading ecologist has stood up for non-native (alien) plants, saying there is little evidence to prove the majority have any negative effect on the environment.

Speaking at the third RHS John MacLeod Annual Lecture in London at the end of last year, Ken Thompson, Senior Research Fellow at the University of Sheffield, said natives and non-natives can happily co-exist – many exotics add to the diversity of the UK's natural flora as well as its gardens, he believes. He invited scientists, gardeners and conservationists to look at the merits and flaws of each non-native plant on a case-by-case basis. 'Just because a plant is an alien, it doesn't mean we shouldn't like it and, more importantly, it doesn't necessarily make it invasive,' he said. He went on to explain that some British natives are as, if not more, aggressive than many aliens – bracken and nettles, for example. 'If bracken wasn't native, it would be classed as a national emergency,' he said.

Although many biologists studying invasive species believe that non-native plants are undesirable, conservationists and gardeners take a different view. Some of the UK's most beautiful 'wild' plants such as snake's head fritillary and arable weeds including corn cockle are subject to conservation efforts despite being introduced to Britain. 'They have been here long enough to become "honorary natives",' said Ken.

In gardens, aliens can provide benefits too, he said. Many are welcomed (including some that fall out of favour when they escape to the wild) because they improve aesthetics through a variety of colour and form, and provide a 'pollinator heaven' (a broad food source for a range of fauna).

> "If bracken wasn't native, it would be classed as a national emergency"

# Why Grow Heritage?

TOBY MUSGRAVE, FEBRUARY 2012

Do you ever wonder when, and from where, our favourite fruits and vegetables originated; who first grew them; how they got their names; and which cultivars are still available today? The fascinating answers are perhaps one reason why there is resurgent interest in cultivating heritage

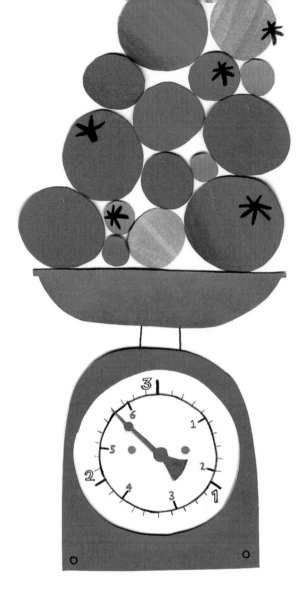

fruits and vegetables. And as to the definition of 'heritage' – there isn't one. Most proponents agree that the cultivar should not be used in large-scale commercial cultivation and that it must be propagated by open-pollination (in the case of seed) or by grafting and cuttings (in the case of fruit). Age is another criterion, but there is no set cut-off date: some believe a heritage cultivar must be at least 50 years old, others 100.

However fascinating the stories are, we would be entitled to ask if nurseries and seed catalogues are not filled with enough new and enticing selections to render old-fashioned cultivars redundant? The first part of the question is without doubt accurate, but many gardeners choose to grow heritage crops because they possess favourable characteristics, such as superior taste and a lengthy ripening period (in contrast with F1 hybrids, which all ripen simultaneously and result in gluts of produce). Even so, there is more to the answer.

"Europe has lost perhaps 2,000 fruit and vegetable cultivars since the 1970s"

Europe has lost perhaps 2,000 fruit and vegetable cultivars since the 1970s. In the USA, the Center for Biodiversity and Conservation estimates that 96 percent of the commercial vegetable cultivars that were available in 1903 are now extinct. This cultural loss is abhorrent, but perhaps more worrying is the loss of genetic diversity.

To put the potentially devastating consequences of such losses in context, the main reason why the Irish potato famine was so devastating was that potato cultivation was a monoculture – only one cultivar, 'Lumper', was grown. And when one plant succumbed to blight, so did the entire crop. More recently, in 1972 in America, several genetically similar cultivars of sweet corn succumbed to blight. The national loss of the harvest was 15 percent, and as high as 50 percent in some southern states. It is therefore imperative for future diversity that we lose no more cultivars.

The loss of so many cultivars in the 20th century was the direct result of two linked factors. Firstly, plant breeders, in response to changes in consumer behaviour, have created cultivars which possess characteristics that our great-grandparents would never have considered. For example: robustness, in order to reduce damage during harvest, handling and transport; uniformity of size and shape; and longevity of shelf life.

The second factor was ill-considered legislation enacted in the 1960s and 1970s to protect plant breeders' investments. It became illegal to commercially sell seeds that were not included on a UK (or other EU country) national list. To 'list' a cultivar was expensive and only worthwhile if commercially viable – something many heritage crops are not. Fortunately, as a result of intense lobbying, the UK Government now recognises a 'Vegetable Conservation Variety', which it defines as 'a landrace or plant variety, which has been traditionally grown in particular localities or regions and is threatened by genetic erosion'. There is, of course, still a cost to list a cultivar, but it is reduced.

In recent years the commercialisation of production and retail has stimulated a wide-ranging debate about what we eat, its provenance and cultivation. 'Organic' is more mainstream rather than 'alternative' and 'growing your own' continues to enjoy a renaissance.

There are organisations dedicated to preserving heritage cultivars, but what can the general public do to help? As individuals and consumers we can make ourselves and others aware of the issues and support institutions that preserve heritage cultivars. As gardeners, we can grow heritage crops and make a positive contribution to ensure the long-term survival of our horticultural heritage and genetic diversity, while enjoying the rich tastes and stories of the past.

# Growing Along the Edge

LYNNE MAXWELL, AUGUST 2013

As an island nation, the sea is all around us; it has helped chart the course of British history and has a great influence on our climate. No one perhaps knows this better than gardeners who cultivate a patch where land meets sea.

"One of the main recommendations coastal gardeners give is to work with the conditions, and use plants that want to grow there"

Coastal gardens include many of Britain's most celebrated: Trebah (among many in Cornwall), Inverewe in the Scottish Highlands and Abbotsbury Subtropical Gardens in Dorset have all been developed to make the most of the specific conditions and microclimates found there.

Gardening on the coast can be challenging. Desiccating, salt-laden winds (gales, all too often) ensure only the toughest plants grow unless shelter is provided. In winter, bitter continental air may at times invade, and blast the east coast of the UK, making it far colder than the western seaboard. Soils tend to be sandy, salty and light, nutrient poor and unable to retain much moisture, a particular problem on the east coast with its lower rainfall.

By contrast, west-coast British gardens benefit from a great advantage. Here the sea harbours a rich treasure – the North Atlantic Drift – which massages our coastline with a conveyor belt of relatively warm water, lending coastal regions milder climes than inland areas. Temperatures can differ, even across an island such as Mull, Scotland, by as much as 7°c (12°F) from west coast to east.

At the other end of the UK, on the Isle of Wight, the warm current comes from the south-west, creating a microclimate at Ventnor Botanic Garden, which sits in a valley nestled next to the warm sea. Records dating to 1850 there show a lowest recorded temperature of only -5.8°c (21.6°F).

For coastal gardeners, establishing a windbreak is the first priority, as it is salt-laden winds that do most damage. *Cupressus macrocarpa*, *Pinus radiata*, or *Olearia traversii* are favoured first lines of defence, with *Tasmannia lanceolata*, *Pittosporum* and *Griselinia* forming the rearguard. Sweet chestnut and sycamore are also wind- and salt-resistant.

A windbreak should not be dense, but allow winds to filter through rather than hitting it like a 'wall', as that can cause turbulence as it slides over the top. Protected sites may not need windbreaks to the same extent; at Ness Botanic Gardens on the Wirral, for example, some screens proved unnecessary and have been removed to open up the view. Holm oaks (*Quercus ilex*) favoured when the gardens were established remain, but Leyland cypresses have gone. In smaller spaces, sorbus and elder (pruned annually) are effective.

The exposed nature of many coastal sites means soil tends to be thin. Mulching is often an answer, although vegetable matter will not stay put on windy, sloping sites. Local pebbles, crushed stone and gravel can be placed around plants to retain moisture, and weigh down organic mulches beneath.

Coastal gardeners do have access to a useful mulch and fertiliser: seaweed. Bladderwrack and related kinds dry out quickly, but mixed with damp leaves and incorporated into borders and vegetable plots, they break down fast.

Sometimes extreme conditions demand extreme measures, such as 'reverse gardening' where the grass is stripped off, revealing skeletal, nutrient-poor soil. This technique has been used at Overbecks in south Devon to create a garden where proteas, leucadendrons and restios thrive, all of which do best on poor soils.

Once shelter and soil have been dealt with, it is time to look at plants. The beauty of coastal gardening is that plants will often grow here that will not thrive further inland. Even gardens on Britain's east coast enjoy the warming effect of the nearby seas, rendering frosts rare and usually short-lived. Around the UK coast, a tempting range of species of subtropical and Mediterranean plants can be considered – from *Eucalyptus*, *Callistemon*, *Cistus* and *Echium* to agaves, *Puya*, *Aloe* and even – if sheltered – bananas.

One of the main recommendations coastal gardeners give is to work with the conditions, and use plants that want to grow there. Plant small trees and bushes, and silver-leaved plants, which naturally reflect the bright sun and resist drying winds. Push the boundaries of what is possible, especially over temperatures and hardiness. Accept there will be losses, but balance these against wonderful surprises. Above all, enjoy the one coastal perennial that survives everything – the view.

# What Future for Peat?

SUSIE HOLMES, MARCH 2010

Peat-based composts are, for a generation of gardeners, synonymous with gardening. Almost all the plants we buy are grown in them and they constitute the vast majority of composts sold – in fact home gardeners account for about 70 percent of all UK peat use.

"Our reliance on peat is fairly recent – gardeners have adapted to changes before, and so can again"

Our love affair with peat-based compost began in the 1970s when peat took over from loam-based John Innes mixes, transforming the horticultural industry in the process. Until recently most 'multipurpose compost' and growing bags were 100 percent peat, with lime and fertiliser added, although many products now contain at least 10–20 percent other materials as manufacturers (encouraged by the UK Government) try to reduce peat use.

So why can we not carry on using peat to grow plants? There are two major concerns over peat extraction.

The loss of biodiversity from rare lowland peat habitats has historically been the main problem, and Government targets for peat extraction are part of the UK Biodiversity Action Plan, developed as a response to the 1992 Convention on Biological Diversity, encouraging sustainable development.

The second and more recent concern is the loss of peat as an important store of carbon, once bogs are drained and peat extracted. This peat, over time, gradually breaks down, giving off $CO_2$, a greenhouse gas. As a result, new Government targets for peat replacement will be linked to the 'Act on $CO_2$' campaign. As such a large proportion of horticultural peat is used by home gardeners, there is pressure on the gardening public to do their bit, in addition to efforts by the professional sector.

Although a UK Government target set some years ago to make 90 percent of composts peat-free by 2010 will not be met, limited progress has been made – a reduction of around 25 percent has so far been achieved.

Arguments that far more peat is burned in power stations globally than used in horticulture are unlikely to make any difference, either – in the battle to reduce greenhouse gas emissions, every bit saved helps.

We should not assume replacing all or some peat in a mix is bad. Blending in materials such as bark and wood fibre can improve drainage, while green compost or loam improves water and nutrient holding, creating mixes which are actually better for growing in than pure peat. However, there is no mix ideal for every situation, and gardeners will find some blends are better for certain uses; a coir-based mix is good for seed sowing and propagation, for example, but a blend with bark or wood fibre will probably suit outdoor planters.

There is nothing new about this, in essence – gardeners have long blended their own media for specific uses, but the materials manufacturers are adding to shop-bought media may be in some cases unfamiliar. Moreover, it is not always easy to ascertain the precise ingredients in a bag of 'compost'.

Manufacturers, however, are now improving labelling so it should soon be easier to see what the peat content is – and which other materials are used in the mix. Some are even adopting a bar-chart system in much the same way packaging of certain foods shows the fat and salt content. The Government is also encouraging more in-store information to make it easier for gardeners to make 'greener' growing media choices.

Often, the biggest problem gardeners have when changing to a new growing medium is with watering. Some reduced-peat or peat-free media dry quickly on the surface yet are still moist below, making it all too easy to overwater plants. However, an advantage of this drier surface is reduced moss and liverwort growth compared to peat mixes. It may also be necessary to feed plants differently in reduced-peat or peat-free media. Coir-based mixes may need feeding earlier and mixes containing green compost may last longer without feeding because of the slow-release nutrients in the compost.

No one material can replace peat, but the quality of alternatives has improved hugely and, as a result, the RHS is committed to helping gardeners reduce peat use. If you are not confident, try a reduced-peat mix first, especially for specialist plants. For tubs of shrubs or summer bedding, quality peat-free media should perform well.

The key to success with new growing media is managing watering and nutrition, and not expecting them to behave like peat. The Government will continue to encourage gardeners to use less peat, which should mean a wider choice of reduced-peat and peat-free products, with better information on packs and in store. Our reliance on peat is fairly recent – gardeners have adapted to changes before, and so can again.

# Shades of Green

HELEN YEMM, MAY 2009

If nothing else, the garden media blitz of the past 25 years or so has improved the understanding of gardening basics – and most recently has made us look at the part we gardeners play in protecting the environment. When I started out, chemical-free, truly organic gardening was the province of a tiny minority with gardens usually marred by unsightly props (recycled car tyres and swirly-patterned carpets as I recall).

> " ...were it not for the odd spot of glyphosate I would still be struggling with bindweed"

For the rest of us, garden pests could be miraculously wiped out with drenches of malodorous wonder-gunk developed primarily to benefit agriculture – never mind, apparently, the natural predators and bees that got caught in the firing line. A lawn-perfectionist's wormcast problem was 'solved' using chlordane, while slug pellets containing methiocarb were most often chucked around by the fistful. If this sounds like a horror story from yesteryear, it is worth remembering that it was not that long ago.

Passionate about my garden, I sat firmly on the fence. I still blush at the recollection of an exchange I had with a chap who, it transpired, was a major luminary from what is now Garden Organic. Asked whether I gardened organically, I replied – thinking of my compost heap and frog-filled pond – that yes, I did 'partially'. This was clearly the wrong answer and he told me so. You couldn't be a 'partially' organic gardener then, and of course by Garden Organic standards, you still can't. The word 'organic' has perhaps become devalued in strength and meaning since, but thankfully the stick is rarely wielded by the purists – and a carrot is now dangled by the horticultural retail trade with an ever-expanding range of new products.

While I still don't belong to the increasing, completely 'green' minority, and I am still sitting on that fence, I have gradually changed my ways. Whereas before I played at it, now I compost and make leafmould on a truly epic scale – common sense and a basic organic-gardening must-do. But I still simply cannot bear watching thriving ornamental garden plants being eaten, and the natural predators I encourage – frogs, hedgehogs and birds – seemingly just can't keep up. So I still target leaf-munchers (and fungal infections, too) using a range of contact and systemic products that I find provide the best, longest-lasting protection. Ironically perhaps, what was clearly just a shrewd marketing move – selling ready-mixed garden chemicals in convenient, expensive and un-green disposable trigger-spray bottles – has limited my use of them.

Without using chemicals, controlling our two most reviled pests – slugs and snails – is tricky. 'Dog-eat-dog' biological pest controls are good news for gardeners, but expecting us to rely on slug-busting nematodes is unrealistic: slugs canter around my borders well before the soil is warm enough for nematodes to be effective. So I resort as well to a mixture of copper and grit barricades, environmentally-friendly slug pellets and nocturnal hunting armed with torch. Yet by August my hostas are in shreds.

And on my allotment? In common with many new veg growers, I feel it makes little sense to grow crops and then douse them with chemicals. I use nematodes to control slugs around my spuds, use barriers and meshes to keep pests off crops, and grow cultivars known to resist pests and diseases, since control using organic methods is hit and miss. Despite initially keeping much of the weed-infested ground under black plastic for almost a year, were it not for the odd spot of glyphosate I would still be struggling with bindweed. In short, I suspect that I carry on much the way other gardeners do: at the moment we choose a shade of 'green' that suits us, simply because we can – but for how long?

One by one, the chemicals on which a whole gardening generation became dependent are being withdrawn, replaced by alternatives deemed to be less damaging. Many of us find this irksome. How much environmental damage do we actually do with our increasingly occasional, responsibly-aimed insecticides, fungicides or carefully-targeted weedkilling? I read that in the next decade more stalwarts may disappear – such as glyphosate (as in Round-up) and bifenthrin (as in Bug Clear) – yet we won't know how effective their replacements will be until we get them.

So whither 'partially organic' gardeners like me? Faced with fewer and fewer choices, we will have to accelerate a process that for most of us is already under way – that of weaning ourselves off dependence on products deemed to be environmentally unsound and adopting alternative ways of doing things. We are now better informed about gardening generally. So, as a result, we will have to make sensible planting decisions and (this will be hard for me) not pack our plants in to our gardens so closely, to realise that less is not just more – but that less is also healthier and not so pest ridden. It is not going to be easy.

# High Chaparral

NIGEL DUNNETT, DECEMBER 2010

Climbing down the three-metre ladder from David Matzdorf's green roof on the top of his curved London house feels like the botanical equivalent of descending several thousand metres down a South American mountain in a few seconds. The rooftop is similar to a sunlit Mexican hillside studded with agaves. Below, the narrow space to the front of the house feels like a shady tropical forest floor. The house is so enveloped in vegetation that from above, and from much of the street, it is camouflaged to the point of invisibility.

This was, in part, a necessity: a green roof helped persuade the local authority to grant planning consent for the house, on a tiny 'infill' site in the London Borough of Islington, with strict controls on the type, character, and amount of new-build in an established neighbourhood.

To minimise visibility from the street, a stipulation was that the west end of the house, the most visible, could only be one storey high and the east end two. David, who has an architectural background, worked with architect Jon Broome to develop the novel solution of a curved roof linking the two storeys, covered by the green roof.

A further planning condition required that the house be set back 5m (16ft) from the road; this tiny area became the only available space for a garden on the ground, so the green roof more than doubles David's garden space. A passionate horticulturist, he wanted to take advantage of the ecological and environmental benefits that green roofs offer. His particular interest was to attempt to create a roof with significant biodiversity value, but planted predominantly with exotic or garden plants. The roof is mainly an experiment, testing which plants succeed and which fail in this sheltered site, benefiting from London's urban heat island, as it is likely less hardy plants can survive on the roof compared with other parts of the UK. Failure of plants from Mediterranean climates (such as southern Europe, South Africa, Mexico, and south-western USA) in the UK is not so much winter cold itself, but winter cold, persistent wet soils and damp air.

"...it may be easier to grow many Mediterranean-climate plants on roofs than in the ground"

'Little expires directly from the cold,' says David, 'but plants are weakened, and damaged roots succumb to rotting in spring.' Green roofs, with free draining substrates and good air movement, provide ideal opportunities for growing such plants. Being elevated, they also avoid frost pockets.

## Planting with a passion

David first became interested in plants in the 1980s. Living in a London housing scheme, he offered to look into planting options to liven up the dreary, depressing landscape outside his windows. Once he started researching planting options for the site, he was hooked – it led to him studying for an RHS certificate in horticulture, which developed into a passion for exotic gardening.

By the mid-1990s David was looking for some garden space of his own. 'I wanted to live as close to central London as possible, and the only way that I could afford to do that was to build my own house on this postage-stamp of a site.' Having a green roof on the house was a given. David planted the roof himself. 'I imagined I could plant the whole roof immediately in the summer of 2000 with beautiful and interesting exotic plants,' he says. The sheer number required was daunting, however. He first ordered a bulk supply of sedum 'plug' plants for ground cover. Planting was arduous: slits had to be cut through an erosion mat, the underlying soil removed, the plant installed, then the hole backfilled. Every evening after work in summer 2001 he came home and planted batches of plugs until the whole roof was covered.

Initially there was some adverse reaction from neighbours: the newly planted roof appeared stark, with patches of plants poking through the matting. 'People expected it to green and mature immediately,' says David.

The sedum cover was only the starting point – David always intended to experiment with his plantings. Early woody additions, in 2001/2002, included magenta-flowered *Cistus* x *pulverulentus* 'Sunset', pale pink *C.* x *skanbergii* and rosemary. Above all, he wanted to try out new plants in this environment. 'I am at heart an experimental gardener,' David says, 'and quite prepared to have successes and failures – I don't lose too much sleep over something that dies.'

In 2006, prompted by the proliferation of weeds, David wanted to try a wider range of drought-resistant plants. First were three *Dasylirion wheeleri*, with radiating whorls of narrow, grey-green leaves, established on raised mounds. 'This wasn't a deliberate technique initially,' says David; 'the rootballs were simply too big to fit in the 10cm depth of soil.' Now, this is his main technique to establish larger plants. The mounds lift the plants' crowns above the 'general sog' of the roof, giving extra protection against winter wet. To start with, David used gravel around the rootballs, but now he uses a more lightweight mix of sharp sand and perlite to add depth to the growing medium in places. The yucca-like dasylirions established well (he recommends them for anyone wishing to try something exotic on a green roof), and gave him a mental picture of a Mexican hillside, as did the acquisition of other appropriate species such as *Agave* and aloes. Of the 18 agaves he has grown, the most dependable are *Agave* x *nigra*, *A. filifera* and *A. montana*. Bold, structural plants are placed carefully, first positioned in their containers, and observed from all angles at street level and each adjusted until it looks just right before planting.

Between the sedums – David's favourite is *Sedum kamtschaticum* var. *floriferum* 'Weihenstephener Gold': it has good evergreen foliage and flowers twice a summer – and larger plants is another layer, a diverse mix of perennials. Attractive self-seeders are encouraged. He treasures *Euphorbia myrsinites* with its snaking stems and densely-packed, grey triangular leaves, but top of the list is intensely blue-flowered *Sisyrinchium* 'E.K. Balls', which flowers at the same time as the cistus. Although it is supposedly sterile, on David's roof it does seed itself sporadically. Bronze-leaved *Carex comans* is also a successful self-seeder, although seedlings are variable, so David weeds out all but those showing the best orange-brown colour. Variegated sedge *Carex oshimensis* 'Evergold' and *Luzula nivea* are other grass-like plants he grows on the roof.

Also successful in the herbaceous matrix are succulent *Delosperma cooperi*, a hardy ice plant with radiant, purple daisy flowers; a few different *Echinopsis* cacti (which would be unlikely to survive outdoors outside urban areas); long-flowering *Persicaria affinis* 'Donald Lowndes'; *Armeria maritima*; and *Lysimachia nummularia*. The curve of the roof allows some differentiation of planting across the surface: at the base of the slope the soil dries out less quickly, and it is here that plants such as the sedges tend to prosper.

Looking after the plot is straightforward. 'I don't weed the whole roof, I weed around plants that need to be kept clear,' he says. 'If growth is getting dense at ground level I tend to put in something competitive that can smother surrounding weeds. I see little point in straining to keep this as a pristine garden.'

David advises installing a simple irrigation system at the outset, even if it is seldom used. Typically, he irrigates for 20 minutes perhaps only three or four times a summer, and only during exceptionally dry periods when the roof plants are visibly suffering. Otherwise they rely on natural rainfall.

There are some problem invasive plants, particularly annual meadow grass and other weedy grasses. He says his biggest mistake was planting *Vinca major* on the uppermost, flat part of the roof. It has proved to be an aggressive coloniser. Some woody invaders are tolerated: a few *Cotoneaster horizontalis* and *Leycesteria formosa*, for example.

David has been a pioneer in trying out exotic plants in a challenging urban environment. He now jointly manages an international web forum devoted to cultivating exotic and xerophytic (drought-tolerant) plants. More than this, he has gone further than anyone else in testing such plants for use on green roofs in the UK, pushing the horticultural boundaries in practice. He has had failures, but says he would change little if starting again, except to use less fertile soil – the loam he used was too rich in the early stages.

Green roofs offer much potential, yet most examples stick to a limited range of tried-and-tested plants. By varying the depth of the growing medium (the single biggest influence on biodiversity according to some researchers), a surprisingly wide range of species can succeed. Indeed, it may be easier to grow many Mediterranean-climate plants on roofs than in the ground. David's bold, adventurous spirit has pointed the way forward for other urban green-roof pioneers to try out yet more promising plants, species and cultivars that may become increasingly important in a changing climate.

# Commonplace Conservation

JOHN SALES, OCTOBER 2000

Most gardens are small, often much less than half an acre, yet usually only the large ones are taken seriously enough to be conserved – those of exceptional merit historically, horticulturally and aesthetically. It is understandable that the National Trust should focus its resources primarily on gardens of significance either in their own right, such as Hidcote Manor, Rowallane or Biddulph

> "Until recently, little deliberate attention has been paid to preserving the small and the ordinary in gardens"

Grange, or as part of a greater whole such as Stourhead, Killerton and Wallington. But what of small gardens and those typical of their time, rather than exceptional? Would we not like to know what an ordinary, 18th-century town garden looked like and contained? Not everyone owned a landscape park.

Some historic gardens of lesser importance have been conserved or re-created, usually because of the significance of the property as a whole – but these are nearly always large and rural. By chance the National Trust has acquired a few comparatively small gardens that could be considered as representative of their time, such as the 0.8-ha (2-acre) Victorian garden of Peckover House in Wisbech. But these are not 'small gardens' in the modern sense.

Until recently, little deliberate attention has been paid to preserving the small and the ordinary in gardens. But there are a few straws in the wind – one quite literally: Mr Straw's House, Worksop. This Edwardian, semi-detached villa has been preserved as a 'time capsule' and the garden is also being restored. Another is 20 Forthlin Road, Liverpool: hardly typical in its association with Paul McCartney of the Beatles, but nevertheless a run-of-the-mill 1950s terraced council house with a garden to match. More significant is that the Trust has recently acquired and restored Sunnycroft, a late-Victorian suburban villa and garden in Wellington, Shropshire, not because of its especial merit but because it represents a genre, reflecting a way of life that has gone forever. For future generations the ephemera of our working lives and leisure time are vital in forming a clear picture of our values and the way we live. As with houses and their contents, the commonplace in gardens is just as important as the unusual. We preserve, conserve and cherish elements of the past for many important reasons: not least to see our own lives, values and accomplishments in the context of those of our predecessors. As well as being able to admire and enjoy the great achievements of the past, we need to be able to understand the ideals of ordinary people, how they lived and how they gardened.

A century from now what picture will gardeners and garden historians be able to glean of the everyday small gardens of our era? Most television gardening programmes, if anyone bothers to preserve them, would not give an accurate impression, either because they tend to concentrate on what is perceived to be exceptional or because of the fashion for makeovers. Flower-show gardens, which are well recorded, do indicate trends but their circumstances are artificial. With the welcome development of garden design as a profession, many more gardens are planned on paper, indicating the designer's intentions, but this minority would on their own convey an entirely distorted notion. Moreover there is frequently an unrecorded gulf between the intention (even if practicable) and the ultimate reality – a potentially interesting study for any serious student of garden design.

Books and magazine articles are likely to be a helpful source but these, too, tend to dwell on what is perceived to be exceptional or different. Furthermore, all those atmospheric photographs taken at 5am on a misty summer morning can alter colour schemes and give an entirely false impression of the quality of the place.

## Candidates for conservation

Would it be possible to identify a representative selection of archetypes of small private gardens and conserve them in perpetuity as part of our cultural heritage? Objective conservation of historic gardens is a recent phenomenon and it is not long since many people believed it impossible for gardens such as Knightshayes, Sissinghurst and Hidcote to survive in the absence of their makers. Inevitably something is lost but clearly what has been retained gives pleasure, interest and inspiration to thousands every year.

While it is equally feasible to conserve small, private gardens, the challenge increases as size diminishes because of the dilemmas thrown up by continued growth and development of the larger plants. This would be particularly true of 'plantsman's gardens', which rely on a stream of novelties passing through them. Conversely, it would be easier with gardens that have a more architectural structure.

For each garden a long-term conservation plan would be needed to anticipate over-maturity and ensure timely renewal of some elements, especially the planting; it would also have to cater for visitors, too many of whom could destroy the place.

Still more difficult would be to agree the selection of small, private gardens typical of our day and age. Even discounting personal taste, which is bound to enter the argument, it is hard to judge the products of one's own time without prejudice; far easier after 50 years, by [which time] the essential qualities of most small gardens would be lost. To choose gardens objectively would be more difficult than to adopt the National Trust's practice of considering acquisition only after being offered a property.

All gardens, particularly small ones, relate in some degree to the house and the needs and aspirations of those who live there. It would be unwise and unreal to try to conserve gardens in isolation, disconnected from their intended use and setting. Ideally the gardening styles (even the life styles) of those who made and owned them would need to be conserved. Gardens consist of a complex web of interrelated processes. Their character in the long term, as well as their immediate appearance, is determined by the style of their upkeep and renewal.

And there's the rub. How would one find capable people to cherish gardens in perpetuity according to a precise style and design without imposing their personalities? The National Trust is a world leader in this sensitive, demanding task and has the necessary continuity of purpose. But who would procure the inevitably essential endowment funds? Could the 32 county garden trusts, which are linked by a national association, arrange the long-term conservation of small gardens equally effectively?

Whether or not the conservation of small, private gardens is feasible, the least we can do is make full and accurate records of gardens of all kinds in their prime. By recording past achievements honestly, that which we value has a chance of being part of our future.

# PLANTS

*Note from the editor*

Descriptions of plants have, inevitably, been a very important mainstay of the RHS publications, since plants are the indispensable elements of gardens. They are also extremely dynamic – new plants are either being found or bred continuously, while old ones have a way of coming in and out of fashion. Indeed, *The Garden* is possibly unique in the depth and quality of its coverage. This may be a response to the founding aims of the Society, but more obviously it is due to the fact that British gardeners are fortunate enough to make gardens in a country whose climate and soils encourage the thriving of many thousands of species and cultivars.

In this chapter there are articles on, inter alia, roses, auriculas, phormiums, iris relatives, snowdrops and the jade vine – but, as I was so spoilt for choice, they could as easily have been on philadelphus, wintersweet, lilies, crocuses and crinums.

Indeed, it seems likely that most people who join the Royal Horticultural Society have an interest in plants as well as gardens, and are at least reasonably happy with (or not badly put-off by) botanical Latin names and in-depth descriptions. Many well-known enthusiastic specialists of their day have written about their favourite or most deeply studied plants, and some of these are represented here. The most famous is the Edwardian gardener, E A Bowles, who coupled a wry sense of humour with an inquiring mind and adventurous spirit, but Val Bourne, Bob Brown, Nigel Colborn, Stephen Lacey, Roy Lancaster, Anna Pavord and Graham Rice, for example, have also made very valuable contributions in recent years to our knowledge of both newly introduced plants and the garden-worthiness of the ones we know already. Roy Lancaster, in particular, has continued to carry the flag for interesting trees and shrubs, at a time when they have become less generally popular – although not if Tony Kirkham gets his way. The RHS does not, after all, have slavishly to follow fickle fashion; it can take the long view.

**URSULA BUCHAN**, editor

# Hardy Cacti and Other Succulents

E A BOWLES, APRIL 1908

When I undertook to lecture upon the Cacti and other succulent plants that had proved hardy here in Middlesex on a specially constructed bank of my rock-garden, I thought the size of my collection and the healthiness of the plants warranted my so doing.

"Considering the trouble, are they worth growing? I think so, for I greatly admire their strange beauty of form, the symmetry and beautiful arrangement of their protective spines"

Then came one of the most destructive winters I have ever experienced in the garden. Bitter winds with sharp frosts – as much as 26 degrees [Fahrenheit] one night – and a cold spring, after the sunless cool summer of 1907, have between them decimated the ranks of my Cacti. The ground was cold and damp so early in the autumn that I believe the roots of many rotted away instead of drying up when I put on the overhead [glazed] lights in November.

I have in consequence a long list of the slain to read to you, and this afternoon's meeting partakes so much of the nature of a memorial service that I feel somewhat chary of giving any advice as to the cultivation of these plants for fear you will class me with the good lady who, resenting a kindly hint from a district visitor upon the management of her babe, answered, "Me not know how to bring up children indeed! Haven't I buried twelve of 'em?"

Two wheelbarrows full of rotten pieces of Cacti are, then, my qualifications for addressing you.

There are, of course, many succulent plants, such as the Sedums and Sempervivums of northern latitudes, that are absolutely hardy in Britain; but I wish to speak of kinds that are generally considered tender and more fitting for greenhouse cultivation than for the open air.

It is, I think, twelve years since I began growing a few Opuntias on a raised bank of the rock-garden. They flourished so well that I extended the bank, building it up with special drainage to suit xerophytic plants.

It lies facing due south, and is backed by a hedge of evergreens, and I placed a layer of brick rubble and coarse gravel of about the depth of 18 inches under the soil throughout, constructing gullies to carry off the rainfall, and placing drain pipes, leading into these gullies, in some parts. The soil is chiefly turfy loam mixed liberally with old mortar rubble, silver sand, sandy peat, and some well-weathered cinders from the furnaces.

I consider that, provided the plants are well watered in very hot weather, and fed with a little guano [fertiliser from bird droppings] during their early growing period, the general soil cannot be too light or too poor.

I keep some glazed lights from an old vinery on purpose for covering this Cactus bank in winter. They are placed overhead from November to April, resting on posts driven into the ground, but having the sides open to the air. In ordinary seasons the early part of November is sunny enough to allow this bank to become quite dry, and the plants shrivel a little, and thus are ready to withstand the cold of our ordinary winters.

Many of the Cacti are so beset with barbed spines that they are terrible to handle. Gloves are worse than useless, for the spines penetrate them and enter the flesh of one's hands; and in removing the gloves the greater portion of a spine is broken off, leaving the barbed end buried, very hard to see, and often exceedingly painful.

I arm myself, for attending to these spitefully ungrateful plants, by donning a pair of wicker cuffs, and I find a couple of long-handled steel forks, known as 'Cook's forks', one in each hand, very useful for extracting weeds or rotten pieces of Cactus. In planting a large specimen I use a small pair of tongs, such as one puts on coal with, to hold the plant and place it in position. Even with these careful preparations I seldom escape without a few spines in my hands.

Considering the trouble, are they worth growing? I think so, for I greatly admire their strange beauty of form, the symmetry and beautiful arrangement of their protective spines. I know many people think them bizarre, or even positively ugly. But if only they could carefully examine a few, and note how we have, by gradual transitions, every state of development, from the leafy Pereskias, with slender cylindrical stems bearing a few spines, through the almost leafless and spiny Opuntias, to the melon-shaped and ridged *Echinocactus* and *Cereus* forms, their dislike would turn to admiration.

The flowers are often of the most brilliant colours, and in the genus *Opuntia* the anthers are sensitive, and close when touched in a somewhat spiral manner, reminding one of a sea-anemone seizing food; and many kinds freely produce handsome red fruits that remain for two years on the plant. So that I find them attractive and interesting at all seasons.

# Out of the Bleu

ROY LANCASTER, NOVEMBER 2011

Commonly met by first-time viewers with a look of disbelief, the fruits of *Decaisnea fargesii* have the appearance of something produced by a child from a lump of blue Plasticine. Colour apart, the fruit in shape resembles a long (up to 15cm/6in), curved, lumpy sausage with warty skin. Some observers liken it to a swollen broad bean, which is slightly nearer to the mark, for it is packed with flattened, disc-shaped, black seeds embedded in a greyish pulp. However, it is more than the fruit's appearance that is of interest. The plant's botanical name commemorates two people: Belgian botanist and horticulturist Joseph Decaisne (1807–1882) and French Lazarist missionary and naturalist Père Paul Farges (1844–1912).

"Some 40 years later in western China, in 1891, Père Farges found a second *Decaisnea*..."

Although *Decaisnea* (pronounced 'decayneeya') belongs to the *Lardizabalaceae* family, the same as rampant climbers *Akebia* and *Holboellia*, *Decaisnea* is shrubby in growth, forming a multi-stemmed bush with stout, upright, pithy stems 4–5m (13–16½ft) high bearing, in their upper parts, large, handsome, pinnate, glaucous-backed leaves, about 50–80cm (20–30in) long, which produce clear yellow tints before falling in autumn.

The greenish yellow flowers, with six slender-pointed, spreading segments, are produced on the new growths in spring in arching or pendulous sprays. Male and female flowers are borne separately (monoecious) though occasionally some flowers are perfect (of both sexes). Given its size, *D. fargesii* is suited to a larger woodland garden where its handsome foliage can easily be observed.

Brussels-born Joseph Decaisne was interested in horticulture from an early age and when he reached 18 in 1825, he began work as a gardener in the garden of the National Museum of Natural History in Paris. His special talent for plants and his academic prowess was such that in 1851 he was appointed Professor and Director of the garden, a position he held with great distinction until he died in 1882.

It was, however, British botanists Joseph Hooker (1817–1911) and his colleague and friend Thomas Thomson (1817–1878) who in 1855 named a new shrub found by them in the Sikkim Himalaya after him. This was yellow-fruited *Decaisnea insignis*, which is rare in cultivation.

Some 40 years later in western China, in 1891, Père Farges found a second *Decaisnea*, which was to bear his name, though some authorities now consider it to be a variant of *D. insignis*. Farges, who was born in Monclar-de-Quercy (Tarn-et-Garonne) in southwest France, was despatched to China by the Société des Missions Etrangères de Paris (a Roman Catholic missionary organisation) in 1867 and then to his post at Chengkou, in an extremely rugged and isolated region of northeast Sichuan, where he remained for the next 29 years.

Partly to help relieve the monotony of a frugal living, rough travel and minimal contact with other Europeans, he was persuaded to collect and supply dried plant specimens and seeds in the neighbouring mountains for the Paris museum. His collections were rich in new species, many of garden ornament and he is particularly remembered for being the first person to successfully introduce the beautiful *Davidia involucrata* var. *vilmoriniana* (handkerchief or dove tree).

*Decaisnea fargesii* is native to the mountains of western China, where I have seen it on several occasions, in both Yunnan and Sichuan, growing in thickets and on woodland margins. On sacred Mt Omei (Emei Shan) in western Sichuan, I collected its fruits in October 1980. They are said to be eaten by monkeys and when ripe are collected by local people for the pulp, which is edible and slightly sweet. The fruits have acquired several fanciful English names including 'blue slug plant' and 'dead man's fingers'.

# Spots or Stripes?

STEPHEN LACEY, DECEMBER 2011

Variegated plants are currently out of fashion. Garden designers concentrate more on perennial and shrubby plantings of natural character, flower colour, and the clipped green shapes of yew, box, beech and hornbeam – variegation does not really fit in.

While I see the charm in a landscape of bare branches and sweeps of dead grasses and seedheads, five months of it at home and I would be climbing the walls. Besides, to dismiss any group of plants out of hand is never sensible. Each has its uses, virtues and gems of beauty, if you take the trouble to investigate. In the case of variegated plants, winter is an ideal time to make a survey, because it is at this time that so many really shine, adding colour, detail and warmth to a bleak and monochrome season.

Variegation is often displayed as marbled, striped or spotted patterns on foliage, usually in white, cream or yellow, and there are several causes. Plants with variegation work best when placed with deliberation and used sparingly – being showy and extrovert, they set a restless mood if scattered about – unless you go all out on a border of variegation, such as at the University of Oxford Botanic Garden, which can be exciting.

One of the chief assets of variegated plants is that their white and yellow markings introduce illumination, even the illusion of sunlight, into a border. So, it is in the shadier parts of the garden that they have the most obvious role to play. Against the north-facing wall by my own front door I have planted *Euonymus fortunei* 'Silver Queen'. It has made a lively self-clinging panel of white-edged, grey-green foliage about 2m (6½ ft) high, growing in tandem with *Cotoneaster horizontalis*, the red berries and autumn tints of which contrast well. Until a few years ago, the shades of the euonymus were echoed in the adjoining border by luscious clumps of white-striped evergreen *Iris foetidissima* 'Variegata', sadly wiped out by a virus now stalking this species. I have installed a white-variegated holly – *Ilex aquifolium* 'Silver Queen' – in its place.

"The other dark spot where I use variegation for lightening purposes is at the end of my garden under a high wall"

I remember once visiting noted florist, the late Sheila Macqueen, in the depths of winter. The shady rear wall of her Hertfordshire cottage was covered in two different selections of large-leaved ivy: cream *Hedera colchica* 'Dentata Variegata' and – my favourite ivy – emerald and yellow *H. colchica* 'Sulphur Heart'. In two places, a waterfall of grey catkins tumbled out, provided by *Garrya elliptica* 'James Roof'. The effect was of a snug overcoat. Nearby, a huge stand of *Viburnum farreri* was contributing a thick honey and almond scent.

Teaming up variegated plants can be effective but they usually benefit from also having some plainer leaves between them as contrast. The other dark spot where I use variegation for lightening purposes is at the end of my garden under a high wall. Green ivy and silver birches are principal players here, and two evergreens I planted are *Rhamnus alaternus* 'Argenteovariegata', loosely conical in growth and curious for having its veins prominent on its upper rather than lower leaf surface, and white-splashed *Prunus lusitanica* 'Variegata'. Both have grown pretty fast into substantial shrubs.

In contrast to white- or silver-variegated plants, which can be quite icy in impact (testified by names such as *Hedera helix* 'Glacier'), golden-variegated plants contribute a warm glow. On the east-facing wall of my house grows non-clinging, ivy-fatsia hybrid x *Fatshedera lizei* 'Annemieke' in tandem with prickly, gold-edged holly *Ilex aquifolium* 'Golden Queen': on a chilly winter day it is like passing a radiator.

At Kerdalo in northern France, a whole slope of the garden above the house has been planted with sunshine tints of gold and golden-variegated plants to counter the grey winter skies. It is a bold piece of design, especially in winter, but some might find the bling a bit much in summer, when other plants and effects deserve the focus. I have made sure that my brashest, golden evergreen, gold-edged holly *Ilex aquifolium* 'Golden van Tol', is screened by a beech tree in summer to suppress its ebullience. I am cautious also with *Ilex* x *altaclerensis* 'Lawsoniana', a vigorous, almost spineless holly with yellow-centred leaves handsomely washed in pale and dark greens. Its botanical name is a corruption of Highclere, the Berkshire castle where it originated (now famous as the set for ITV's *Downton Abbey*). Though it is magnificent in winter, in summer I part hide it behind a 2m (6½ ft) high stand of *Boltonia asteroides*: the holly is a terrific foil for its clouds of white autumn daisies.

"White flowers and golden variegation are often effective together: white clematis through gold-splashed ivy is also pleasing"

White flowers and golden variegation are often effective together: white clematis through gold-splashed ivy is also pleasing. Sometimes, however, you want to seize upon the fact that a variegated shrub is eye-catching year-round. The late plantswoman Rosemary Verey used spineless, gold-edged holly, *Ilex* x *altaclerensis* 'Golden King', clipped into two-tiered balls, on all four corners of her knot garden. They commanded attention across the lawn like beacons, drawing you over to admire the knot. The same holly was planted as the centrepiece of the knot garden at London's Garden Museum, set rather like a jewel in the middle of a green brooch.

Silver-variegated box (*Buxus sempervirens* 'Elegantissima') can be used as corner-posts to runs of green box hedging; they play an attractive variation on the box theme, but are not overly showy. Friends of mine have a large silver-variegated pittosporum clipped as a dome in the centre of their terrace. Also effective is attractive *Azara microphylla* 'Variegata' – while not for clipping, it creates a haze of small leaves on a larger plant, and has the bonus of vanilla-scented winter flowers. Both it and the pittosporum are rather tender and away from milder areas will need the protection of a wall.

I like variegation to be bright, even and sharply defined; some plants do not fall into this category. I feel only sympathy for plants suffering from spots, as on *Aucuba japonica* 'Crotonifolia' – of course, there are 'spotted laurels' with clear yellow markings such as *A. japonica* 'Picturata' – and for plants such as *Viburnum rhytidophyllum* 'Variegatum', which have varied if vibrant splashes of colour. Others have speckling, such as *Osmanthus heterophyllus* 'Goshiki' (*O. heterophyllus* 'Variegatus' is nicely clean) and curious *Fatsia japonica* 'Spider's Web' with leaves that look as if dusted with flour. Problems can arise if variegated plants have coloured flowers, such as with *Ceanothus* 'Pershore Zanzibar'. Out of flower its lime and emerald variegation may be admirable but, for me, once the blue flowers appear there is just a little too much going on. One I do enjoy is *Daphne odora* 'Aureomarginata' for the sake of its fruity scent; it is probably the easiest daphne to grow, and being confined to the leaf edges, the gold is not too disturbing with the pink blooms, although selections such as 'Rebecca' have stronger leaf colour.

Striking leaf colour and shape can be a splendid mix. Last winter killed *Phormium cookianum* subsp. *hookeri* 'Cream Delight' and *P.* 'Yellow Wave'; I am tempted to grow replacements in pots, to be wheeled under cover in cold snaps. Variegated yuccas can be treated in a similar way. A friend grows them like this by her back door, with a medley of other potted evergreens amid an assortment of colourful objects. It all makes for a chirpy winter welcome.

# Little Belles

BOB BROWN, JULY 2009

B lue is a sought-after colour for borders and growing campanulas in your garden is one of the most reliable ways of including it. These herbaceous plants mostly flower in early summer, though some continue to bloom for longer. Several of the best cultivars have been around for some time and have proved themselves to be good garden plants; this is inevitably less true of some of the newer cultivars. Apart from looking good, my personal criterion for selecting the best is that the clump should only need reducing in size after the third (or fourth or fifth) year. Some, especially *Campanula rapunculoides*, may be invasive and are best in wilder areas of the garden.

There are three campanulas with similar-sounding names that need to be distinguished: *Campanula latifolia, C. latiloba* and *C. lactiflora*. These three include the most useful cultivars for UK gardens. *Campanula latifolia* (greater bellflower) is a native of Europe (including the UK) and western Asia where it grows in woods. It is a tall (1.2m, 4ft), large-flowered, upright plant. The flowers appear, like most campanulas, in summer (June to August where I live in the Midlands), and are deep blue, white or smoky-grey blue. These can be magnificent plants and propagate well from seed or from large chunks split from growing plants. However, when a particularly desirable seedling in smoky amethyst occurs, the nurseryman is tempted to reproduce it from basal cuttings. This seems to weaken the stock, so not every cultivar is a strong grower.

"Although I am as susceptible as anyone when it comes to gazing into a flower close-up, it is the garden impact that I really respect"

Species that naturally grow in woods must be able to cope with shade and dryness. This ability is advantageous where planting is needed between shrubs or under trees. At Spetchley Park outside Worcester, *C. latifolia* has naturalised in a difficult environment, forming great drifts of colour in June and July among grasses in thin pine woodland on gravel.

*Campanula trachelium* is also naturally a plant of woods and clay soil with a similar natural distribution to *C. latifolia*. This is a shorter species (to 1m, 39in) with smaller flowers, 2–3cm long (1in) but in greater numbers. The normal mid-blue type seems to generally have reddish-brown stems. White *C. trachelium* f. *alba* usually comes true from seed. If you leave the seedheads on it should naturalise in your garden. There are also two *C. trachelium* doubles – a deep purple-blue called 'Bernice' and a double white called 'Alba Flore Pleno'. 'Bernice' is tissue cultured and plants are strong, persistent growers. I shy away from 'Alba Flore Pleno', however, as the dying brown flowers are more obvious than on other selections.

Of similar appearance are *Campanula persicifolia* and *C. latiloba* (once named *C. persicifolia* subsp. *sessiliflora*). Both species form mats of evergreen foliage only 10cm (4in) or so high but send up tall, narrow flower stems with outward or slightly up- or down-facing, cup-shaped flowers. *Campanula latiloba* has flowers without the short pedicel (flower stalk) found on *C. persicifolia* but the most important difference for gardeners is that *C. persicifolia* and *C. trachelium* are both subject to rust disease while *C. latiloba* is not. As a result it seems to do better in gardens in the UK than *C. persicifolia*, but sadly it has fewer cultivars. The best is *C. latiloba* 'Highcliffe Variety', which quickly forms relatively large clumps with deep blue flowers appearing from 1–1.5m (3–5ft) stems. This blue is wonderfully intense but sufficiently greyed to sit happily in its surroundings.

*Campanula persicifolia* has many luscious cultivars. I am particularly fond of the doubles, which come as flowers-in-flowers including the wonderfully named 'Blue Bloomers', loose doubles such as 'Azure Beauty' and 'Fleur de Neige', and tight doubles with petals packed like halved cabbages. For a blue tight double I would pick 'Pride of Exmouth' and for a white, 'Powder Puff'.

Although I am as susceptible as anyone when it comes to gazing into a flower close-up, it is the garden impact that I really respect. Therefore I tend to avoid bicoloured flowers such as *C. persicifolia* 'Chettle Charm', beautiful though it is. If I want a smoky-blue, 'Cornish Mist' is as good as any. Both *C. latiloba* and *C. persicifolia* will grow easily in most UK conditions including moderate dryish shade, and are even naturalised in places. Of the three that sound so similar, *C. lactiflora* is perhaps the easiest to distinguish because its flowers are always a milky-blue (or pink or white) – that is, they have a dash of grey-white in them. The petals are fetchingly reflexed and the flowers held in massive heads. The colours are never quite as intense as remembered. I wonder whether the descent into rather muddy colours is the result of cultivars being raised by seed (not by me) or of stock plants seeding into themselves – or are the memories at fault? So, I have more or less given up the quest for what others think of as the true 'Loddon Anna' (pink), 'Prichard's Variety' (deep blue from black stems) and 'Superba', and accept them as a group of softly coloured, blowsy perennials that need strong shapes around them like alliums to relieve the collapsed-chintz-sofa effect.

If the preceding plants are suitable for the middle or even back of a flowerbed, then the following are more suited to the front. *Campanula glomerata* (30–75cm, 12–30in) like *C. latifolia* and *C. trachelium*, is another UK native. It is a clustered bellflower – a plant of open limy, well-drained soils in sunny sites. This plant dies for me of winter wet and impacted clay soil and shade, whereas for people with more ordinary gardens it is sufficiently invasive that they complain. I suspect that, because it is shallow-rooted, pulling it up by hand could easily control it. It has tight clusters of upward-facing flowers, naturally blue but also in white and, in 'Caroline', with big, smoky amethyst flowers edged deeper amethyst-pink.

*Campanula punctata* (to 40cm, 16in) and *C. takesimana* have much in common. Both have reddish flowers, and are from eastern Asia. Both are adored snail and slug foods, and seem to dislike limy soil (unlike the rest of the genus) and winter wet. Both are invasive if you do not have enough slugs and snails to control them. In a hot summer they can excel, in cool summers they do not. To distinguish them remember that *C. punctata* has hairy leaves with heart-shaped bases, whereas *C. takesimana* is glossy. I can only grow them in pots. Sadly, many recent introductions are cultivars or hybrids of these.

*Campanula* 'Pink Octopus' is a recent pink cultivar with a shapely split corolla. It needs to be seen up close, so pot culture will suit. *Campanula* 'Burghaltii' and *C.* 'Van-Houttei' are old hybrids with large, exquisite, smoky amethyst and blue flowers respectively. In my experience neither is persistent enough in garden conditions. They are also the only campanulas I have ever had to stake. *Campanula* 'Sarastro' is a newish introduction from Sarastro Nursery in Austria. It claims to be a hybrid between *C. punctata* and *C. takesimana*. I believe it is a *C. punctata* x *C. latifolia* hybrid because of its colour, non-running habit and softly hairy foliage. It has plentiful, large, deep violet-blue bells like other campanulas in June and July, but re-flowers neatly on new shorter flower stems in the later flowering season which carries on until the end of autumn. For this reason I plant it forward in the border or the later flowers are hidden. *Campanula* 'Kent Belle' is a similar hybrid that preceded 'Sarastro'. It is taller at 75cm (30in) but similarly gets shorter as it re-flowers (equally late into the autumn). Its flowers are shiny and exactly match the look of the wrapper of a bar of Cadbury Dairy Milk chocolate.

For sheer blue, pink or white exuberance the biennial campanulas, *C. medium* and *C. pyramidalis*, cannot be beaten. I have raised them in two-litre pots and planted them in September to flower the following May to July. One plant of either will fill a large space; between 1–2m (3–6½ft) high and about half as wide in good soil. I think that many people have stopped growing them. Biennials are easy if they are neat self-seeders but troublesome if they are not. I cannot vouch for their ability to self-seed because I remove them at the relatively messy seed-setting stage.

There is no doubt that the most reliable campanulas are cultivars of either native or naturalised species that have adapted to UK conditions. They are so useful in our gardens because they freely give wonderful colour and height in a wide range of different gardening situations.

# Making Tulips Better Mixers

ANNA PAVORD, APRIL 2002

With one brilliant, early marketing ploy at the end of the 19th century, tulip-grower E H Krelage of the Netherlands changed forever the way we look at tulips in our gardens. At the Great Exhibition of the Work of Industry of All Nations (a kind of world trade fair) in Paris in 1889, he launched the new tulips that he had christened

"There are only two shades a tulip cannot provide – a true blue and a true black – but in between is a subtlety of range probably unmatched by any other flower on earth"

'Darwins'. These monster blooms, held proud on long, strong stems, were planted in vivid great swathes under the Eiffel Tower, and the nearby Luxembourg Gardens were filled with them. In that one public relations coup, Krelage changed the tulip from a 'jewel' flower, appreciated more for the individual, exquisite marking of each bloom, to a flower of high-impact massed bedding; brightly-coloured garden wallpaper. It has taken a long time to recover. Krelage's Darwins were weatherproof and tough. They had shoulders like heavyweight boxers and were uncompromisingly 'butch'. Park keepers all over the world fell in love with them. In New York City, the public parks of the Bronx blazed with red tulips, and London's Regent's Park, the Sheffield Botanic Garden and many others glowed with swathes of Darwins.

Such was the success of Krelage's marketing ploy that for decades many gardeners thought of Darwin hybrids such as *Tulipa* 'Beauty of Apeldoorn' and 'Orange Queen' solely as flowers of mass effect and forgot that they were elegant mixers in the late-spring border. The brilliant red-yellow-orange shades that characterised Krelage's Darwins blinded many growers to the glorious potential of tulips' other tricks.

There are only two shades a tulip cannot provide – a true blue and a true black – but in between is a subtlety of range probably unmatched by any other flower on earth. Tulips are classified in 15 groups according to flower shape and flowering time. Take *T.* 'Magier' in the Single Late Group, one of the 10 tulips that all gardeners should grow before they die. In a normal season, it blooms in early May, the colour of rich clotted cream, each petal edged with a fine feathering of deep mauve. As the flower ages, which it does gracefully and well, the darker colour leaches through the petals, staining the cream with flames and veins of purple. This mesmerising performance lasts for about three weeks.

Last season, I had 'Magier' growing in a pair of narrow borders running either side of a pergola. They were mixed with English bluebells and fountains of creamy cow parsley. When they finished, tall bearded irises took over the stage, followed by annual *Nigella damascena* (love-in-a-mist) which held the space for the rest of summer.

## Partner with irises

When planting tulips in the garden, bear in mind that, generally, they cannot cope with strong competition. In the wild, they grow on bare, shale-strewn slopes with little other vegetation around them. This is partly why it is difficult to get tulips to settle permanently in crowded herbaceous borders or in lush grass. But they consort well with irises, which share a taste for hot, baked conditions and perfect drainage. Tulips have the good grace to put themselves away tidily when they have finished flowering and so do not get in the way of the iris' rhizomes, which need to be well exposed to the sun.

Tulips also look beautiful against the fresh new foliage of hostas. Try Fringed Group *Tulipa* 'Blue Heron' or the gorgeous 'Bleu Aimable' (old-fashioned shade of greyish-mauve) in front of the elegant grey-leaved *Hosta* 'Krossa Regal'. Or set drifts of caramel-coloured *T.* 'Ballerina' between spears of lime-variegated hostas such as *H.* 'Moonlight' or *H.* 'Emerald Tiara'.

Belonging to the Lily-flowered Group, 'Ballerina' is an elegant, rather small-flowered tulip with markedly pointed petals. It blooms in lovely sunset shades, netted together in the most complex way. Outside, the flower is flamed with blood red on a lemon-yellow ground and has an orange-yellow veined edge. The inside is marigold-orange feathered with bright red. At the base is a buttercup-yellow star smudged with pale green.

It is particularly beautiful in bud, underpinned by greyish foliage, not too heavy. And it is scented. What a paragon! Nearly all the Lily-flowered tulips, such as 'Queen of Sheba' and 'Aladdin', have similar grace, although not many are scented.

No one can pretend that tulips and hostas like the same growing conditions, so for these combinations, I get the best results by planting the bulbs in plain black plastic pots at least 30–37cm (12–15in) across.

The planting mix is half John Innes No. 3 and half sharp grit, more to the tulips' liking than my damp clay soil. When the tulips are about to come into flower, position the pots wherever you want them in your beds. There is no need to bury the pots as they will be sufficiently disguised by foliage from surrounding companions and will scarcely show. Using this method you get the plant combinations you want, without hurting the tulips in the process.

When the bulbs have finished flowering, store the pots somewhere bright and dry, perhaps at the back of a cold frame with the lid propped open. If the sun shines, the bulbs will get well baked. In late summer, clean them up and replant in early November using fresh compost mixed with grit.

Trickier to deal with are bulbs that have to be tipped out of decorative pots or tubs in order to make way for another display. One of the disadvantages of this regime is that the tulips do not have the chance to die down naturally and withdraw all the goodness from stem and leaf back into the bulb. Even if they are replanted immediately, the intimate relationship of roots to soil has been disturbed and the critical process of gathering in resources for the bulb disrupted.

> "...choice brings its own problems. Do you stick to the tulips you know you love? Or do you gamble and invite a whole load of strangers into your garden?"

But we all need to clear out pots in this way and I get the best results with tulips from the Single Late Group ('Blushing Lady', 'Queen of Night'), which seem to hang on in the garden in a way that other types of tulip do not. Sadly, tulips rarely seem to increase in the way that narcissi do. In our garden at least, replanted bulbs do best in the rain shadow of our driest, hottest walls. They also seem to thrive under fruit trees, where the tree roots help keep the soil on the dry side.

Resettling tulips is always an uncertain business, but of course they do far better in the sandy soils of Lincolnshire than they do in the damp clay of the West Country. They aren't mad about chalk either, though at least chalk drains well. Our passion for watering everything in summer does not suit them at all. They like to be dry and hot from June-September, as the heat initiates the flower bud for the following season.

There are more than 5,000 different species and cultivars of tulip to choose from, which flower from late February to early June, and more are being introduced all the time. But choice brings its own problems. Do you stick to the tulips you know you love? Or do you gamble and invite a whole load of strangers into your garden? Generally, I do both.

I can't imagine spring without 'Groenland' (syn. 'Greenland') in the Viridiflora Group, or Triumph Group 'Couleur Cardinal'. That comes out in late April like a sultry Gina Lollobrigida: scarlet, but the kind of deep voluptuous, sensuous scarlet that no virtuous cardinal would ever dare wear. The outside of the tepals is washed over with a plum-coloured bloom, giving the flowers the dull richness of ancient satin.

But if I had not gambled on a stranger, I would never have unearthed 'Annie Schilder', the great new find of this last tulip season. It is an old-fashioned tulip, not enormous, but well-shaped and a gorgeous toffee-orange colour, slightly paler round the edges of the petals. On the back is a curious pinkish-purplish sheen, which takes the edge off the orange. The petals are not marked, as they are in the similarly coloured 'Prinses Irene', a Triumph Group tulip, but washed over in a more subtle way. Try it against the rich green leaves of *Geranium maderense*.

'Prinses Irene' generally flowers towards the end of April. It is a sport of 'Couleur Cardinal' and shows its parentage in the complexity of its make-up. The background colour is soft orange, but up the outside of the outer sepals the orange is flamed in an extraordinary way with purple and hints of green. Much narrower flaming licks up the outside of the inner tepals. Plant it against the light, so the sun sets it on fire. It goes well with spurges, either *Euphorbia* x *martini* or, if you are really brave, the brick-red heads of *E. griffithii* 'Dixter'.

For best effect, fill in with dark ajuga, primula or purple-leaved *Viola riviniana* Purpurea Group. *Myosotis* (forget-me-not) remains one of the best companions for tulips and if a trick is as good as this one, there is no reason not to repeat it. The forget-me-not (which should be a tallish species or cultivar) will probably self seed. All you have to do is add different tulips each season. Try Double Late Group 'Angélique' or Fringed Group 'Bellflower', pale rose pink with a fine crystalline fringe of the same colour round the edges of the petals. It flowers from early May and looks even more enchanting if you mix old-fashioned tight double *Bellis perennis* (daisies) in white, pink and red with the underplanted forget-me-not. The Triumph Group cultivar 'White Dream' gives a similar but even paler effect.

If purple is the theme, tulips give it to you in variety. Excellent 'Negrita' is a Triumph Group tulip with flowers astonishingly full and blowsy. Growing to about 45cm (18in), it flowers in early May. 'Purple Prince' is another winner, slightly earlier and shorter than 'Negrita' but with the same rich, lustrous colour. The lilac-purple blooms of Single Late Group 'Greuze' are also outstanding, especially teamed with tawny brown wallflowers such as *Erysimum cheiri* 'Fire King'.

Generally, bicoloured and patterned tulips are more interesting than plain ones, but everything depends on the way the colours are combined. In

'Akela', a Single Late Group tulip, the markings are variable, but in a clean combination of deep pink and white. The white runs up the centre, with deep pink at the edges. 'Anna José' (Triumph Group) is similar but the pink is in the centre, flushing out to yellowish cream at the edges. As the flower ages, the cream bleaches, which makes the flower look as though it is fading.

But don't dismiss the 'plain' tulips, as there are exceptions. Take 'Blue Parrot', not blue at all, of course, but a rich, old-fashioned Victorian purple, which also runs down the top of its flower stem. The base, hidden beneath the curling tepals, is a surprising peacock blue. This 'plain' yet handsome, elegant and classy tulip flowers in May. You may find it zooms straight into the category of Tulips You Cannot Possibly Live Without.

# 'Galanthomania' to Follow Tulips?

NEWS, APRIL 2010

Galanthophilia – the love of snowdrops – has been sweeping the nation this winter, with prices for the rarest bulbs reaching well over £100.

> "...the phenomenon has gradually been building over the last five or six years"

During bidding on the online auction site, eBay. co.uk, a single bulb of rare, pure white *G. reginae-olgae* 'Autumn Snow' sold for £162. Other high prices include *G. nivalis* 'Ecusson d'Or', at £145.03 for one bulb, and yellow *G. plicatus* 'Wandlebury Ring', at £123. At the annual Galanthus Gala – where snowdrop connoisseurs exchange bulbs and a hotly-contested auction takes place – prices have also been steadily rising. This year a bidder paid £150 for *G. plicatus* Poculiformis Group 'E.A. Bowles'.

Joe Sharman, gala organiser and owner of specialist nursery Monksilver Nursery, Cambridgeshire, said the phenomenon has gradually been building over the last five or six years. 'It's been getting more and more intense,' he said. The record UK price is thought to currently stand at £265, paid in 2008 for a bulb of *G. nivalis* 'Flocon de Neige'.

# We Need More Trees

TONY KIRKHAM, DECEMBER 2009

Imagine a garden without plants, or worse still, a landscape without trees. It is hard to picture, yet despite being a nation of avid gardeners, we seem to run scared of tree planting, afraid of the potential problems they might give us as they mature. Perhaps we are too easily deterred by the bad publicity trees get from obsessed insurance companies and building surveyors, or the gripes of neighbours over shade or falling leaves and fruit. But put the right tree in the right place and it can provide many more benefits than problems. Positive aesthetic attributes that each tree can provide in any sized garden include its size, shape and habit, flowers, fruit, leaves and trunk. In my view these alone far outweigh any negatives.

"By any measure, planting a tree is good value for money and a long-term investment compared to ephemeral bedding plants and even most perennials"

Even in the smallest garden, many species such as the maidenhair tree (*Ginkgo biloba*) and Japanese maples can be grown successfully for years in containers (and many tree species have cultivars specifically selected for their compactness).

Trees give three-dimensional scale to gardens and landscapes large or small. They can provide the backbone to a border, or a focal point in the lawn, while at the same time softening hard-edged neighbouring buildings. Mixtures of deciduous and evergreen species planted as hedges demarcate boundaries, absorb noise and provide shelter. Studies show that hedges planted on north boundaries reduce wind speed substantially – and can cut heating bills in winter by between 10 and 25 percent, an important contribution to more sustainable living.

Unfortunately trees get a raw deal and bad press, being blamed for damage or nuisance, such as cracked and obstructed pipes, subsidence or gutters blocked with leaves and fruits in autumn – not to mention the potential for damage from falling trunks and limbs in storms.

Even television gardening programmes appear to steer clear of trees in favour of shrubs, perennials and vegetables. Where trees are the subject, presenters too often provide viewers with outdated information on planting and establishment techniques, and fail to 'sell' the substantial long-term benefits trees can provide to gardens. In garden centres, trees are often relegated to the farthest corners with little information to guide customer choice. With more positive PR or 'spin' from television and retailers, buying a garden tree could be less arduous.

We must not be misled or put off by potential problems: they occur much less frequently than is often thought. Where do we sit outdoors in the garden on a hot day? Usually, under the shade of a tree. Why? Because the air is cooler – estimates suggest a mature tree can reduce the local air temperature on a hot summer day by up to 10°C (18°F). Asthma rates for children fall by a quarter where tree populations are high. Trees are 24/7, living, air-conditioning systems, absorbing carbon dioxide, dust, pollen and other particulates and releasing oxygen from photosynthesis.

In much of the USA, large deciduous trees are commonly planted around houses. Their shade is valued for reducing air-conditioning costs in summer, while by dropping their leaves in winter they allow sunlight in, enabling the opposite, a warming effect. With climate change, we are experiencing more unusual, extreme seasonal weather patterns and we are only too aware of more frequent downpours causing flash flooding. Trees in front gardens and streets reduce and slow surface runoff from storms, limiting soil erosion, and reduce and delay peak volumes of storm water reaching drains, helping to reduce the potential for flash flooding.

Just as importantly, trees are valuable habitats for a wide range of creatures both in rural and urban settings, increasing biodiversity and bringing wildlife into built-up areas. And it is not necessary to plant only British natives for wildlife, for many exotic species are beneficial, too.

By any measure, planting a tree is good value for money and a long-term investment compared to ephemeral bedding plants and even most perennials. Properly cared for throughout their life, trees will give the planter and their neighbours many years of satisfaction and pleasure. Try to imagine a treeless city – dull, harsh, noisy, dirty and boring. Trees in the garden and streets definitely improve and enhance town dwellers' quality of life and for this alone we need to plant more in both situations.

# Changing Roses for Changing Times

SARAH COLES, JUNE 2009

In the last few years, rose breeders have been through a wall of fire; growing garden roses decreased dramatically in popularity, due partly to changing fashions, coupled with perceived problems fighting pests and disease. However, many growers have now come out smiling, due in part to the huge range of roses available, many newer ones developed specifically with the modern gardener in mind.

> "French breeders Delbard say it takes 12 hours for a rose such as Claude Monet to play all its fragrance notes"

Today, we can grow roses that vary from displaying five petals to many more than 100. They can grow 15cm (6in), or to more than 15m (50ft). Their flowers may be rosette, quartered, cupped, coned, quilled or domed. Plants can be upright, or informal and relaxed. Their colours span the rainbow. And roses are less disease prone than ever. Blackspot-resistant, but a martyr to mildew, *Rosa* 'Zéphirine Drouhin' may still sell, but better modern-day equivalents include Jasmina ('Korcentex') and also Cinderella ('Korfobalt'), much as Duchess of Cornwall ('Tan97157') is a better rose than old Whisky Mac ('Tanky').

The earliest garden rose is thought to be *Rosa gallica* var. *officinalis*, grown in Roman gardens. Cerise and semi-double, it was called the apothecary's rose in medieval England. White or pale pink Alba Roses are another ancient group and also once-flowering, while highly scented Damask Roses are said to have been introduced from Damascus during the Crusades.

With the introduction in the early 19th century of repeat-flowering roses from China, the quest began to produce a continuous-flowering rose. Hybrid Perpetuals combined European rose forms with fresh colourings and two or three flowerings per season. In the late 19th century French breeders, Guillot & Fils, introduced 'La France', the first Hybrid Tea (HT). It was not a healthy rose, and of dingy pink, but its distinctive pointed buds and flowers dominated breeding for decades.

Brighter colours arrived courtesy of vibrant *R. foetida* and *R. foetida* 'Bicolor'. Never easy to grow, cross or propagate, it was used by French breeder Pernet-Duchet to produce 'Soleil d'Or' in 1900, the first yellow and orange, large-flowered rose. Today most bright colourings (oranges, salmons, golds and crimsons) come from these selections of *R. foetida*, which unfortunately makes many roses unduly susceptible to blackspot.

In the 20th century, Floribunda Roses and HTs became the ideal. Most needed spraying to fight disease, and scent was not a priority, although plants bloomed through the season. They were, and often still are, grown in block beds, displayed and sprayed together and pruned in a single operation. Often garish in flower, disease-ridden at the season's end and dull for the rest of the year, these plantings played a part in the fall in popularity of garden roses.

Some gardeners still grew Old Roses. In 1972 the late plantsman Graham Stuart Thomas's collection became the basis of the National Trust's collection of historic roses at Mottisfont Abbey, Hampshire, and their grace, scent and flower form, in limited but subtle colours, showed gardeners that roses could still make fine garden plants. They continue to be sold by nurserymen, notably rosarian Peter Beales.

Demand from gardeners was changing to old-fashioned-style roses with long flowering periods and good disease resistance. This inspired David Austin, a breeder who broke the HT mould. His English roses, introduced from the 1980s, have varying flower shapes; many are scented, reminiscent of roses of yesteryear. They are repeat-flowering with a relaxed habit, allowing them to mix with other plants. Each year brings additions to the David Austin stable, some in soft colours, some brilliant, but never harsh.

So what makes today's ideal rose? Michael Marriott of David Austin Roses says the aim is to produce 'a rose that is beautiful, healthy, fragrant and long flowering – generally a tough and reliable rose'.

Part and parcel of this is resistance to pests and disease. Gardeners who grew roses in the 1970s will remember it was considered needful to spray in summer if roses were not to be martyred by blackspot, mildew or, an increasing scourge, brown downy mildew. However, with the rise of organic gardening, awareness of the environment and concern about killing beneficial insects, gardeners grew more reluctant to spray. Today, as more and more garden pesticides are withdrawn, the issue has never been more pertinent. As Thomas Proll of Kordes Roses puts it, 'wanting healthy roses is much more than a trend – it's a permanent demand'.

The earliest 'disease-free' roses were developed by Kordes and Noack Roses in Germany. Noack introduced Flower Carpet roses, but while these with their glossy leaves and cheery flowers are welcome by car parks, like many other roses vaunted for health and ease of growing, they lack scent and a certain finesse. There are, however, splendid exceptions – violet-pink-flowered Jasmina ('Korcentex') and pink Laguna ('Kormulen') are two. For the rest, most breeders today still recommend occasional spraying against disease.

David Austin's English-rose breeding programme pays attention to vigour and health; some of his introductions such as The Mayflower ('Austilly') and Wild Edric ('Aushedge') are good for organic gardeners. Michael Marriott says that he never sprays roses in his private garden, and that with proper soil preparation, balanced feeding and careful choice of cultivars, beautiful scented roses can be grown with no spraying whatsoever.

Gareth Fryer of Fryer's Roses says, 'as far as our breeding is concerned, we are using only disease-free parents in our hybridising and have adopted a "no-spray" programme in the outdoor trials area. As a result, cultivars with well-above-average disease resistance are introduced. To start with, these tended to be boring, dull-coloured selections, but as we progress more interesting types are showing through and this has become extremely exciting.' Recent introductions from Fryer's with excellent disease resistance include Tickled Pink ('Fryhunky'), which was Rose of the Year 2007.

So which other modern roses have good fragrance and a long season with never a single spray? With magenta-pink blooms, Special Anniversary ('Whastiluc') is super; Munstead Wood ('Ausbernard') is velvety-crimson; and Crown Princess Margareta ('Auswinter'), apricot and fading to cream at the edges, can be grown as a climber. Golden-flowered climber Gardeners' Glory ('Chewability') has strong disease resistance. Most Patio Roses have little scent, but Rosy Future ('Harwaderox') is an exception, while lilac-pink Scented Carpet ('Chewground') is a break-through in previously scentless Ground Cover Roses.

Gone for the most part are days of beds filled solely with roses. Gardeners today have a more naturalistic approach, growing roses with grasses, shrubs and other flowers. As Michael Marriott says, 'The way roses are used in gardens has changed hugely. They are being accepted back into the general garden scheme rather than the classic rose garden, and used with other plants. I design rose gardens round the world and more people are asking me to design a mixed border with perennials – biennials and annuals are great mixers with roses too.'

At RHS Garden Harlow Carr, the Rose Revolution Border (and proposed planting around the new Learning Centre) mixes roses with perennials, and has never been sprayed. Old and species roses such as 'Roseraie de l'Hay' and *R. glauca* are grouped with modern, disease-resistant selections sold by Harkness Roses and David Austin, such as Armada ('Haruseful') and Wildeve ('Ausbonny') in a matrix of perennial planting. Interestingly, Peter Beales Roses sells a range of these companion plants suitable for use with their roses.

Scent is another crucial factor – what is a rose without perfume? As Michael Marriott says, 'fragrance is crucial, and roses have wonderful potential. There is no other plant that has such a range of completely different fragrances.' There is traditional Old Rose scent, but also scents recalling myrrh, musk, blackcurrant, lemon, herbs and more. French breeders Delbard say it takes 12 hours for a rose such as Claude Monet ('Jacdesa') to play all its fragrance notes.

Long viewed as soulless and scentless, cut roses have come into their own. Fragrant bouquets can be bought from David Austin and The Real Flower Company, and scented cutting selections are available. Cloud Nine ('Fryextra') and Congratulations ('Korlift'), both pink, last well indoors, and intriguing First Great Western ('Oracharpam') with ruffled lilac and magenta blooms, and Terracotta ('Simchoca'), brick-brown, show well in a vase. Unusual colours are popular cut flowers, many developed by growers such as Bill LeGrice. Sadly, few are good garden plants.

So the rose is back, certainly according to the rose breeders who have brought this flower up to date. 'With advances made in breeding super, healthy, abundant types, roses are back in fashion,' reports Gareth Fryer. As fellow breeder Rosemary Gandy told me, 'the future of the rose is secure because of its beauty, elegance, and romance'. Long may this continue.

# Lasting Impressions

PHILIP CLAYTON, MARCH 2009

Some plants inspire wonder in all that see them; one such example grows at Cambridge University Botanic Garden, producing its bewitching blooms between March and April. Rare outside the tropics, *Strongylodon macrobotrys* (jade vine) is a member of the pea family from the Philippines and demands high temperatures and space – plants reach 30m (100ft) –

"What sets this climber apart are its glowing, blue-green flowers carried in 1m (39in) racemes" so only the largest, warmest glasshouses will do. What sets this climber apart are its glowing, blue-green flowers carried in 1m (39in) racemes.

My first encounter with the Cambridge plant was unforgettable. In most glasshouses the blooms dangle tantalisingly out of reach. Here it is a different story: the plant grows in a low corridor; to pass at flowering time you must tiptoe between 90 or so racemes, most dangling to chest height; a curtain of shimmering green. Up close, the flowers indeed seem crafted from finest jade, and glow as if miraculously lit somehow from within.

# Stalls or Circle?

ELSPETH THOMPSON, APRIL 2010

Some plants are terrible flirts, making you fall in love with them at first sight. I experienced this when I first encountered Show auriculas on Pop's Plants of Wiltshire's display at an RHS London Show years ago. Like many others crowding the stand, I was smitten. I spent ages gazing at their pretty painted faces, with their endless and unlikely combinations of green and grey, old gold, burgundy, brown and even black, deciding which to take home. I planted them up in vintage terracotta pots and grouped them on my garden table, where they made me happy each time I looked at them. I showed them off with pride to all who visited and loved them with a passion. However, while many auriculas are good, sturdy plants, and overwinter outside without problems in well-drained borders, I had been seduced by the trickiest, most entrancing types; as a result I lost them all in the first winter. Choose from the less-fussy, named Border auriculas and you soon find many make good sturdy plants: they do not droop in the rain and overwinter without problems; even the fancy-looking doubles are reasonably reliable. Most also give a good display of flowers in the first season. By contrast, many of the plants with green, grey and white-edged flowers I fell for are too demanding for the beginner, and may desert you for neglecting their needs.

Although hardy, most must be grown in a shady, north-facing cold frame for much of the year, or an airy alpine house will suit them well. They do not like to dry out, and protect from sun and too much warmth – plenty of ventilation is required. Water from below as any splash will cause their colourful petals to run and destroy the delicate 'farina' (the mealy, powdery coating) on their leaves.

There is also the need for regular dividing and re-potting, as well as their vulnerability to vine weevil. These cultivars can also be slow to flower well; you need to be able to hang on to them for at least a couple of years to see them at their best. In short, when caring for auriculas remember that originally they were alpine mountain dwellers, happiest in fresh, cool air with their roots never sitting in wet soil.

> "You would think auriculas, with their rarified colour combinations seldom seen in other flowers, would have an aristocratic history. Far from it"

The ancestors of cultivated auriculas can still be found growing wild in the European Alps – most are yellow, but there are the occasional red or purple sports that first caught breeders' imaginations, although the plants we grow have complex bloodlines originating from several species rather than simply being selections of *Primula auricula*. It is thought that cultivated plants were introduced to Britain in the 1580s by Flemish weavers. By 1659 Thomas Hanmer's *Garden Book* mentions whites, yellows, 'haire colour', orange, cherry, cinnamon, crimson, purple, violet, 'murrey', olive and dun auriculas, while his contemporary Mr Peter Egerton had bred the first peachy doubles and smartly striped forms. By the end of the 17th century auricula fancying was on a par with tulipomania, prized plants changing hands for the equivalent of thousands of pounds. There are other intriguing parallels, as the first Green Edge, like the coveted feathers and flames in tulip breeding, may have been caused by a disease – in this case the mutation of the petal into leaf material. This was 'Pott's Eclipse', reputedly bred in 1757, and the ancestor from which all Green Edge, Grey Edge and White Edge auriculas have been bred.

You would think auriculas, with their rarified colour combinations seldom seen in other flowers, would have an aristocratic history. Far from it. They were popular plants with fanciers from all walks of life, competing for cash prizes in 'Florists' Feasts' in halls and pubs all over the country. Some of the most fanatical collectors and breeders were the northern silk weavers and lacemakers working in tiny cottages in Cheshire and Lancashire. Where space was at a premium the diminutive size of the plants, as well as their colours, must have been part of the draw. However, two world wars and industrialisation almost put paid to these advances, and it was not until the 1960s that interest in auriculas revived, with literally hundreds of named selections now available, and new ones being bred every year by amateur enthusiasts and nurserymen alike.

The range may seem bewildering at first, but familiarising oneself with the basic classification will help you to make more informed choices and avoid the mistakes I and many others have made when beginning. The National Auricula and Primula Society has identified the following groups: Alpine auriculas are the closest to wild *Primula auricula*, with no dusting of farina on their leaves. Usually divided into pale- and gold-centred kinds, they have cream, gold or yellow centres and petals that are darker nearer the centre, fading evenly to a paler shade at the edge. They are generally tough and easy, flowering well in the garden provided the soil is not waterlogged in winter. They can also be grown in pots. 'Adrienne', 'Ancient Society', 'Dilly Dilly', 'Joy', 'Daniel' and 'Sophie' are good examples.

> "Double auriculas resemble the trimmings on Victorian hats, with pretty bunched petals and no visible centre"

## Best for borders

Border auriculas are sturdy plants bred for growing outdoors, and their flowers do not droop in the rain. Blooms tend to be larger than other types, less delicate, and there is no shading on their petals, though some have farina on their foliage. Most are scented. 'Old Mustard', 'Eden Blue Star' and 'Eden Greenfinch' are among the best. They do well in pots.

Double auriculas resemble the trimmings on Victorian hats, with pretty bunched petals and no visible centre. Many such as 'Nymph', 'Trouble' and 'Piglet' come in shades of cream, buff, faded pink or mauves. Despite their more complicated appearance they are good for beginners and easy in the garden or in pots. Show auriculas can be divided into four types:

Edges are the queens of the show table. In these a mutation replaces outermost petal tissue with leaf tissue. They are divided into Green Edges (plain green edge) such as 'Prosperine', Grey Edges (dusted with farina) and White Edges (thick coating of farina). Though the colour combinations can seem infinite, all have a black body and a white centre, known as the 'paste' for its paint-like appearance. These are fusspots, best under cover where rain cannot spoil the flowers and farina. Grow in alpine house conditions; they thrive in fresh, cool air and semi-shade in summer. 'Prague' is the best Green Edge to start with; 'Grey Hawk' the easiest Grey Edge.

Fancies are Show auriculas that do not conform to any category. They usually have an edge to the petals and a white paste centre but, unlike Edges, their body colour is never black. Some, such as 'Astolat', have distinctive, flat-edged petals; others have mottled or farina-dusted petals.

Stripes have been reintroduced over the past 20 years and are vigorous growers and prolific flowerers, with 'Nil Amber', 'Fluffy Duckling', 'Likely Lad' and 'Henry's Bane' all sought after. Best grown in pots under cover, but easier and more floriferous than Edges.

Selfs are dramatic and stylish, with a white paste centre and plain body colour (divided into yellow, red, blue, black and other Selfs). As the paste centres are ruined by rain these are also best grown in pots under cover. 'Sharon Louise' is a good yellow Self, though scarce and slow to reproduce; while 'Joel' is a good blue Self for beginners.

Cultivation of auriculas is best dictated by their category. While Alpine, Border and Double auriculas should grow in a well-drained border, they need space to thrive. Best placed where taller plants will give them some shade in summer, they will rot if dripped on or out-competed by other plants. They are pretty at the edge of beds, where their flowers can be appreciated, or by the edge of a path as long as it's not too hot or dry. They also lend themselves to troughs, raised beds and collections of plants in pots.

More demanding Show auriculas are best in pots and moved into the garden in summer; protect from rain. For display, open-air 'auricula theatres' popular in the 18th century have never been bettered: there is a fine example at the National Trust's Calke Abbey in Derbyshire, dating back to the 19th century but restored in 1991 and home to hundreds of show plants when in flower. If an auricula theatre sounds too grand, a shallow shed or open-sided lean-to with shelving will do, painted a dark colour to let the bright colours of the plants shine. Garden designer and writer Mary Keen glazed an outdoor privy at her Gloucestershire home and painted the interior black to create a beautiful auricula house, while David Wheeler, editor of *Hortus*, houses a fine display in what looks like a wooden bookcase, with *objets trouvés* added for a contemporary cabinet of curiosities.

Looking through catalogues, and fuelled by knowledge acquired in intervening years, I feel temptation stirring again. Take 'White Wings', with its grey-green petals, blotched black at the centre and edged in dusty white; 'Pharaoh', gold-centred with glowing orange petals smouldering into brown; or one of the dramatic dark red Selfs such 'The Raven'. True, it could all end in tears again. But plants that demand a little more from you, like some people, are often the most rewarding. Whoever said the path of true love ran smooth?

# Shout Sunshine

GRAHAM RICE, JUNE 2010

The very phrase 'California poppy' seems to shout sunshine. Blazing in short grassland and rocky habitats from the Pacific shore to high in the Rocky Mountains, California poppy, *Eschscholzia californica*, is among the most brilliantly coloured of all annuals.

"...creating a dazzling display so easily, without using a lot of extra water, is an attractive idea"

Wild California poppies tend to have flowers in vivid yellows and orange shades, with lacily-divided green leaves, but they vary enormously. More than 90 wild varieties and subspecies have been described. Characteristics occasionally found in wild plants have been combined with new features by plant breeders in creating the recent impressive range of exciting cultivars.

Easy to grow, drought-tolerant and now available in so many more colours and flower forms – California poppies have been transformed into stylish summer flowers. Many cultivars, with unusually attractive, prettily-dissected bluish or silvery foliage, appeal even before they bloom.

Most annual poppies can be fleeting in flower, but altering the way California poppies are grown can extend their flowering season from weeks to months. They can be treated as hardy annuals all over Britain. Traditionally they are sown in the open ground, where they are to flower, in spring, then thinned out and, after a blaze of colour, cleared away.

Two or three successive sowings can extend the period of flower, but larger, longer-flowering plants develop from seed that germinates in late summer or early autumn. As with many annuals from Mediterranean-type climates, starting to develop a root system in the autumn promotes more prolific flowering the following year.

Also, these plants may behave as short-lived perennials, developing a deep taproot and a semi-woody structure at the base, allowing them to persist for two or three years. A downside of this tap-rooted structure is that it is tricky to raise from seed indoors: compost tends to fall from the roots while potting on.

Sowing seed outside, in late summer or autumn, provides the most prolific display on well-drained soil, in gravel gardens or the edges of drives, in annual meadows, even on rough limestone or sandstone walls. They often tend to self-sow in such spots, but rarely come true for more than a few years.

Spring sowing is advisable on heavier soils, but the taller cultivars in particular may develop a less bushy habit when sown in spring. Seedlings should be thinned out when small.

For mixed container planting, direct sowing is impractical, as they tend to be overcrowded by their neighbours. Sow a few seeds in a 7cm (3in) pot, thin to three seedlings, and plant into the container when a good-looking mound of foliage has developed.

California poppies love sun and tend to close their flowers in shade or on dull days, so always give them plenty of light; in containers, their companions may need to be lightly trimmed. They are, however, drought-tolerant once established, especially if sown in autumn.

Breeders have brought the sleek, satin sheen of the wild plants to semi-double flowers and selections with rippled petals, covering the full colour spectrum except for green and blue. Blue-grey foliage is an especially welcome addition. Most new cultivars are compact, 23–30cm (9–12in), and their increased branching leads to longer flowering.

The Thai Silk Series has mainly semi-double flowers with up to 13 fluted petals. Combining a dwarf, bushy habit (20–25cm/8–10in) with bluish green or greyish foliage, many are bicolours, such as 'Apricot Chiffon' (usually sold as 'Apricot Flambeau'), 'Strawberry Fields', 'Appleblossom Chiffon' and the mixture 'Champagne and Roses'.

Mixes are useful for an informal look. Single-flowered, fluted 'Fruit Crush' (20cm/8in) has just four colours (pink, orange-scarlet, butter yellow and carmine), some with grey-blue leaves. Slightly taller, semi-double 'Mission Bells' has fluted flowers and a wider palette of colours. 'Monarch Mixed' also has a wide range of scintillating, flat, single and semi-double blooms.

One recent introduction to look out for, with a distinctive growth habit, is *E. californica* var. *maritima* 'Golden Tears'. Having vivid yellow flowers over bluish leaves, it reaches only 15–23cm (6–9in) high, but spreads to about 60cm (2ft).

All have the great advantage of taking dry conditions once established – and in these days of water meters, creating a dazzling display so easily, without using a lot of extra water, is an attractive idea. And whether sunny or subtle, their clear, sparkling colours will always appeal.

# Shrubs of the Season: Summer

NIGEL COLBORN, JULY 2010

One afternoon in late summer I recalled a garden walk that led down a grassy slope towards a Scottish loch. On either side, dozens of *Eucryphia* made an informal avenue. They were in full flower and the large, snow white blossoms, with centres of packed stamens like so many fibre-optic lamps, were so fresh I could have forgotten the season and thought it May. Elsewhere in that garden, however, summer borders were already past their peak.

"Summer shrubs are 'slow burn' rather than 'quick flash', some continuing steadily until autumn. Their colours tend to be more subtle and complex than those of spring flowers, and many have good fragrance"

Most summer shrubs display a comfortable, even slightly melancholy character. The crazy excesses of woody spring flora such as lilacs, mock orange or azaleas are fading memories, and shrubs that flower in July and August are distinctly lower key. They often play second fiddle to riotous perennials or loud summer bedding, but that should not in any way undermine their value.

Apart from mophead hydrangeas and bigger buddleias, few summer shrubs are showy enough to be spectacular, but they can make extremely valuable contributions. The height and width of plants such as *Fuchsia magellanica* and *Phygelius* can raise the colour profile of mixed plantings, tempting your eyes higher and wider. Most bloom much longer than their flash-in-the-pan spring counterparts. A select group flower for so long that they tend to be taken for granted.

But by no means all summer shrubs are so low key. In isolation, *Hibiscus syriacus* or *Abelia* x *grandiflora* can be magnificent. But they have to work much harder than spring's weekend wonders: when forsythia erupts into golden bloom in March it has little competition. For the contribution it makes over 12 months, however, it would be found wanting, compared to many.

Summer shrubs are 'slow burn' rather than 'quick flash', some continuing steadily until autumn. Their colours tend to be more subtle and complex than those of spring flowers, and many have good fragrance. Everyone knows *Buddleja davidii* attracts butterflies, but the big lacecaps of *Hydrangea aspera* draw insects to the pollen and nectar of the fertile florets – food for birds such as blackcaps, chiffchaffs and whitethroats.

It is more useful to section summer shrubs by character rather than divide them into botanical groups. 'Foot soldiers' flower low key through the season; 'show stoppers' provide shorter term drama; and 'spring-like', a third group, have more subtle charms that capture the sweetness and purity of spring, but well out of that season.

The most long-distance plodders among the foot soldiers have lasting value, but will not cause passers-by to stop and gasp. They flower almost indefinitely, with pleasing foliage, and most have convenient growth habits. Fuchsias are probably the best examples. Forget the overbred monsters with flowers resembling ballet dancers – fine for patios or pot displays. There are simpler fuchsias hardy enough to grow into big plants across much of the UK.

Best known is slim-flowered, red and damson *Fuchsia magellanica*. It is often used as a hedging plant, but selections such as near-white 'Hawkshead' and purple, red and cream-flushed 'Lady Bacon' are superb summer shrubs for sun or part shade. A closely-related hybrid, *F.* 'Riccartonii' has plumper buds in the same colours as wild *F. magellanica*. Larger-flowered hardy fuchsia hybrids include pink-sepalled *F.* 'Chillerton Beauty', indestructible red and blue *F.* 'Mrs Popple', and superb, semi-double *F.* 'Margaret'.

*Phygelius capensis* (Cape figwort), technically a shrub but usually grown as a perennial, needs moisture and good light to perform well. Keep plants vigorous by occasional hard pruning. They are dubiously hardy and may succumb in a bad winter. *Phygelius* x *rectus* 'African Queen' is a good, strong pink while *P. aequalis* 'Yellow Trumpet' carries primrose-coloured tubes.

Among more low-key plants, some folk love *Leycesteria formosa* (Himalayan honeysuckle), while others regard it as being rather coarse. The flowers hang attractively on this suckering shrub, followed by berries with purplish bracts, but it seeds everywhere. A yellow-leaved selection called *L. formosa* Golden Lanterns ('Notbruce') will brighten a dry shady spot. I prefer marginally hardy *Cestrum parqui*, which, in fertile ground and sun, produces flushes of night-scented, creamy yellow flowers, attracting moths.

*Potentilla fruticosa* (shrubby cinquefoil) is an often-overlooked foot soldier. It was fashionable during the 1960s and for decades new selections kept turning up. Unfortunately, it became associated with car parks and hotel landscaping but, despite its overuse, it is valuable. It flowers almost constantly, on tidy bushes, and relishes a miserable climate, thanks to its subarctic origination. Good *P. fruticosa* choices are yellow-flowered 'Katherine Dykes' and scarlet 'Red Ace'.

If you walk up Battleston Hill at RHS Garden Wisley in late summer, expect to be impressed by the late-flowering *Hydrangea paniculata*. Wisley gardeners cut them hard back in late winter to promote vigorous new wands, which terminate in huge, creamy panicles. You can do this with all selections of *H. paniculata*, such as greenish white 'Kyushu', and *H. quercifolia*, provided they are well grown in fertile ground. The results can be sensational, especially mixed with late-summer perennials such as *Actaea*, *Echinacea* or blue *Aconitum* (monkshood).

## Lacecaps and butterfly bushes

With space and drier conditions, *Hydrangea aspera* can introduce more drama. Dinnerplate-sized, flat-topped flower clusters are held above big, hoary leaves on stiff, 3m (10ft) stems. As the flowers mature, the fertile parts become purple, surrounded by pale, pink-tinted sterile florets. This is a lanky plant with ugly legs, but do not condemn it for that – just site it with tact.

Almost everyone has *Buddleja davidii* growing within a stone's throw and, as butterfly attractors, few shrubs are better. Prune buddleias hard at winter's end for the biggest and best flowers. To encourage further blooms for late butterflies, remove flowerheads once they have faded (deadheading also eliminates troublesome self-seeding). In his blog, plantsman Graham Rice reports that *B. davidii* 'Miss Ruby' was recorded as one of the best butterfly attractors at a recent trial, but *B. davidii* 'Purple Prince' also works well.

Hybrid *Buddleja* x *weyeriana* is also great for butterflies and will produce ever-later blossoms if constantly dead-headed. Its cultivar 'Golden Glow' has apricot flowers with a mauve centre.

Lasting glory in late summer comes from *Hibiscus syriacus*. Some colours work better than others but, in full sun and fertile soil, they will bloom profusely from late July until October. Colours range from white, as in 'Diana', through pink (try 'Woodbridge'), to 'Marina', bright, near-unnatural blue. The flowers are striking, but lack the elegance of tender *Hibiscus rosa-sinensis*.

Some summer shrubs are just as fresh and delicate as spring flowers. For example, *Indigofera* (from the pea family) have soft, ferny foliage and rose-purple or pink flowers, often produced constantly over the second half of summer. The most widely grown is *Indigofera heterantha*, which has arching branches furnished with perky pink flowers, but *I. potaninii* has longer, more slender racemes.

Spare a thought, too, for close relative *Lespedeza thunbergii*. Though best treated as a perennial, this is a sub-shrub, the 2m (6½ft) lax stems of which are smothered with magenta flowers and are perfect for draping over tired neighbouring plants. *Abelia* x *grandiflora* can reach 4m (13ft) and bears blush-pink, two-lipped, tubular flowers, but is only suitable for warmer areas or a sheltered, warm wall.

The orange-scarlet blossoms of *Punica granatum* (pomegranate) are produced all summer long. If our winters become milder, it will be less risky to grow such plants outdoors, but they want a long, hot summer to fruit well. Low-growing *P. granatum* var. *nana* forms a compact, pretty, free-flowering evergreen bush.

> "...you could plant *Acca sellowiana* for its curious, inside-out, myrtle-like flowers and edible fruits"

One of the great mysteries is why so many excellent summer- and autumn-flowering shrubs are not more widely grown. Eucryphias, though most are trees rather than shrubs, are a spring-like delight in August. By a warm, sheltered wall, you could plant *Acca sellowiana* for its curious, inside-out, myrtle-like flowers and edible fruits. Or, for brooding leaf colour and modestly appealing sprays of greenish yellow flowers, try *Diervilla rivularis* 'Troja Black'.

*Calycanthus occidentalis* (California allspice) is another slightly weird shrub with stiff-petalled, maroon flowers that smell like apples. It is worth seeking out, as is its white-flowered Asian relative, *Sinocalycanthus chinensis*. Smaller white flowers, 1.5cm (½in) across but in small groups, are produced by upright hydrangea-relative *Deutzia setchuenensis* var. *corymbiflora*.

*Clethra alnifolia* (sweet pepper bush) reaches about 2.5m (8ft), bearing dense, upright panicles of flowers up to 15cm (6in) long, pink in the cultivar 'Rosea'. Choice, white-flowered *Hoheria* are New Zealand evergreen shrubs with lance-shaped leaves, most often encountered in the UK as *H.* 'Glory of Amlwch' and *H. sexstylosa*. Sadly, although frost hardy, they need protection from freezing winds so are unlikely to thrive outside mild and coastal areas.

It is too easy to overlook summer shrubs when herbaceous garden plants are to the fore, but their contributions should not be underestimated. The most useful tools in the hands of a plant enthusiast are a notebook and a digital camera. So, on your travels this summer, look at shrubs and trees that bloom in July and August, and make a note of any you would like to see in your own garden. You might be surprised, come Christmas, at the number on your list.

# Meet the Relatives

JULIAN SUTTON, FEBRUARY 2010

Iris and crocus are old stalwarts of British gardens, joined over the last century or so by *Crocosmia*, but there is far more to *Iridaceae* (as members of the iris family are known), and more of them are becoming widely available.

"...be warned: early success with this beguiling plant family can lead to serious addiction"

Many hail from South Africa or South America and, as memories of harsh mid-20th-century winters fade and our collective experience of growing fairly tender plants expands, more gardeners are giving them a try.

The sun is higher in the sky at the equivalent season anywhere in South Africa than in Britain. In addition, most of these plants are from open habitats, many concentrated in areas with a dry season. They avoid its rigours with a period of dormancy, retreating below ground to a bulb-like corm (swollen stem); this is a speciality of the family and understanding when plants go dormant is central to growing them well. As a result, it is clear that in UK gardens most need full sun and good drainage.

Corms and bulbs that become fully dormant are offered through nurseries and bulb merchants. For those that never die down, look for growing plants in nurseries. Seed is sometimes the only way to acquire unusual species, however. Sow winter-growers in autumn, summer-growers in spring. But be warned: early success with this beguiling plant family can lead to serious addiction.

African *Gladiolus* species show the two main patterns of dormancy. Most of southern Africa has rainfall during the hot summer, with a cooler (or positively cold) dry winter. Corms from this area tend to grow in summer. Only the extreme southwest of Africa, a zone within roughly 250 miles of Cape Town, has a Mediterranean-type climate, with a hot, dry summer and a cool, moist winter. Frosts, even snow may occur at higher altitudes. In the UK, corms from this area generally come into growth in autumn after a summer rest.

*Gladiolus flanaganii* is proving a fine garden plant, though it was scarcely known in gardens 20 years ago. Found on cliffs high in the Drakensberg mountains, its corms grow deep among rocks and so stay moist all summer. In Britain, it suits the front of a border or a pot, where its low, arching stems carry red flowers in summer. Though tolerant of frost when dormant, gardeners in cold areas or with wet soils should lift it in autumn, and store the dry corms somewhere cool but frost-free.

Originating from the winter-rainfall area, *Gladiolus tristis* is a well-tried garden plant, with palest yellow, lightly scented flowers on 1m (39in) stems in spring. In warmer UK gardens, grow it where the soil dries out in summer. Elsewhere, it is safer in a pot that can be moved into a cold glasshouse during cold snaps to protect the leaves.

For the adventurous, the range of winter-growing *Gladiolus* is immense. I enjoy growing scarlet-flowered *G. splendens* in a pot of gritty compost, stored completely dry at the back of the shed in summer. Drainage is key for plants in the open garden, especially in colder areas – I know of plants thriving in garden soil on the Cornish coast, and on a stony raised bed near Gloucester.

*Tritonia* also has both summer- and winter-growing species. I admired a fine crocosmia-like clump of *T. disticha* subsp. *rubrolucens* covered in pink funnel-shaped flowers last August, grown as a hardy perennial in Lancashire. Winter-growers include *T. crocata*, a much lower-growing plant that quickly makes colonies on fertile, well-drained soil in mild areas. The up-facing, saucer-shaped flowers in May are mostly in shades of orange, although pinks and whites also exist. Gardeners in cold areas have had some success growing them on a summer cycle, but I prefer to keep them potted, giving protection in cold spells.

Winter-growing *Ixia* have open flowers clustered near the tops of flexible, wiry stems. Grown with good drainage in full sun, they multiply well although our dimmer, high-latitude light can lead to them flopping over when in flower. Like *Tritonia*, they flower best in fertile soil. Named hybrids are easy to obtain but, of the species, *Ixia viridiflora* is a must with its turquoise, dark-eyed flowers in May: best in a pot and dried out in summer.

Still from South Africa, the colourful, even gaudy flowers of *Sparaxis* typically have a contrasting central zone. Selections of *S. elegans*, *S. grandiflora* and *S. tricolor* are available in many colours for Mediterranean climates, but can also be used with care in the UK. Dry corms sold for spring planting perform well in their first summer, but maintaining them can prove tricky as they are naturally winter growing.

The same can be said for the many hybrid freesias available in the bulb trade, although I have rarely seen them grown well for long without winter protection. Of the wild species, *Freesia alba* or *F. lactea* are good choices for large white flowers and strong perfume. To me, their scent is most welcome in early spring when grown over winter in a cold glasshouse.

Closely-related *Anomatheca laxa*, sometimes included in *Freesia*, is a more reliable plant for an open gravel garden or even the front of a well-drained border. A smaller plant, reaching just 12cm (5in) with dainty sprays of little pink, white or even (but rarely) bluish flowers in summer, it is sadly scentless.

*Babiana stricta* with intense violet flowers and hairy leaves is, again, often sold as dry corms, but really needs winter protection to do it justice – try growing it in a cold frame. Some crocus-like *Romulea* species are hardy in rock gardens: *R. bulbocodium* from the Mediterranean, with flowers in shades of violet, seems unjustly to have fallen from favour. Of the many winter-growers I would highlight red-flowered *R. sabulosa* and *R. monadelpha*, both best in pots under cold glass.

Central and South America are home to some distinctive iris relatives. The genus *Tigridia* is known for one colourful species, *T. pavonia*. Its large but short-lived flowers vary from orange and red through yellow to white, often spotted in the central bowl. Its bulbs (not corms) should be planted in spring and lifted once dormant in autumn, to store frost free in sand. Rare *T. orthantha* has a bright future in gardens. Its backswept orange tepals give this hummingbird-pollinated flower a different look. Each lasts two days, but they appear for weeks. *Tigridia orthantha* 'Red-Hot Tiger', found in Mexico by Bleddyn and Sue Wynn-Jones of Crûg Farm Plants, seems cold tolerant. Grown in a pot, stored dry in an unheated glasshouse in winter, it survives and re-flowers better than *T. pavonia* with us in Devon.

*Cypella herbertii* is a more open, wiry plant. Its orange-yellow flowers resembling small tigridias are borne all summer. In a pot overwintered under glass, it is in growth almost all year.

On the scale of a crocus is *Herbertia lahue*. A panful of this violet-flowered bulb is lovely in a cold glasshouse, but it is hardy enough to try in a sink or raised bed that dries out in summer.

A few species of American *Sisyrinchium* have a bad name – such as useful but invasive *S. striatum*. I like *S. macrocarpum* with large yellow, brown-ringed flowers. At 30cm (12in) tall, it suits a well-drained border front or rock garden. Grey-green-leaved *S. palmifolium* bears heads of yellow flowers that open after lunch, on 60cm (24in) stems. It makes a fine clump in a gravel garden.

Once part of *Sisyrinchium*, *Olsynium* are lovely summer-dormant plants for a rock garden. *Olsynium douglasii* has nodding purple bells in spring, while *O. douglasii* 'Album' has white flowers.

*Libertia* are evergreens forming clumps of stiff, upright foliage. Bearing white flowers on 75cm (30in) stems, New Zealander *L. grandiflora* tolerates more shade and wetter ground than most. I favour *L. procera*, essentially a tall

*L. grandiflora*, reaching 1.5m (5ft) on our clay. With its orange winter foliage, *L. peregrinans* is impressive, although it spreads freely. In coastal gardens, heads of metallic-blue flowers give an exotic look to Chilean *L. caerulescens*; inland, a warm, sheltered spot is advisable.

From Australia, *Diplarrhena moraea* and *D. latifolia* are hardy in a sunny bed, with beautifully marked white flowers on low clumps in summer. For those with a near-frost-free glasshouse, I recommend *Dietes bicolor* for a big pot, moved out for summer, grown in sun and kept quite moist. The creamy, chocolate-blotched flowers are held above the leaves on tough green stems.

> "...semi-evergreen *Watsonia* species can have real structural presence in the garden"

Many of these plants could be dismissed as garden toys, pretty things to play with at the margins. However, semi-evergreen *Watsonia* species can have real structural presence in the garden. Established clumps of *W. pillansii* are packed with broad, 75cm (30in) long leaves, over-topped in early summer by 1.5m (5ft) spikes of orange-red flowers. It makes new growth in autumn, yet never loses its leaves – tidy gardeners might cut out old growth in late August. Congested clumps can be split and replanted with plenty of compost or manure at the same time. New corms are formed in summer: in dry soil they can be too small to flower, but in cold areas good drainage is sensible. Many hybrids, mostly nameless, vary from pink (such as *W.* 'Tresco Dwarf Pink') to red and orange. A well-known feature of Tresco Abbey Gardens, Isles of Scilly, they are hardy enough to be grown much more widely. Sugar-pink *Watsonia borbonica* is nearly as tough, and equally impressive, as is *Watsonia borbonica* subsp. *ardernei* 'Arderne's White'.

The biggest *Moraea* species also make an impact through sheer bulk. Summer-growing *M. huttonii* bears a succession of yellow iris-like flowers in May on stiff 1m (39in) stems, over glossy green leaves. Large clumps make an imposing sight at The Garden House, Buckland Monachorum, Devon in the company of *Dierama* and *Agapanthus*. Trimming back old leaves in late winter lets one admire emerging flower shoots. Arching flower stems and sheaves of evergreen leaves make *Dierama* easily recognisable. As a rule, a sunny site that does not dry out in summer suits them best. Species hybridise freely, and many garden plants are impossible to name. Among the wild species, I am especially fond of mauve-flowered *Dierama medium* and purple-red *D. reynoldsii*. Obtaining exactly the plant you want can be tricky, but take heart: the only bad *Dierama* is a dead one.

# Reinventing the Dahlia

VAL BOURNE, SEPTEMBER 2010

Dahlias are once again high in popularity, and Mark Twyning, who looks after the National Plant Collection of Dahlia held by Winchester Growers at Varfell Farm in Cornwall, is one of the reasons why. He has bred a host of new dahlias that enthral gardeners – their small, mainly single flowers fit easily into any garden and give a gentle presence from July until the first frosts. They are poles apart from the dinnerplate-sized monsters gardeners distanced themselves from 30 to 40 years ago.

Mark became interested in breeding dahlias more than 10 years ago, after watching David Brown – a key figure in the dahlia world – at work. David rescued many cultivars in the 1970s when he became alarmed by their declining popularity, and he set up the first National Plant Collection of dahlias (the foundation of the present collection). Without his intervention many good plants would have been lost.

"Perhaps the best-known of Mark's cultivars is Dahlia 'Twyning's After Eight', a classy, ivory-white Single dahlia"

One of Brown's own seedlings, *Dahlia* 'Blewbury First', a muted pink, yellow and peach Waterlily cultivar, inspired Mark to have a go himself. 'It was a bit of fun to start with, I just collected seeds at random from the collection's dahlias and grew them on,' he says. 'Most seedlings come up as singles, as it's the basic form of the wild flower and most easily pollinated.'

Dahlias have been known, and grown, as decorative plants for centuries. There are around 35 species of dahlia, found in Mexico, Columbia and Central America. Only a few species have as yet been used in hybridisation, so there remains a large gene pool to draw on. The Aztecs grew double dahlias – when Francisco Hernandez, physician to the King of Spain, visited Mexico in 1570 to study medicinal plants he found and drew a double-flowered example.

Their heyday was probably the Victorian and Edwardian eras; in 1970, Paul Sorensen wrote in *Arnoldia* (the bulletin of the Arnold Arboretum, Harvard University) that an average of more than 100 new cultivars were named every year between the 1790s and the 1930s. In the UK, competitive dahlia growing and showing in the 19th and 20th centuries stoked a wave of hybridisation. The natural variability of the plants is part of the attraction for Mark: 'I find dahlias exciting because you can produce many differences from the same head of seed. It's like doing the lottery, you never know what will pop up; genetically they are amazing.'

In addition to the natural variability in flower form, shape and colour exhibited in seedlings raised from the same flower head, dahlias also show a spontaneous tendency to 'sport', producing shoots that have flowers with yet more variation. 'You have to grow sports on,' says Mark, 'to make sure that they are stable. Some can revert back to their parent, losing their desirable traits.' Many do prove stable, however, and have been named. Seedlings can be in flower just a few weeks after sowing, making breeding dahlias quick and easy, and most prove easy to 'bulk up' from cuttings when a good selection has been produced.

Perhaps the best-known of Mark's cultivars is *Dahlia* 'Twyning's After Eight', a classy, ivory-white Single dahlia. It is floriferous with wide-open flowers on strong stems held above almost-black foliage. Flowers last well and the plant is a perfect height for the border, reaching 90–120cm (3–4ft). 'Gardeners love it,' says Mark. It arose as a seedling of *D*. 'Clarion', a bright-yellow Single with dark foliage, bred by New Zealander Keith Hammett. Most of Mark's dahlias are named after chocolate brands, puddings or sweets; the first named was *D*. 'Twyning's Candy'. This pink-and-white-striped Single is a seedling from *D*. 'Asahi Chohje', a red and white Anemone-flowered Japanese cultivar. Eye-catching 'Twyning's Candy' attracted much interest when first displayed at the RHS Hampton Court Palace Flower Show in 2003. *Dahlia* 'Twyning's Smartie' has bright pink and white flowers, but the proportion of each colour varies randomly, making it appear to shimmer in the border. Reaching an average of 140cm (4ft), it is a seedling from a miniature Ball dahlia with the same variable colour trait, 'York and Lancaster', but classed as Miscellaneous.

Mark admires classic *D*. 'Bishop of Llandaff' (bred in 1922 by Treseder Nurseries) for its dark, ferny foliage and warm-red, peony-like flowers. His copper-leaved *D*. 'Twyning's Aniseed' is a seedling from it, with vibrant pink-red single flowers and dark foliage, though not as dark as "the Bishop". It reaches 120cm (4ft). *Dahlia* 'Twyning's Black Cherry' is a seedling from butterscotch-orange, miniature Decorative *D*. 'David Howard' (raised in 1958 by the Norfolk nursery owner of that name, and another seedling from 'Bishop of Llandaff'). With dark foliage and fully double, cherry-red flowers, 'Twyning's Black Cherry' can reach 150cm (5ft). It and two interesting sports (one has white-tipped red flowers, the other is deep purple, both still un-named) are classed as Decoratives.

Not all of Mark's plants have dramatically dark foliage, however. *Dahlia* 'Twyning's Chocolate' has lightly bronzed green leaves and dark red flowers, the same sultry reddish-brown as chocolate cosmos (*Cosmos atrosanguineus*) flowers. Of unknown parentage, 'Twyning's Chocolate' will reach 120cm (4ft). Single, white-flowered *D.* 'Twyning's Peppermint' is a little taller, and can reach 150cm (5ft). Its parentage is also unknown, but its petals have fimbriate edges, possibly indicating a Cactus dahlia was one parent. *Dahlia* 'Twyning's White Chocolate' is a white Collerette grown from seed collected from a creamy yellow Collerette dahlia, *D.* 'Clair de Lune'. The outer petals of Collerette dahlias surround a ring of shorter petals, and 'Twyning's White Chocolate' has a yellow ring around the heart of each flower. Another Collerette, with a name that bucks Mark's confectionery theme, is *D.* 'Twyning's Pink Fish': pink-flowered, it reaches 120cm (4ft).

Having collected seeds and sown them for many years, Mark inevitably started making deliberate crosses by selecting both parents. Although interested in the science of genetics, he does not keep strict written records, and when crossing two cultivars, he does not bag the flowers to exclude pollinators, so the bees may intervene. Of the hundreds of seedlings grown on, an average of only five or six will be kept. If they prove good enough, they are bulked up by cuttings ready for sale.

Mark describes his hybridising process as follows: 'First, decide on your goal then select two parents, making sure, if double or semi-double, that the flowers actually have pollen and stamens. Select a single-flowered dahlia as your pod plant (the seed producer). Wait for the flower to open on the pod plant, then select an open flower from the pollen parent. Pick it and bring it indoors, remove the petals, then wait until the pollen is dry. Tap it onto the pod plant's stigma. The fertilisation rate is generally high.'

From hundreds of seedlings planted out in the show garden at Varfell Farm, two new dahlias were released at the RHS Chelsea Flower Show in 2010. *Dahlia* 'Ian Hislop', a Single with cupped, warm-orange flowers, and *D.* 'Rachel de Thame', a tall, orangey-pink-flowered cultivar from a cross with a species, *D. sorensenii*. For the future, Mark's main ambition is to breed a dark-leaved Cactus dahlia: 'something that has evaded breeders so far,' he says.

# A Strapping Good Leaf

JAMES WONG, MAY 2013

What do South Pacific seafaring, bulletproof vests and extinction of a giant flightless bird have in common? Strange as it may seem, it is *Phormium* leaves – yes, that ubiquitous landscaping plant loved by designers of car parks and roundabouts everywhere.

"Resistant to salt water, phormium fibres could be woven into fishing nets and were even used with deadly accuracy to create elaborate tripwire and snare devices..."

Yet to the Maoris of its native New Zealand, the plant's long strap-like leaves, filled with strong yet super lightweight fibres, made it such a central part of life that it was considered sacred. They used it to make everything from soft ceremonial gowns to walking sandals and basketry, all dyed in myriad yellows, reds, browns and blacks from pigments obtained from the plant's flowers.

Traditionally extracted by scraping the cut leaves with a mussel shell, the fibres were durable enough to make the sails and rigging that allowed inter-island travel on rafts and boats – themselves constructed by stitching together the plant's hollow flower stalks. Resistant to salt water, phormium fibres could be woven into fishing nets and were even used with deadly accuracy to create elaborate tripwire and snare devices that helped hunt giant moas (enormous ostrich-like birds) to extinction.

The antimicrobial chemicals and blood-clotting enzymes that naturally occur in the leaves also made these fibres ideal to use as sutures for injuries sustained during frequent inter-tribal skirmishes. For another piece of warfare kit, the leaves were woven into mats to camouflage buried forts and lookout holes. Remarkably, the Maoris wove leaves into tough, panelled jackets that reduced the impact of the colonialists' musket shot: the world's first bulletproof vests.

In more cordial times the starchy roots were used to brew an intoxicating ritual drink, sweetened using the plant's nectar-rich flowers. With so many applications it is such a shame that us Brits only think of it as an exotic border perennial. Phormium beer anyone?

🌿 🌿 🌿

# PEOPLE

*Note from the editor*

Of course, gardens do not make themselves, as Jane Brown makes clear in this chapter, and the gardening world has always boasted its fair share of eccentrics, charlatans, geniuses, artists, enthusiasts, loners, team players, workaholics, trendsetters and visionaries, whose influence both on their own gardens and other people's has been substantial, if incalculable. In my opinion, the pleasure in reading *The Garden* lies as much in the accounts of the garden makers as the gardens themselves.

In recent years, the RHS has placed emphasis on its educational programme for schools, but the Society knows that much of the success of a school in inspiring its students to take up gardening depends on the enthusiasm and knowledge of individual teachers. Most inspirational, for me at least, is the story of the Writhlington School Orchid Project, the brainchild of a particularly energetic and dedicated physics teacher, Simon Pugh-Jones. With the co-operation of talented and committed pupils, he has made the school known across the world for its contribution to orchid conservation.

This chapter includes two short obituaries, such as appear regularly in a publication concerned with people who often become more distinguished the older they get, as well as a long and affectionate profile of Sir Harold Hillier, by his friend and colleague, Roy Lancaster. These all show what interesting lives many garden-lovers lead.

Also in this chapter is an article by a larger-than-life gardener, Sir Roy Strong, writing about re-inventing The Laskett 25 years on from making it with his late wife, as well as a letter by John Sales, one-time Gardens Advisor to the National Trust, concening his close friend and collaborator, Richard Ayres, which also shows the benefit of teamwork.

I could not resist ending with what I believe is the only poem ever included in the RHS' publication, the ballad of a seed written by Alice Oswald – an erstwhile professional gardener – for the millennium issue of January 2000. The seed is both the end and the beginning.

**URSULA BUCHAN,** editor

# Fashion Victims?

JANE BROWN, FEBRUARY 2000

It somehow seems appropriate that Westminster, our seat of government, should mark the year 2000 with a ferris wheel, for we go around in circles all the time. Fashions in gardens used to revolve slowly with the measured tread of history's taste-makers, from Islamic emperors to European monks, via English squires and Victorian villa values. For every century's turn of the wheel there was a style, or at least a variation on the basic styles that nature allows, either a straight or a curvy edging to the flower bed; after that it is all a matter of degree. But we have accelerated the wheel of taste in the most recent 100 years and discovered how to run it backwards, allowing us to pluck whatever bauble we fancy from the supermarket shelves of history. As choice and crowding have dictated smaller and smaller gardens, so the supply of goods and ideas that we might put in them has multiplied. The ease of choice, hailed as a consumer's right, has become overwhelming: the ability to choose is manifestly not so easy after all. What are we to do?

Some 20 years ago, I wrote a book about the Edwardian gardening partnership of Edwin Lutyens and Gertrude Jekyll. It was just as their revival bandwagon began to roll and, from a fairly safe distance, I have watched them lionised, Lutyens as a great, though expensive architect and the doyen of garden-seat designers, Jekyll reprinted, restored and recycled as the patroness of thousands of column inches on colour and planting design. 'A Lutyens house with a Jekyll garden', a catchphrase in their day, is a house agent's dream in ours, with a premium attached: their best houses and gardens, perhaps 50 built from 1890–1914, finished and planted for a few thousand pounds then, now sell for equivalent millions. And here I am doing just what I deplore: in equating their extraordinary artistry with money, I feel we have missed the point.

They were the first to give design and planting ideas for medium-sized and smaller gardens, confounding the assumption of history that for a

> "...we have accelerated the wheel of taste in the most recent 100 years and discovered how to run it backwards, allowing us to pluck whatever bauble we fancy from the supermarket shelves of history"

garden to be good, it also has to be enormous and preferably aristocratic. Lutyens and Jekyll did not deal much with the land-owning classes; their clients were self-made men, lawyers, businessmen, a lucky gambler or two, or women of independence (like Miss Jekyll herself) who chose to spend a high proportion of their income on gardens. It is so easy to confuse quality and scale, and in fact the majority of their gardens, including some of the very best – the courts of Folly Farm, the Deanery Garden at Sonning, the elegant and scented outdoor rooms that surround Les Bois des Moutiers near Dieppe were worked onto spaces ranging from one third of an acre to an ideal of three to four acres.

Their secret weapon was their restraint: they stuck tenaciously to what Jekyll called the 'sanity and sobriety' and the straight lines of their Arts and Crafts movement context. Lutyens had a dictum that 'there was no such thing as a free curve' and everything he designed was formed by his obsession with geometry and his brilliant mathematician's mind. He was a stickler for accuracy, there being no such thing as 'about right' either; it was right or not at all.

Jekyll had no truck with serpentine lines of beauty, classical porticos, or seas of grass, indeed little faith in anything of the 18th century. Her planting was all devised, through some 350 commissions, within a finite range of plants, which she loved and propagated in her garden nursery on Surrey sand. This controlled repertory of straight lines, pure geometry and sympathetic planting allowed them endless solutions to individual design problems, all in complete harmony with the tastes of their time.

The tastes of their time, but not ours. The use of English oak, two-inch bricks and finely crafted natural stone gave their gardens an essence of Edwardian luxury: but all that should have vanished with the First World War. Some of their best gardens belong in a museum with other works of art. Their day was over in the 1920s but we have allowed them to trespass down 80 years. We should have acquired their restraint and understanding of scale, but left almost everything else, and moved on. Jekyll's plans were only ever 'starter kits' and moving on is what she intended her gardeners to do.

In the 1920s the world of domestic design adopted Modernism. The Moderns subscribed to contemporary solutions for modern lives, and their theories applied to gardens as well as houses. They were rebels in regard to scale but in love with materials: they rejected formal symmetry in favour of lop-sided abstractions, steel and plastics, and adored concrete, *objets trouvés* (rocks and pebbles, sea-washed timbers) and plants of spiky, sprawly, personable forms. In fact, they came to the rescue of people who hated herringbone-brick paths and straight lines: they recalled the 18th-century romantic picturesque that Jekyll had dismissed. In the cyclical nature of gardens the 'modern' must be the style for the 21st century.

Or is it possible that we have outgrown our need for labels, big-name designers and 'styles'? In writing about gardens I find the analogy with the fashion industry is recurrent: couture creations that win catwalk applause have little relevance to real lives, which are lived in the High Street adaptations. Our affections are formed in feeling just right.

So the gardens that I love best are where our all-too-short tenancies on this earth have been celebrated with flowers, trees and dappled groves. Where others' lives shine through what is merely a framework of restraint or 'style'. Favourites which come to mind are: the E H 'Chinese' Wilson garden at Chipping Campden in Gloucestershire with so many of the plants he collected; Sir Frederick Gibberd's modern, 'selfish' indulgence at Marsh Lane, Harlow; Derek Jarman's Dungeness beach garden; and Nick Burton's restoration of the flower walk at Kelmarsh Hall, which recalls the ghost of Norah Lindsay. Modern theorists have been praising gardens as the 'people's art' for 50 years. Now is the time for all good men and women to make gardens of their own.

# He Had a Dream

ROY LANCASTER, JULY 2011

For a nurseryman keen to spread his wings, with a young family and a long-cherished dream of establishing a major collection of trees and shrubs from the cool temperate regions of the world, it was a tempting offer: 'an attractive country residence with walled garden, glasshouses, bothy, garage and outbuildings surrounded by pasture and arable land, in all about 41 acres'. His wife had drawn his attention to the sale notice in the September 1951 issue of *Country Life*, and the more he considered it, the better he liked it. Further enquiries revealed that the

"In 1977, having assembled a woody-plant collection of world renown, Harold made a decision of huge significance and generosity..."

property lay close to the London–Bournemouth road (A31), and the soil varied from London clay to Bagshot sand.

The residence in question was Jermyns House and the man who was determined to, and in fact did, purchase it was Harold Hillier, then aged 46 and head of the world-famous nursery firm Hillier and Sons of Winchester.

For some time Harold had been looking to move from his Winchester home, surrounded by chalkland, to a site with acidic soil where a wider range of his favourite plants might be grown, especially rhododendrons, camellias and magnolias. Given the poor state of the house and the improvements required to make it suitable, it was another two years before the family moved in, which they did on 3 June 1953, the morning after Coronation Day. One of the first trees planted by Harold, on a site close to the house, was a dawn redwood (*Metasequoia glyptostroboides*), plants of which Hillier's had raised from the first introduction of seed to Britain from China, via the Arnold Arboretum, in 1948.

Once begun, planting of trees and shrubs proceeded at an ever-increasing pace, first in peripheral areas then on newly acquired neighbouring land. In 1961 the 4ha (10 acre) 'parkland' that Harold initially planted as a nursery ceased production. More land became available and remaining trees formed the centre of an ambitious arboretum. This was consolidated with gifts from like-minded friends and nursery contacts and eventually by introductions from his travels in North America, Mexico, Europe and the Far East.

In the 1960s and 1970s, the arboretum became a magnet to dendrologists and woody-plant enthusiasts who came to study and admire the botanical and ornamental 'treasures' that found a 'home from home' in this verdant slice of Hampshire.

In 1964 Hillier Nurseries celebrated its centenary with a press day at the arboretum, during which an earnest young journalist asked Harold for his thoughts on the newly fashionable subject of conservation. 'While others are talking about it, I'm doing it,' he replied, 'putting roots in the ground.'

In 1977, having assembled a woody-plant collection of world renown, Harold made a decision of huge significance and generosity, forming a charitable trust and offering his arboretum to Hampshire County Council, accepted on their behalf on a glorious day in May the following year by the late Queen Mother.

In 1983, Harold Hillier received a richly deserved knighthood, only the second nurseryman after Sir Harry Veitch in 1912 to have been so honoured. Then just two years later the horticultural world was saddened by news of his death, aged 80.

Today, the Sir Harold Hillier Gardens, as the property is now known, covers an area of 73 ha (180 acres) and is promoted as a 'garden for all seasons' boasting a collection of 42,000 plants from the world's temperate regions including 11 National Plant Collections. It also runs an ambitious educational programme for all age groups. Beyond the statistics, impressive though they are, there lies a simple fact that from one man's dream a world of plants grew.

On a warm, sunny day the week before Easter this year I had occasion to visit the Sir Harold Hillier Gardens with friends. We found it busy with visitors old and young, and families relaxing on the grass. At one point we passed a group of youngsters contemplating a tree labelled *Tilia* 'Harold Hillier'. 'Who was Harold Hillier?' asked one of the children. 'He was the man who created these gardens,' their teacher replied. 'He must have been pleased,' the child observed.

# From Tiny Protocorms...

JON ARDLE, MAY 2003

It may have become something of a cliché, but 'catch their interest when they are young' remains a truism. Quite how far a spark of inspiration can be developed depends largely on the skill and enthusiasm of individual teachers. In this respect, many of the pupils who attend Writhlington School, a rural comprehensive in north Somerset, seem well aware they are fortunate to count Head of Physics, Simon Pugh-Jones, among the staff.

"Flower show rosettes and certificates cover a blackboard in Simon's classroom"

During the past 10 years, Simon has developed an after-school Greenhouse Club from a small nursery growing bedding plants into a programme that has taken his pupils as far afield as the Brazilian cloud forests, seen them mount displays at local and national orchid shows, raise their own hybrids, and grow wild orchid species from seed for re-introduction at home and abroad.

Simon's involvement in extra-curricular horticulture at Writhlington began in 1990 when he agreed to take on the glasshouse at the school. He began Greenhouse Club for interested pupils to raise bedding plants, freesias and to plant up hanging baskets. Orchids, for which he has had a passion since childhood, first arrived as a cymbidium collection donated by a pupil's grandmother.

Like Simon, some of the club members were quickly smitten by their exotic new charges, and more orchids soon followed, many donated by Wiltshire and Somerset orchid societies and specialist nurseries, until they had elbowed aside all the other plants.

The main glasshouse now accommodates four temperature ranges, and each member of the club has responsibility for a different genus. Greenhouse Club has convinced Simon it is important for his students to learn quickly about orchids as he finds their success and enthusiasm is fired by their expertise. Giving each pupil real responsibility in caring for the plants of a selected genus or two encourages them to learn more.

## Life skills

The discipline of regular care (the pupils often start in school at 8am), preparing and sowing plants, and dealing with the public's questions, help develop pupils' confidence and improves key skills like communication. The club is open to students of all abilities, and Simon believes working with orchids has prevented several pupils from being suspended or expelled, while opening new career paths and aspirations to many more. 'A lot of students now *know* they are going to university to do botany or plant science, and they will often be the first generation of their family to do so,' he says proudly.

Simon has also found that the school's recent high profile in the media, including appearances on BBC TV's *Blue Peter* and the news coverage of pupils supplying orchids to the Prime Minister at 10 Downing Street have important effects. 'It shows the students that they can be amongst the best in their field, and this has had huge knock-on effects for the aspirations of the whole school,' says Simon.

He also believes that the club is important in helping its members challenge stereotypes in their appreciation of such 'uncool' (to their peers) factors as flowers and perfume. There is a certain amount of 'stick' from other pupils, but this does not seem to bother the club members. The breadth and depth of their knowledge, their pride in the school's collection (and their own plants in particular) is obvious.

Simon says the 12–14 year olds in the group have 'lab skills at undergraduate standard, putting them in a position to develop some fascinating projects over the next few years'.

Flower show rosettes and certificates cover a blackboard in Simon's classroom. The school's most recent exhibit, at the European Orchid Show in London, received a silver-gilt award from the RHS, plus the trophy for the Best Small Exhibit. Several specimen plants were given much-coveted Certificates of Cultural Commendation (CCCs). 'It's so much better for a judge to acknowledge formally that a pupil has done well than just a teacher saying it,' says Simon.

The show was also a notable event for 15-year-old Chris Ashman, one of Simon's keenest students, who joined the British Orchid Council's judging panel [as a] Trainee Judge. His speciality is *Dendrobium* and one of his charges gained a well-deserved CCC.

> "...the school's impressively well-equipped orchid-raising laboratory contains shelf-space for more than 2,000 flasks..."

If growing for showing can be regarded as part of the National Curriculum's 'Vocational Science', the project work Writhlington's higher science pupils undertake at post-16 is much more applied. Often, it involves them with an increasingly wide range of partnership organisations and co-operative ventures.

Central to most of these is the school's impressively well-equipped orchid-raising laboratory, set up with the help of Greenaway Orchids, Bristol Zoo and the Royal Botanic Gardens, Kew (among others). It contains laminar-flow cabinets for sowing seed, sterilising facilities and shelf-space for more than 2,000 flasks – most of them showing signs of seedling life, or at least a thin film of newly-germinated green protocorms.

Each higher-science student studies applied genetics by making a cross with plants of their own choosing, researches the parents' origins, and attempts to grow-on their own seedlings to flowering.

Not all projects take place within the UK; in April 2000, having raised nearly £12,000 from a variety of sources including the Merlin Trust, Writhlington mounted an expedition to Mata Atlantica, 1,800m (6,000ft) up in Brazil's cloud forests. Hosted by the Rio Atlantic Forest Trust, over three weeks pupils investigated the relationships between specific orchid species, their habitats and pollinators, and carried out a 'rescue' operation to move a vulnerable *Masdevallia infracta* colony to more secure sites.

Fund raising for a similar trip in 2005 has already begun, but in the meantime Simon is forging links to set up *ex situ* conservation projects in Brazil, together with Costa Rica's Lankester Botanic Garden and communities in Sikkim, northern India. The aim is that local people harvest seed from their native orchid species and send it to Writhlington, where it is flask-grown, then the seedlings are sent back to be grown and sold by the locals, giving them a source of income without having to wild-harvest plants.

Simon's latest partnership is with the Eden Project in Cornwall. 'We will be establishing deflasked seedlings from appropriately-collected seed in some quantity, on pieces of wood to be attached to trees in Eden's tropical biome, to grow as epiphytes as they would in the wild.'

Writhlington has become closely involved in the conservation of the Mendip Hills' own hardy-orchid species. Simon suggested changing the management of the school's rugby field in 1994, effectively turning it into a hay meadow during the closed-season summer months, and only cutting it at the end of August. In 1999, *Ophrys apifera* (bee orchid) began to flower there, quickly developing into a colony, recently joined by *Anacamptis pyramidalis* (pyramidal orchid).

The school's micropropagation laboratory is now raising native hardy orchids with the aim of re-introducing plants into nearby areas. Several projects are under way, focused on increasing the success of re-introductions. This also forms the basis of the Master of Philosophy thesis that Simon is somehow finding time to prepare.

Beyond the heating bill for glasshouses and laboratory, orchid growing takes nothing out of the school's coffers, and is largely self-financing through selling plants, gaining outside sponsorship and grants and fund raising (another of Simon's specialities).

The school has recently been awarded Business and Enterprise status as a centre for business studies, and the Year 10 growers are perhaps best-placed to capitalise, as they already have their own Young Enterprise company, Stem Labs. Again, their pride in the cymbidium seedlings that are their major product is palpable, for these are plants into which each of the students has already made considerable personal investment.

The breadth, international scope and sheer volume of work undertaken at Writhlington School is frankly astonishing, and shows just how far it is possible to take children once they have been bitten by the growing 'bug' – provided they are motivated by an exceptional teacher. The respect with which Greenhouse Club members treat 'Sir' speaks tellingly of their appreciation for his commitment to them.

Simon is justifiably proud of his pupils' achievements, but modestly cites the support of the school's head, Marie Getheridge, as 'crucial; a teacher without support can't make things happen'. His enthusiasm was recognised, however, with the 2001 award for Teacher of the Year for the west of England. [He was awarded an MBE in 2013.]

When pressed as to why he commits so much of his own time to the projects he juggles, he confides 'my job isn't like work – I enjoy it so much. Seeing the interest and successes of the students is just brilliant.'

# Obituary of Princess Sturdza

FEBRUARY 2010

Princess Greta Sturdza, who died aged 94 on 30 November 2009, was a gardener and plantswoman of international repute. Her garden Le Vasterival, near Varengeville-sur-Mer, Normandy, became a magnet for gardeners seeking to learn skills and gardening know-how.

> "...she grew up without a garden but with a keen interest in natural history"

A passionate, hands-on gardener, she was once described as a woman of demonic energy, regularly rising at 6am to work all day in her garden which, from the original 3ha (7.5 acres), expanded to the present 12ha (30 acres).

Born Grete Kvaal on 30 April 1915 in Oslo, Norway she grew up without a garden but with a keen interest in natural history. She studied English at Oxford where she met Prince Georges Sturdza of Moldavia whom she married in 1936. In Moldavia during the Second World War she cared for orphans and was involved with the Red Cross, later becoming its President. At the end of the war she and her family fled to Norway, then to France where, in 1955, they bought Le Vasterival.

Here her interest in gardening really took off, clearing scrub and draining marshland before beginning an ambitious planting scheme. She was a member of the International Dendrology Society, serving as President from 1997–2002. In 1992 she was made an Honorary Life Member and President Emeritus. A long-term member of the RHS, she was awarded its Gold Veitch Memorial Medal in 1987 and became a Vice President in 1992.

She published two books: *Le Jardin d'une Passion* (1997) and *Le Vasterival – The Four-Season Garden* (2006). In 2008 she was awarded the Worshipful Company of Gardeners' trophy for her contribution to Courson Flower Show, near Paris.

# Obituary of Mavis Batey MBE, VMH

JANUARY 2014

Mavis Batey, who died aged 92 on 12 November 2013, was a garden historian, author and former President of the Garden History Society. She was also a codebreaker during the Second World War.

Born Mavis Lever on 5 May 1921, she studied German in London and became an interpreter at Bletchley Park when war broke out. She broke a code that enabled the Royal Navy to defeat a convoy of Italian destroyers at Cape Matapan off the Greek coast.

In 1942 she married Keith Batey, with whom she had three children, and later began to research 18th-century garden history. Mavis served as Secretary and President of the Garden History Society, and was a Vice President until her death. She was involved with the restoration of the Royal Pavilion Brighton gardens, and lobbied [successfully] for the formation of the Register of Historic Parks and Gardens.

In 1985 Mavis was awarded an RHS Veitch Memorial Medal and in 1987 received an MBE. She wrote a several books, including *Oxford Gardens* (1982).

# Reinventing Your Garden

SIR ROY STRONG, OCTOBER 2012

I've just reached 77 (not that that's saying anything), but it has made me reflect on one aspect about gardening and old age. What is it that happens to gardeners as they get older? We all know about the burden of the work, and ailing and failing limbs, but people seem to get stuck. Somehow after 60, mummification sets in, along with an inability to look at their garden with a critical editorial eye. I often visit the gardens of friends who are more or less in the same age range as myself. I will look at a tree and say 'Why don't you take that out, it's awful?' It may have had a purpose 30 years ago when it was little more than 1 m (39 in) high, but now it is 15m (50ft) or more. It is sucking nutrients from the soil. It dominates the garden and blocks views. At least, I say, try limbing it up.

The recipients of this advice look stunned as though I'd uttered some appalling blasphemy. 'But we planted it,' they protest as though that absolved them from the horror it has become. It doesn't. Instead it reveals them as failing to understand one of the basics of horticulture: that gardens are about change, about perpetually adjusting a picture, which will never be finished.

> "What is it that happens to gardeners as they get older?"

Such a reappraisal is particularly true after a garden is more than 25 years old. It will be littered with planting mistakes of your own making and garden styles will have moved on, offering exciting new possibilities. Moreover, many of your garden's most cherished features will have attained maturity, calling for reassessment and setting off to best advantage. But I notice that on the whole a blindness sets in.

In my own garden [The Laskett, Herefordshire] I'm at the end of such a radical re-editing. If one quick-growing conifer has gone so have 50 others. The light suddenly pours in, calling for new planting, and the topiary – lovingly sculpted for more than 20 years – stands revealed as never before in all its glory. Hedges are lowered and recut, providing new vistas. Ornament is resited to advantage. It is exciting. The Laskett Gardens are now open to visiting groups who tend also to be of that certain age. Time and again I tell them that the current message from this garden is 'Go home, chop something down, and start again'.

# Winter Walk

JOHN SALES, MARCH 2012

In 1996 [as Chief Gardens Advisor], I designed the Winter Walk at Anglesey Abbey with Richard Ayres, then Head Gardener. The design arose in response to the need for a winter feature leading from the car park.

The garden at Anglesey Abbey consists of a series of bold strokes across flat landscape, recalling transitional formal layouts of the early 18th century, still geometric in overall structure, while also incorporating semi-natural features within it.

The challenge for the Winter Walk was to produce an original scheme, considering the first Lord Fairhaven's bold and clear-cut approach, but incorporating opportunities for developing a series of effective winter-plant combinations. I remember drawing a wiggly line for the path in my notebook and showing it to Lord Fairhaven and Richard Ayres. With their approval we developed the scheme on the lines you see today.

"I remember drawing a wiggly line for the path in my notebook and showing it to Lord Fairhaven and Richard Ayres"

The presence of a gardener like Richard to guide the process on site is indispensable to the continuing success of any complex layout of this kind. Their attention is vital: garden-making is a creative process, demanding imaginative and perceptive input at every stage. The process never stops.

# Ballad of a Seed

ALICE OSWALD, JANUARY 2000

This is a poem about a seed – that physical emblem of beginnings – to mark the new millennium. Some people say the year 2000 is no different from any other year; and perhaps that is particularly true for gardeners. Plants keep their own time.

So this poem, while celebrating beginnings, is not really about their befores and afters. It is not about what a seed, or a millennium, becomes, but what it is already.

"Some people say the year 2000 is no different from any other year; and perhaps that is particularly true for gardeners. Plants keep their own time"

That's why, instead of using conventional ballad form, it uses the sounds of a ballad but breaks them out of their verses. In ballad form, the verse is a kind of time-keeper to push the story forwards. In this broken ballad, you do not move beyond the seed's first phase.

In the final image, the seed is seen not as the progenitor of the plant, but as something in itself monumental and mysterious – like a sculpture by Barbara Hepworth or Peter Randall-Page.

I was born bewildered
at dawn, when the rain ends;

uniquely no-one in particular, a pauper in a shack of a flower.

At dawn, when the rain ends,
things drift about seeking shape.

I saw pollen pass through trees
in no rush,
possessing nothing, not even weight.

I set out, taking my whole world with me,
wrapping myself round in my own identity as thin as a soap-film,

and all that day I was a wind-borne eye.
I couldn't put myself
at rest, not even for one second:

increasingly unfocused, spinning
through the disintegrating kingdom of a garden,
and going nowhere
and seeing myself at all angles;

and I was huge,
like you would make a stone guitar,
a cryptic shape of spheres and wires.

# GARDEN DESIGN

*Note from the editor*

In 1954, to celebrate 150 years of the
Royal Horticultural Society's existence,
Geoffrey Jellicoe, the foremost garden
and landscape architect in Britain, wrote a
long and wide-ranging article in which he
surveyed the history of garden design, and
where it intertwined both with the history of
the United Kingdom and that of the Society.
Although much garden research has
been done since 1954, the Garden History
Society has been founded, and a number
of important gardens renovated and
conserved, this still remains a readable
and perceptive introduction to the subject.

He mentions Sir Edwin Lutyens' collaboration
with Miss Gertrude Jekyll – of course – and
I here include one of the rare contributions
Miss Jekyll made to the Society's journal,
in this case in the way of a talk (which
someone else delivered for her) towards the
end of her life and on a favourite subject of
hers, colour planning. Adrian Bloom has a
modern take on the Jekyll idea, while I myself

ponder the enduring attractions of the playful use of water.

The other pieces in this chapter represent a melange of more contemporary preoccupations in design: for example, the pros and cons of 'garden makeovers', 'living walls' in cities, and how much we as a nation truly value design over cultivation in our gardens, a subject enthusiastically argued at an RHS Bicentenary Debate in early 2004. The last words go to Tim Richardson, who looks at how those killed in the Twin Towers have been memorialised.

**URSULA BUCHAN**, editor

# Geoffrey Jellicoe's Survey of Garden Design in England 1804–1954

GEOFFREY JELLICOE, OCTOBER 1954

## Part One: Introduction

Eighteen hundred and four [the year the RHS was founded] was the year before Trafalgar, when England secured for herself the freedom of the seas. Eleven years later Waterloo was to provide a hundred years of peace and prosperity, a period during which the arts of civilisation were to be developed freely and in association with commercial power. With Napoleon's armies encamped ominously at Boulogne, it would seem an odd moment to found a society that is almost wholly known to the world at large as being concerned with the peaceful and enjoyable art of gardening. But in the first place the Society was founded to encourage and develop the growth of fruit trees; and in the second, country life in England for the well-to-do went on very much undisturbed by the Napoleonic wars.

"With Napoleon's armies encamped ominously at Boulogne, it would seem an odd moment to found a society that is almost wholly known to the world at large as being concerned with the peaceful and enjoyable art of gardening"

It was a moment of great significance for the philosophy that gives rise to the arts, for the eighteenth century had been the culmination of the age of reason. But reason had produced the machine, which in turn was the cause of the Industrial Revolution, and by 1804 the single stream of creative power that had produced such magnificent works in the previous century became divided into two streams that have never wholly rejoined. The one was preoccupied with the intellectual, and in particular with all the sciences, while the other was concerned with the romantic or poetic, possibly expressed most forcibly in this country by William Blake. It was the age when Wordsworth was extolling the virtues of nature by an appreciation through the senses, when the poetic imagination would read into nature anything it wished. It was the age of the great English landscape painters.

In one way it might have been better for the pure arts of garden design in England had there been no decisive Trafalgar, and no absolute freedom of the seas. There can be no doubt that the logical development of garden design was thoroughly unhinged by the import of a world's palette of plants, and by the use of the greenhouse that made their growth practicable even if climate were against them. But to understand fully the problems of design that existed during the beginning of the Society's existence it is necessary to go back in history.

The course of English garden history ran smoothly enough from medieval times to the beginning of the eighteenth century. The cloister and the castle garden were open-air rooms, the box- or stone-edged flower bed holding its limited range of flowers in a firm architectural setting. As the land became safer, so the walls were thrown down and the garden extended into its environment; sometimes, as at Hatfield, it was simply an extension or echo of each façade. As ideas filtered from Italy, so the garden became more formal and shapely. The influence of Holland with its emphasis on domesticity was friendly to the native instinct, but in the early eighteenth century the greatest power in the western hemisphere was France. The power was echoed in the great gardens and avenues of Le Nôtre, and for a short while the English aristocracy created avenues on their estates that went beyond native reason. A revolution then took place in English landscape that was no less dramatic in its way than the social revolution in France at the end of the century. The change in outlook upon nature that caused the rise of the English School of Landscape Gardening was no momentary child of fashion. It was a revolution that reversed the whole previous philosophy of western man that had been based on that of the Greeks. For the Greeks set out to conquer the resources of nature and to impose intellectual man upon his environment as surely as the avenues of Badminton imposed the house upon its surroundings. The revolution of the eighteenth century was to satisfy the urge of biological man, and was the father of all the return-to-nature movements from that time to the present day. There is much in common between this art and that of the ancient Chinese. It is interesting to read in Gertrude Jekyll, for instance, how she endeavours to create a woodland scene based upon the natural laws, interest being given by accident; for it was the accidents of nature, of waterfalls, thunderstorms, twisted trees, and so forth, that were the essential contrast with the smoothly working laws in a Chinese garden.

Although the arts of the English School of Landscape Gardening were based on the painters, and the essence was to allow the imagination to wander at will, the art as originally practised by Capability Brown was extraordinarily simple. He first idealised the existing country landscape of the time into the groups of trees and undulating grassland that is the particular glory of England. Nothing indicating man's labours (such as a hedgerow) or reasonable means of sustenance (such as a cow) was to be visible; but the landscape could be enhanced by ruins, temples, church spires and browsing deer because these created lofty sentiments. No boundaries were to be seen. So with these simple principles, Capability Brown, who was a genuine artist, could visit and decide upon the development of landscape in a shortness of time that leaves breathless a modern age that has every transport facility at its disposal. As the century developed and drew to a close, the landscape world came to be dominated by Humphry Repton, who brought to a climax the design of the estate having a great Palladian house set in its English park, providing possibly the unique contribution to the visual arts of the world made by this country.

## Part Two: 1804–1854

The three adventures in the layout and ownership of gardens by The Royal Horticultural Society itself approximate to the early part of each half-century of its existence. There is first the simple scientifically planned orchard gardens at Chiswick (1824); then comes the astonishing architectural adventure in Kensington in 1862; and finally the acceptance and opening of Wisley in 1904, which may properly be said to be a cross-section of all gardens and gardening taking place contemporaneously in the country. The Chiswick garden is perhaps symbolic of the fact that below the fluctuating surface of the fashionable and well-to-do gardens, the kitchen garden and the ordinary cottage garden continued without much

"The characteristic of the age was the chopping up of grass into small beds of doubtful shape, and the planting of these in a way similar to that of a child with sudden access to a box of paints"

change. [William] Cobbett, who was trained as a gardener, paints a realistic and beautiful picture of rural England not only in his *Rural Rides*, but in less known works such as *The English Gardener*, first published in 1827. The cottage garden has been a consistent characteristic of England. It is significant that when England finally became a land primarily of town and slum dwellers, the love of nature was only temporarily suppressed, and in due course created the garden suburb and the New Towns, themselves based on the individual home and garden. With the knowledge of this secure and common-sense background we can explore the tumultuous course that landscape design as an art has taken from 1804 to the present day.

Up to Trafalgar and Waterloo there is little sign of confusion. It is true that architecture had already become divided within itself with the advent of the Gothic Revival, but [John] Nash and [Humphry] Repton were sweeping on in a combination of classical architect and romantic landscape architect in a way unequalled before or since. Kew had been opened in the previous century for the scientific study of trees, and in fact in 1810 contained 11,000 species; but the import of plants generally from abroad, while on the increase, had been absorbed in the same way that foreign architectural styles had always been absorbed. Then came the full impact of flowers from all parts of the world, and it was as though the increasingly wealthy country had consumed an artistic feast it was unable to digest. People called for more and more flowers, and to lengthen the period of colour, as well as to harbour tender and exotic plants, the greenhouse became an essential for every garden. Bedding out as an element of garden design was paramount until about 1880.

One likes mischievously to think of Humphry Repton endeavouring to grapple with this urge for flowers, for they formed little or no part in his scheme of things. It is interesting to note his use of tubs and great baskets, for the intention is to suggest a transitory vase which is not part of the basic landscape scene; we find a similar idea today in the widespread use of flowers in circular tubs that emanated from Stockholm and is now copied throughout Europe. A very real problem in a broad and noble landscape is how to provide a setting for the individual flower so that a relationship in scale is preserved; the painter has no such difficulty with his fixed foreground, middle and distance. The landscape architect Loudon attempted to reconcile the huge palette of flowers with existing fashions in taste, but he would appear to have had more influence as a writer than as a practitioner. The characteristic of the age was the chopping up of grass into small beds of doubtful shape, and the planting of these in a way similar to that of a child with sudden access to a box of paints.

With increase in wealth after the Napoleonic wars by the middle class, the unprecedented demand for plants of all kinds justified the spirit of adventure that sent explorers all over the world. The sending out of collectors, which began about 1818, was in fact the greatest work of The Royal Horticultural Society, and this was in addition to those sent by private firms such as

Veitch. Nor was it flowers and shrubs alone that were introduced, for soon the conifers of North America were discovered and no garden was complete without them. A pinetum was established at Kew in 1843; the first 'Monkey Puzzle' was described in 1847 as a tree of 'singular beauty'.

It is impossible at this period to concede at the most more than a charming confusion in landscape tendencies, but about the time when Robert Fortune, the most successful of all collectors, was opening up China in 1842, the previously submerged architectural mind once more began to take charge in no uncertain manner. I think the dominant professional figures here are Sir Joseph Paxton and Sir Charles Barry, but by the middle of the century the real influence was probably that of the Prince Consort. The first half-centenary of the Society fell three years after the Great Exhibition and it was under the spell of this that the Society embarked upon its oddest venture, the gardens at Kensington.

## Part Three: 1854–1904

Paxton had a genial personality, a genius for the idea of structural science, and strong leanings towards the classical architecture with which he was so closely associated as head gardener at Chatsworth and which he never properly understood. He designed the Palm House in 1835, and this led to the Crystal Palace of 1851; a single and memorable idea that well summarised the majestic unity of

"...and at Gravetye Manor, it was shown how the geometrical and biological arts can form a happy marriage; Gravetye was in this respect perhaps the first of the modern gardens"

the nation. It was the age of prodigious wealth and expression and in the words of G M Trevelyan 'the world is not likely to see so high a culture again for many centuries'. Such a civilisation called for a more grandiose landscape than historic England could provide, and this was found in the architecture and gardens of the high Italian Renaissance. But the English designers were in their own estimation to surpass the Italians in so far that the formal parterre gardens would not contain the dull coloured stones of Italy or France, but would sparkle with brilliant colour now available through massed and bedded-out flowers. The gardens at Sydenham were like this and were in exact contrast to the Palace itself; for they were as unhappy an example of an engineer's excursion into the humanities as the building itself was successful as an example of the working of the structural laws of nature. The culmination of the architectural garden came about under Barry between 1840 and 1860, and it was this fashion, so far removed from the objectives of The Royal Horticultural Society, that gave rise to the ill-fated Kensington garden.

The Prince Consort was undoubtedly architecturally minded. He had been both President of the 1851 Exhibition, and was President of the Royal Horticultural Society; and there is every indication that he alone was responsible for this classic work. Nothing was to be spared to make it an example to the world. Sidney Smirke, R.A., was appointed architect, Fowke the engineer, and W. A. Nesfield, who had worked with Barry, the landscape artist. The gardens with the colonnades, fountains, and architecture were opened in 1862 at a cost of over £50,000, and made little or no contribution to the study of horticulture; and according to photography, very little towards architecture. But it is a clear indication of the formidable power of fashion at that time to provide an art almost exactly diametrically opposed to the natural indigenous instinct. Nor did the fashion die easily, for works of garden art from Italy were imported on a truly gigantic scale until the end of the century and even later. The most remarkable of all such gardens furnished in this way, in or out of history or anywhere else, are probably those of Hever Castle, in Kent.

It is one of the saddest attributes of the art of landscape that it is transitory. The history of the period is largely gathered from contemporary writing, from drawings, and later from photography. We are led to imagine a rural England of the middle of the nineteenth century scattered with villas of all styles of architecture, and set in gardens of all kinds of planting; the most distant species were available to the modest purse; and always there would be the dark conifer as a visitor from a foreign land. In 1883, just as there had been a revolt against the implications of the avenues a hundred and fifty years earlier, so a new revolt against foreign species of another kind was heralded by the publication of *The English Flower Garden*, by William Robinson. It was a kind of double revolt – to throw off the spurious contemporary architectural garden, and to bring back the indigenous planting belonging to the country.

For a time garden interest was focused upon the struggle between Robinson and Sir Reginald Blomfield, who replied to the wild garden in *The Formal Garden in England*, published in 1892. In retrospect we see that both protagonists stood for the native arts, and in due course, at Gravetye Manor, it was shown how the geometrical and biological arts can come to form a happy marriage; Gravetye was in this respect perhaps the first of the modern gardens. Under Blomfield's influence, on the other hand, gardens were laid out so skilfully in the style of the early formal English garden that they were often mistaken for the original.

Contemporary with Robinson was Gertrude Jekyll, who in her first book set out to make order out of the disordered colour palette of flowers, and to place aesthetic design above horticulture as the objective of a garden. To many of us, however, it is as the collaborator with Sir Edwin Lutyens that she made her greatest contribution to the art of landscape. Since the turn of the century saw the beginning of the unique partnership, we may usher in the third half-century of the Society by a description of their works and significance.

## Part Four: 1904–1954

> "The half century has seen the initiative of good landscape begin to pass from the unorganised gifted layman to the organised professional, but with what result it is as yet too early to foresee"

The best work of Lutyens was done between about 1896 and 1913, but he appears to summarise all the emotions and feelings that were abroad in England between 1880 and 1930. He dominated an era as only Christopher Wren had done before. His genius really lay in house, garden and environment; and in this he stands so far above his able contemporaries that we must explore somewhat deeply to understand why it was that his works were not just a box of tricks that rejuvenated any historic style he wished. Nor does his fame rest upon the fact that his buildings were full of fun in contrast to so much dreary Georgian revival of the period. He was above all an artist, with complete mastery of his trade to express his art. His buildings and gardens emerged from the landscape as naturally as did the planting of Gertrude Jekyll; the word 'naturally' being used to imply submission primarily to the biological laws of nature, rather than the mechanical laws of the universe. The garden was certainly an extension of the geometry of the house, but just as the external shape of the house itself was suggested by the rooms, so was that of the garden by its compartments; a totally different idea from the box-like Renaissance house and garden. Every part of a Lutyens' composition is based upon an appreciation of the basic animal senses, of smell and touch as well as sight. It would be beyond this article to analyse the way his grouping was inspired by the natural shaping of the ground, his stimulating silhouette, his contrast of open and closed spaces, his genius for material both in colour and textures, and all the other arts upon which he played as upon the notes of a piano. But having once heard him deplore the loss of the third dimension in modern architecture, I cannot do better than suggest that he was an architect who appreciated that man has two eyes, and not one eye; instinctively he designed his forms so that the eyes judged the shape stereoscopically, and not solely by shadow or perspective. His work is perceived as sculpture, just as much as a fluted Doric column or the bark-indented trunk of an ash tree. We can and do forgive him the fact that his architecture was too stamped with his own personality to make the union with nature so satisfactory as at Gravetye.

Wisley was presented to The Royal Horticultural Society in 1904, and gives a clear picture of garden tendencies during the past fifty years. It is of interest that while architecture has been through such vicissitudes, the outlook towards nature appears to have changed very little. Here at Wisley is seen the influence of Robinson and Jekyll, and in addition of such men as Reginald Farrer, who at the end of the last century popularised the alpine plant and consequently the rock garden. Here too as a further sequence in the return-to-nature movement we see a development of the study of heath and heathers, a modern landscape exploration into another aspect of the world around us. But landscape is essentially a partnership between the geometric and biological arts, and the revolution in the former that began after the First World War unsettled the established relationship of the previous forty years. Up to that date the handicrafts had resisted the machine, but from then onwards the mechanical and mass production of building materials began to make itself felt. The influences that bore down upon English landscape between the wars were perhaps greater than at any period in history, for they were concerned with an internal revolution where in the past the influence had been from the outside. It is not the last significant element of this period that the Institute of Landscape Architects was founded in 1929, and that a professional course in landscape was established at Reading University about the same time. The half century has seen the initiative of good landscape begin to pass from the unorganised gifted layman to the organised professional, but with what result it is as yet too early to foresee.

## Part Five: The Scene in 1954

The most striking factor in the contemporary scene is the infinite variety of *subjects* of landscape compared with fifty years ago. There are more public parks, gardens and playing fields. There is the landscape of industry, a wholly new art. There are national parks, nature reserves, softwood afforestation, water conservation, mass roadways tearing their way across the countryside. It is elements such as these in a now over-populated but landscape-conscious country that will absorb more and more professionals. Although the high cost of labour and high taxation preclude the making of large gardens, and although a new landscape art of shrinking an existing garden has arisen, the numbers of gardens proportionate to the population is probably higher than at any time. But they are small, and in contrast to the traditional cottage garden, the knowledge that goes to their making is largely obtained though a gardening press that has developed astonishingly since Loudon first issued his journal. The popularity of Chelsea [Flower Show] is itself a sign of the times. The middle-sized garden survives and continues to be made mainly because of mechanical invention that began with the mowing machine at the beginning of the last century. But there is no doubt that the present trend against formal gardens with clipped hedges is secretly stimulated by the problem of maintenance.

"...the numbers of gardens proportionate to the population is probably higher than at any time. But they are small, and in contrast to the traditional cottage garden, the knowledge that goes to their making is largely obtained through a gardening press that has developed astonishingly since Loudon first issued his journal"

The first impact of factory methods of building upon the modern architect seems to have produced the same result as did the impact of flowers upon the gardener a hundred years previously; he was overwhelmed. He lost all that history that he had so carefully cherished and in its place built in a style called international that was at first as de-humanised as bedding-out had been de-naturalised. But as the art matures we begin to see taking place a marriage between the universal mechanical laws that lie behind the making of buildings, and the biological laws that cause the growth of plants; uneasy partners at all times but increasingly so as the world gets older. We see something of this maturity when we turn the pages of Peter Shepheard's *The Modern Garden*, from which the curse of gardens, sentimentality, has been eliminated. The objective would seem to be the acceptance of nature as an equal partner with the works of man, but to arrange her in such a way that we can enter her world and enjoy our origins without clumsily trampling her out.

# Colour in Garden Planning

GERTRUDE JEKYLL, SEPTEMBER 1929

"...when colour is rightly used the various portions of the garden will have the highest pictorial value as living pictures of plant beauty"

Fifty years ago, when the bedding-out of tender plants for a summer display was the general garden practice, if any thought was given to arranging them for colour, it was to produce the crudest and most garish effects; such as a round bed of a vivid scarlet Geranium with a border of blue Lobelia, or a wavy ribbon border of scarlet, blue, and yellow. Now that all that concerns the planning of our gardens is engaging the attention of our best designers, the better use of colour is being carefully considered, and is already being gloriously practised. For when colour is rightly used the various portions of the garden will have the highest pictorial value as living pictures of plant beauty.

An example of the better arrangement may be quoted in the case of a large flower border, nearly 200 feet in length. It begins with flowers of tender and cool colouring – pale pink, blue, white and palest yellow – followed by stronger yellow, and passing on to deep orange and rich mahogany, and so coming to a culminating glory of the strongest scarlet, tempered with rich but softer reds, and backed and intergrouped with flowers and foliage of dark claret colour.

The progression of colour then recedes in the same general order, as in its approach to the midmost glory, till it comes near the further end to a quiet harmony of lavender and purple and tender pink, with a whole setting of grey and silvery foliage. No one who has seen or carried out such a scheme, and whose desire it is to have the best effects that the flowers can give, will be contented with a haphazard mixture. Such an arrangement in harmonies is not only satisfying as a whole picture, but, though perhaps unconsciously to the observer, it follows natural laws relating to sight; for the cool and tender colouring is the best optical preparation for the splendour of the warmer masses, and, when the eye has had its fill of this, it receives a distinct sense of satisfaction when it comes again to the cool and restful colouring of flower and foliage. It is like passing from some shady place of half-light into the brilliant glow of hottest sunshine; and then, when this is almost too burning and oppressive, coming again to the quiet comfort of coolest shade and perhaps the sound of running or splashing water.

Some garden space is often devoted to a special colour, such as the desire for a blue garden. There is some curious quality, not easy to define or to understand, about flowers of pure blue, such as Delphinium, Anchusa, Cornflower, and the useful dwarf Lobelia, that demands a contrast rather than a harmony; for though in a blue garden the colouring can, with more or less success, be made to pass from the pure blues into those of purple shades, such as those of the Campanulas, yet it is a duller thing than if the pure blues only are used, with the companionship of something of white or pale yellow, such as white or yellow Lilies, white Phlox or pale yellow Snapdragon; or the creamy white of *Artemisia lactiflora* or *Clematis flammula*.

Sometimes an objection is made – surely an unreasonable one – that as the garden is called the blue garden, there must be nothing in it but what is actually blue. But surely it is a pity to spoil a garden for the sake of a word. These problems of colour arrangement are becoming an engrossing study; every year some new or better combination suggests itself, with its certain reward in the following season. Something of the satisfaction of a good conscience rewards and encourages the designer; for surely one of the objects of a good garden is that it shall be pictorially beautiful – that it shall be a series of enjoyable pictures painted with the living flowers.

# Go With the Flow

ADRIAN BLOOM, AUGUST 2010

On the face of it, describing a planting design feature as a 'river' may seem overly descriptive (even overflowing) hyperbole. The word 'drift' to describe a meandering strip of plants is perhaps more common, going back to Gertrude Jekyll. Contemporary garden designers have also used the term 'river' to cover

> "...as a way to create drama and effect in a border, I suggest a 'river' of plants is a serious design feature..."

any long ribbon of plants, whether low growing or tall. But as a way to create drama and effect in a border, I suggest a 'river' of plants is a serious design feature worth the consideration of gardeners.

My first experiment in creating a river of planting was actually somewhat tongue-in-cheek, back in 1990 in my garden, Foggy Bottom, at

Bressingham, Norfolk. I planted a 'river of molten lava' using *Kniphofia* 'Bressingham Comet' as the fiery lava among *Heuchera villosa* Bressingham Bronze ('Absi') and smoke-like *Stipa tenuissima*. Later, when Blooms of Bressingham launched *Geranium* 'Rozanne' ('Gerwat') at the RHS Chelsea Flower Show in 2000, I created a well overflowing into a river of the new geranium cultivar that ran through the garden of our exhibit.

Influential Dutch designer Piet Oudolf has also used meandering rivers in some of his informal, large-scale planting schemes, notably at Ensköping, Sweden, in the late 1990s. In Japan, rocks and gravel have been used to represent watercourses for centuries in Zen or 'dry' gardens.

## Planting options

Over the past 10 years, in new plantings at Bressingham, and in the USA and Germany, I have experimented with a diversity of plants in different situations to create rivers with various planting combinations alongside. These, the 'banks', are mainly perennials or grasses, but can also include shrubs or conifers.

What plants you select for the banks depends of course on what is used for the river, both in terms of scale and in the combination of colour, texture and forms. Situation and aspect are also important: sun or shade, hot or cool, dry or moist conditions affect the plant choice. The aim is to create a long-term scheme, with changing interest and drama, so plants that provide colour or foliage contrast through the seasons should be selected and repeated.

Once you start to consider rivers as a design form, some 'landforming' can allow slopes and banks to be made into waterfalls, streams and tributaries. Let your imagination run riot, as long as you keep the plants happy culturally.

Though most applicable to large-scale schemes, a river can be just as striking on a smaller plot. In tighter spaces, scale down your perspective simply by choosing more compact plants.

*Geranium* 'Rozanne' is a perfect plant for a river feature: a tough, long-flowering plant the flowers of which, being violet-blue and spreading into each other, can be realistically imagined as a river or stream. It is an obvious favourite for gardens large or small that receive a fair amount of sun, with large mounds of green foliage, 60–90cm (2–3ft) tall and broad, in bloom until the frosts.

A little more tender than *Geranium* 'Rozanne', but equally long-flowering, is low-growing, soft-pink-flowered *G.* 'Mavis Simpson', especially good for Mediterranean-style gardens. As suitable banks to contrast with the geranium, consider *Crocosmia* 'Lucifer', *Hydrangea arborescens* 'Annabelle', *Miscanthus sinensis* 'Morning Light' or an upright green conifer such as *Thuja occidentalis* 'Smaragd'.

I have used indispensable *Ophiopogon planiscapus* 'Nigrescens' as a dramatic river in sun, and particularly shade, in the UK. Its low-growing, arching, everblack leaves thrive where not too dry, with starry white flowers a bonus. Hostas, as long as slugs can be kept at bay, offer several months of foliage and flower in shade: consider golden-green variegated *H.* 'Shade Fanfare' as a river and, for the banks, taller, larger, blue-ribbed *H. sieboldiana* var. *elegans*. Bright green-leaved *Hakonechloa macra*, or its shorter, variegated cultivar *H. macra* 'Alboaurea' (golden Japanese forest grass), is one of the best grasses to form either a river or edging, depending what other plants are used with it. The cultivar is a favourite of mine for garden or container; it looks attractive for nine or ten months of the year, even when in dormant autumnal beige. The wave-like motion of these grasses in the wind is a valuable added feature. Either of them, perhaps planted on a low bank, makes a perfect contrast surrounding a black pool or stream of *Ophiopogon*. *Heuchera* is another 'dual-purpose' plant for river or banks, available in a range of colours and textures, and many are evergreen. *Heuchera* 'Prince' is a good choice; not all are robust and long-lived.

Using large numbers of plants can be expensive, but many perennials and grasses can be easily divided at the appropriate time, and a river developed gradually over a longer period. I prefer to use hardy, easily-grown perennials or woody plants for rivers and banks to give seasonal change, but annuals can obviously be part of the mix – either on their own, for short-term effect, or as temporary fillers while stocks of perennials are built up.

As I experiment more, I am becoming increasingly convinced that using plants in this way opens the mind to greater creativity and possibilities in garden design. Visually striking, a river can lead your eye into the garden or bed, create varied structure and plant combinations, and be an interesting design feature in gardens of all sizes.

# You've Just got to Laugh

URSULA BUCHAN, NOVEMBER 2009

When I was young and green, I was tremendously stuffy about gardens. They were for the enjoyment of beauty and solitude, for promoting the thinking of deep thoughts and – snob that I was – they were about plants and Latin names. Well, I have got over that now and, although I still think that gardens are about beauty and tranquillity, I also think they can respectably and successfully be – at least in part – about jokes, games and frivolity; gardens can (and often should) amuse, intrigue and distract as well as console, inspire, instruct or impress. In short, that they can be playgrounds for grown-ups.

> "Garden makers have always had a penchant for *jeux d'esprit*, especially where water was concerned"

This is especially so where gardens include the playful use of water. In May, the restored Elizabethan garden at Kenilworth Castle, Warwickshire was opened. Originally made for a Royal visit in 1575, it had an aviary, a fountain and other encouragements to dalliance. My advice is, don't walk too close to the base of the new Carrara marble fountain, if you don't want to get wet.

At The Alnwick Garden, Northumberland, the William Pye water sculptures in the Serpent Garden, although sadly cramped together, are collectively a remarkable group of shiny steel sculptures, from which water rises, falls, bubbles, sprays and reflects the sun; they are an irresistible attraction to visitors. In the Garden of Surprises at Burghley House, Lincolnshire (inspired by the first Lord Burghley's Elizabethan garden), 'divers conceits', such as a 'curtain of water', test one's courage and fleetness of foot.

Garden makers have always had a penchant for *jeux d'esprit*, especially where water was concerned. Kenilworth is one of few Elizabethan gardens that have been recovered. However, from only a century later, and still standing, there is Thomas Archer's Cascade House at Chatsworth, Derbyshire, which provided jets of water up through the floor to soak unwary visitors. Nearby is a 17th-century copper 'willow tree' that still spouts water unexpectedly. The older I get, the more easily enchanted I am by such ingenuity and high spirits. Provided it's a hot day, of course.

# Makeover Madness

MARY KEEN, MAY 2000

Gardeners are by nature down-to-earth people. We call a spade a spade and know what to use it for. Garden makeover designers are different. They say things like: 'I really love this tree, but it is just in completely the wrong place'; or 'I want to bring the ocean to the garden'. Moving mountains, let alone oceans, is not the average gardener's lot. We work in the landscape of molehills. The big ideas, the instant impact and the complete disrespect for the pace and scale of nature are, I suspect, anathema to most readers of this journal. Ask someone who is committed to the long, slow process of developing a garden what they think of 'makeover mania' and you get a short answer and a hollow laugh.

"Show me a gardener who would rather polish steel than take a cutting, and I will eat my hat"

There is no denying the theatre of the makeover. Anyone who has been to the RHS Chelsea Flower Show and has seen the Show Gardens constructed in the space of a few weeks can relish the fantasy of the perfect garden, created on a canvas of mud. Real gardens are never perfect – they are always better last week or next season; they represent years of trials and triumphs. For those of us who dedicate our lives to our gardens, an RHS show is perfect escapism. We enjoy watching the spectacle of something so completely different, so unattainable, especially if it has been put together with the skill of Beth Chatto or Carol Klein. Such gardens are shining examples to the trowellers and truggers. We can accept the unreality of the instant show-garden display. It is a much easier proposition than the fast-forward frenzy of the screen makeover. A whole year of planning, followed by a few weeks of construction, seems reassuringly staid when compared with the hit-the-ground-running, half-hour television programme.

Alan Titchmarsh and Charlie Dimmock in *Ground Force* provide us with the nearest thing we have to a horticultural soap. The endless carry-on, all flap and flirtation, is great fun to watch – as a drama. The tears and tensions give an edge to the programme that keeps even the most cynical viewers glued to the screen. Did Nelson Mandela really like the garden he returned to find after a transatlantic trip? 'I thought we were going to have no secrets,' he said to his wife and he looked bewildered. Was the prison officer who had spent years building a folly at the bottom of his garden genuinely delighted to discover that the *Ground Force* team had finished the work?

The jokes are good, if corny. A piece of broken china turns up. 'Is it Ming?' 'No, Birmingham,' says Tommy Walsh, the laconic builder. All human life is there and Alan Titchmarsh comes across as a real person. Quite apart from his obvious niceness, it is clear that his knowledge of the things that really interest working gardeners is far greater than what he is called on to display. And there's the rub. We would rather watch Titchmarsh showing us how to repot an *Echeveria* than listen to him pronouncing on taste.

Can we justify the programmes in terms of their appeal to the non-gardener? Do they recruit more Members to the RHS and do they teach people who know nothing at all about gardening how to lay out and maintain their plots? Most important of all, do they introduce newcomers to the pleasure of gardening, to the process rather than the product? I fear not. The best gardens respect the genius of the place and put people in touch with the natural world, but this is not the design ethos of the makeover designers. Sheets of plate glass and Perspex can never be sympathetic materials at the heart of the garden. In summer, plants will bake in captured light and all through the year birds will crash against the invisible panels. After a shower of rain, stainless steel loses its sheen, which can only be recaptured with libations of baby oil. Show me a gardener who would rather polish steel than take a cutting, and I will eat my hat. Water features are *de rigueur*, on dry chalk, near streams and in the smallest plots. Does every garden need one?

The ultimate example of the inappropriate must surely have been a diagonally-placed, angular pool down the entire length of a garden designed by *Home Front in the Garden*. When the back of a detached house had been painted lime green and a Perspex ha-ha installed, the owners had only the perpetual chore of admiring the pool and the paint. There was no room for nurturing plants or communing with nature, from which gardeners derive such pleasure.

As a designer, it seems to me that the budgets are often optimistic and the cost of a makeover garden generally seems less that it might be in the real world. This can give viewers a false idea of what can be achieved. The choice of plants is just as perplexing. In the wackier makeover programmes, frost-tender tree ferns and phormiums are used with a reckless disregard for climate and situation. Plants that would not normally grow within miles of one another can happily be shoved shoulder to shoulder into ill-prepared ground. Bamboos, with their in-built territorial imperative are encouraged and modest, local plants are rarely chosen. After planting, gravel or granite chips are spread all over the soil. Is this to hide bindweed and dandelions lurking below?

The saddest thing about makeover programmes is that they are depriving people of the chance to enjoy the kind of gardening that delights the readers of these pages. As we become increasingly unravelled by the pace of modern life, not even sleep is enough to repair our frayed spirits. Gardeners, however, can find peace whenever they step outside. How odd that this feeling, more instant in effect than a makeover, can never be synthesised on screen. Virtual peace is not given to viewers.

# Sightseeing

URSULA BUCHAN, AUGUST 2010

I am a provincial through and through. I rarely spend much time in big cities but, recently, I have discovered (thanks to my city-dwelling daughter's penchant for taking her Aged Parent on buses) the pleasure of seeing London from four metres above street level. Sitting on the top deck of a bus moving sedately down Sloane Street feels like being in a valley between sheer mountains. Best of all, however, is the moment when this bus turns towards Piccadilly and there is a view of Green Park on one side of the road and, on the other, of Patrick Blanc's eight-storey-high 'living wall' (*mur végétal*) on the corner of the Athenaeum Hotel.

"The wall at the Athenaeum Hotel was planted last year and Patrick says he is pleased with the way this sheer cliff of greenery is progressing"

Although you will see a living wall in many an RHS Chelsea Flower Show garden these days, Patrick has been working on them for close on 20 years, and is the acknowledged leader in the field, so to speak. These walls are not just a bravura demonstration of what will survive in hostile conditions, but an artistic expression, with foliage plants used in swerving curves of variable colour. The wall at the Athenaeum Hotel was planted last year and Patrick says he is pleased with the way this sheer cliff of greenery is progressing.

There are about 250 species in all, including those, such as euphorbias, that you might not think would cling so precipitously to the special lining that clothes the wall – a recycled, polyamide, water-absorbent felt, in case you are wondering. Watering and liquid feeding (through horizontal lines of irrigation pipes) is done by turning on the taps for three minutes, five times a day, which uses a mere 5 litres (1 gal). What is more, Patrick thinks it can only get better and better, as plants settle in, and birds begin to nest, safe from threatening cats. This wall makes even a confirmed provincial like me see the point of the city.

# RHS Bicentenary Debate

TOM STUART-SMITH, JANUARY 2004

In early 2004, the Royal Horticultural Society held a lively debate in which 'This House believes that horticultural craft will determine the culture of gardens of the future, at the expense of artistic expression'. At the end of the debate, when a vote was taken, the designers beat the cultivators.

> "...it is perfectly possible to create a garden masterpiece using just one species of plant or none at all"

Tom Stuart-Smith [commenting on the debate] remarked that this question would only be asked in this country, where we are so obsessed by plants that sometimes we cannot see over the leaf to the space beyond. The Barcelona pavilion designed by Mies Van der Rohe for the 1929 international exposition had no plants at all in its terraces, yet it could be said to be a seamless mix of building and garden. At the other end of the historical spectrum, Rousham Park, undoubtedly one of the great masterpieces of British garden making, is almost devoid of exotic plants. A garden that comprises just a series of delectable plant associations without a coherent spatial strategy will always be ultimately unsatisfying, like a meal with too much monosodium glutamate.

It is perfectly possible to create a garden masterpiece using just one species of plant or none at all. Sir Frederick Gibberd said that the true quality of a garden is best judged at the end of February when the froth has gone and the bones are left. As a passionate plantsman, I think this is a little mean, but it properly stresses the importance of design in all the great gardens of the past. In that respect the gardens of the future will be no different.

# New York Fills the Void Left by 9/11

TIM RICHARDSON, SEPTEMBER 2011

Memorials are perhaps the most difficult projects of all to conceive in the world of garden design. This hits home this month as the World Trade Center Memorial Plaza is opening to visitors in time for the 10th anniversary of 9/11.

How do you respectfully encapsulate an act of violence as heinous as the 11 September 2001 attacks on New York? Atrocities of war tend to be perpetrated in secret or where there are few surviving witnesses; this catastrophe was played out, live, on the world's television screens and this memorial will of course be sited on the exact spot.

> "The challenge is to come up with a response that will rehabilitate the space itself while, most importantly, memorialising those who died"

The challenge for a designer is to come up with a response that will rehabilitate the space itself while, most importantly, memorialising those who died. New York's idea was to turn this stricken bombsite into both a place of remembrance and a new business hub even grander than the Twin Towers.

Within a year of 9/11, I visited the Ground Zero area – not to gawp, but to shop in an adjacent department store, which had resolutely stayed open. That 'business as usual' ethic was the most telling response to the attacks, and has clearly informed plans for the new site. Get up, dust yourself off and do it again – that's the American way.

The new site incorporates four new towering buildings as well as two huge, 60 x 60m (200 x 200ft) dark pools on the footprint of the destroyed Twin Towers. A grove of some 400 swamp white oaks (*Quercus bicolor*) will provide shade and a tranquil setting. The names of those who died are to be etched on the pool surrounds.

Creating a space between living and dead is the most powerful way of respecting mourners' emotions. Sir Geoffrey Jellicoe's memorial to John F Kennedy at Runnymede shows that movement through space can lead to a sense of respectful transcendence. I suspect that the real strength of the World Trade Center Memorial Plaza may not lie in the dreadful black pools at its heart, but in the surrounding grove, where the living will quietly try to come to terms with the appalling events that happened there.

# THE KITCHEN GARDEN

*Note from the editor*

I do not believe that any true gardener can resist the appeal of growing their own fruit and vegetables, and the RHS has always taken these matters as seriously as it does decorative horticulture, if the column inches in *The Garden* are any guide. Gardeners know that there is enormous satisfaction to be had in the cultivation of an allotment in the city, or of an orchard of fruit in the country, and the accumulated knowledge on these subjects has been recorded by the RHS since the very beginning. Only recently, however, have cooks such as Nigel Slater reminded us (if we should need it) of the all-important connection between the garden and the kitchen.

Edible produce, particularly at the Autumn Show in London and in the form of wonderful displays at RHS Chelsea Flower Show over the years by Suttons Seeds, the National Farmers' Union, Robinson's Seeds and Medwyn Williams show just what gardeners can do in the way of manipulating the seasons and devising cultural methods to produce remarkable fruit and vegetables.

And amateur gardeners, such as those who enter giant vegetable competitions, are scarcely far behind them, as Joy Larkcom discovered.

In this chapter you will also find the delights of cherry varieties, the supremacy of 'Bramley's Seedling' among culinary apples, the future with blight-resistant potato cultivars, and how the author of *Lorna Doone* was a professional, but not always very successful fruit grower.

The RHS, particularly in recent years, has also sought to give publicity to community projects, which so often involve the growing of edible produce, uniting disparate people whose only connection may be that they are neighbours and they are interested in the process of growing food. The healing nature of kitchen gardening for those with life challenges is also often illuminated. And who could not be touched by Joy Larkcom's throwaway comment that that bible for vegetable growers, the RHS' *Vegetable Garden Displayed*, was translated into German at the end of the war, to help the stricken and starving population of Germany back on to its feet, despite being until recently the sworn enemy.

**URSULA BUCHAN**, editor

# Mr Bramley's Apple

JOAN MORGAN, MARCH 2009

Apple 'Bramley's Seedling' celebrates its bicentenary this year. Not only does it remain our best-known culinary cultivar but, astonishingly, the original mother tree continues to grow and fruit in Southwell, near Nottingham. This tree was raised by Mary Anne Brailsford who, as a child, sowed a few apple pips in a pot in about 1809. One of these pips grew into a vigorous sapling which was planted in the family garden. The tree had been cropping for some years when, in around 1857, it caught the eye of Henry Merryweather, who recognised a potential winner for his fledgling nursery business. By then, the property and tree were owned by Mr Bramley, a local butcher, who gave graft-wood to Merryweather, and his name to the new apple. Sales of grafted trees began in 1862.

"...the brisk fruity taste comes zinging through regardless how much sugar, spices or lemon peel a recipe calls for..."

By the turn of the 19th century, 'Bramley's Seedling' was widely planted in commercial orchards. It helped establish the modern British fruit industry and is a mainstay of today's market orchard. Affection for 'Bramley's Seedling' and its reputation is such that trees are planted by nostalgic Britons and fruit enthusiasts across the world, from southern Spain to California and even Japan. However, the mere fact that 'Bramley's Seedling' is still on sale on supermarket shelves is in many ways more remarkable than this international interest. 'Bramley's Seedling' is a Victorian culinary apple and thus much too sharp to eat fresh with pleasure. Yet, despite our rumoured disinclination to cook, it finds a market year round.

No other country developed a whole group of large, acidic apples specifically for use in the kitchen, as Britain did during the 19th century. Then, the essential requirement for a good 'cooker' was that it would 'fall', that is, cook to a juicy, sharp, smooth and lump-free purée. Generally, the more acidic the apple, the more easily this is achieved. It was the key to perfect apple sauce and, equally, it made an ideal baked apple – the best way to savour the individual flavours of the dozens of different 'cookers' then grown.

The British did not favour the American notion of an apple pie that calls for pieces of apple to spike with a fork, nor the French style with its decorative topping of apple slices, both of which require an apple that keeps its shape when cooked and are therefore less acidic than a proper 'cooker'. Whether the preferences or the apples came first is an open question but 'Bramley's Seedling', with the highest acidity levels of any 'cooker' in my experience, passed the English tests with honours. Plentiful acidity also ensured its continuing use, for the brisk fruity taste comes zinging through regardless how much sugar, spices or lemon peel a recipe calls for, or what mass production abuses it may suffer.

In the 1860s, Merryweather would have been aware of Bramley's culinary merits and recognised its value as a late-season apple that not only stored well (until March) but retained its acidity until spring, making it highly marketable over a long period. Many other late 'cookers', though keeping sound for months, gradually lose their acidity and become flat and insipid when cooked, hence the call for lemon juice to give some bite. Bramley needed no such help. And being a late keeper it suited modern storage and marketing requirements, which now deliver Bramley nearly every month of the year, almost as sharp as first picked.

'Bramley's Seedling' was fortunate in being in the right place at the right time. Although introduced in the 1860s, it did not make a real public debut until the National Apple Congress of 1883, held by the RHS in its former Chiswick garden. The aim was to bring together as many as possible of the different apples growing throughout Britain in order that the fruit experts could resolve the confusion of names, synonyms and identities. Some 1,500 cultivars were displayed, which proved to be an enormous public attraction.

Visitors were amazed by the diversity of apples available at a time when English fruit in the markets was almost overwhelmed by foreign imports. Having already been highly commended by the Society's Fruit Committee in 1876, 'Bramley's Seedling' received an RHS First Class Certificate, and now its worth as 'a very excellent culinary apple' was consolidated. The first large-scale commercial plantings were made in Kent in 1890, setting it on its way to be a major market and garden apple.

In the battle with imports, Bramley apples found a niche, as no other country produced 'cookers'. Even when, years later, the industry faced competition after the UK's entry into the Common Market in 1975 and growers responded with intensive plantations of trees on semi-dwarfing 'M9' rootstocks (that produced the pristine appearance and consistent size demanded by supermarkets), 'Bramley's Seedling' met the challenge.

Commonly believed to succeed only as a standard tree on a vigorous stock, by the early 1980s trials demonstrated it would thrive on any rootstock. It was promoted as thoroughly British along with our most-cherished eating apple, 'Cox's Orange Pippin'. Alas, Cox has diminished in importance but Bramley apples are still planted.

Today 80,000–100,000 tonnes of Bramleys are produced annually: in Kent (39,000 tonnes), the Wisbech area of East Anglia (10,000 tonnes), the West Midlands (6,000 tonnes) and Northern Ireland (35,000 tonnes). About 25 percent of the crop is sold as fresh fruit and 45 percent for processing as pie, crumble fillings and other food products. The remainder goes for juice, and to make cider. Most of Northern Ireland's Bramley apples form a major ingredient of a popular Irish cider.

The triumphant journey of 'Bramley's Seedling', however, has swept aside all other cookers. Grown on 'M9' rootstock, Bramley apples will 'size up' early and fruit can be picked and sold in August. The main crop, harvested in September, can be stored and marketed through to June and July. So, sadly, we have lost the seasonal successions of different culinary apples, their flavours and cooking properties, but thanks to 'Bramley's Seedling' success this British culinary tradition lives on. Anyone wanting to cook a true apple crumble or enjoy a baked apple need only go to the local supermarket, and the enthusiast wishing to sample a wider range of 'cookers' can still track them down at farmers' markets, visit the collections at RHS Garden Wisley, the National Fruit Collections at Brogdale, or better still grow them in their own garden.

# An Urban Harvest

MATTHEW BIGGS, OCTOBER 2009

In 2003, a keen-eyed member of 'Organiclea', a group promoting locally grown organic food in northeast London, noticed that there were lots of apple trees in the area, with fruit that was regularly left unpicked. From this one acute observation, the Organiclea 'Scrumping Project' was born.

The Borough of Waltham Forest is, paradoxically, a perfect place for anyone with a predilection for apples. Over the centuries they have been planted in parks, as street trees and are particularly prolific in gardens.

Locals say that Eden Road E17 was built on an old orchard, and Victorian architect John Warner, who built most of the local houses, put an apple or pear tree in every garden. A red-fruited apple particularly abundant in the area was identified recently by the National Fruit Collection at Brogdale, Kent as a seedling of *Malus niedzwetzkyana* called 'Wisley Crab'. Locally, perhaps inevitably, it has been given the nickname Walthamstow Pink. 'These trees are found in the most unexpected places,' says Marlene Barratt, one of the project co-ordinators. 'One tree we harvest is in a hospital car park, another is in a pub garden, and there are plenty on waste ground. Our latest project is a "linear orchard", planted three years ago alongside a cycle path, which is now beginning to bear fruit.' Fruit is also gathered from a range of more familiar cultivars, from a gnarled old 'Bramley's Seedling' to popular 'James Grieve'. Most cultivars make good juice.

> "Locals say that Eden Road E17 was built on an old orchard, and Victorian architect John Warner, who built most of the local houses, put an apple or pear tree in every garden"

The scheme works in two ways: those who donate their apples are offered a pruning service, not simply to remove dead wood and misplaced branches but structural pruning, to promote balanced growth and prolong the life of older trees, as well as annual pruning to optimise fruit production, too.

In the first year, advertisements were placed in shops and public noticeboards; the local newspaper also ran an article, but word of mouth was most effective.

'Some people now borrow picking equipment to harvest from their own trees and may make use of the press, but the majority register their trees and contact us when the apples are ready to pick,' says Marlene. In the first year two volunteers harvested 10 trees, now 10 to 15 'regulars' take the crops of more than 60 trees between mid-August and early November. Last year's total was almost three tonnes of fruit.

Most of the harvest is taken – in environmentally friendly bicycle trailers, another eye-catching advertisement for the project – to the Hornbeam Centre on Hoe Street, Walthamstow, where it is graded for quality. Unblemished fruit is stored for sale; the rest is juiced.

The project has two presses: a portable one used for 'street corner' pressings where the public are invited to take part, and a larger one stationed at Organiclea's Community Plant Nursery. Larger apples are chopped and crushed before pressing. Any rotten parts are removed; the fruit is then pressed until the last drop of juice is expressed – last year the project squeezed out some 1,000 litres. The 'pomace' (pulp) that remains after pressing is composted.

A quarter of the fruit collected from gardens is offered back to the owner; few take it, but many accept juice instead. Nor is it just apples: cherries, plums, figs and pears are also collected under the scheme and sold as fruit, jams, pickles and juice through the market stall and community café.

There is a voucher scheme for local families in the neighbourhood to buy from the market stall, and fruit and juice also find their way into the local vegetable box scheme. Local people are enthusiastic about the project: it helps them to appreciate the value of locally sourced produce, and reminds people in a 21st-century urban environment of the tradition of processing and storing food for winter – and their ultimate dependence on the land for their survival.

Organiclea wants to develop improved storage so fruit can be kept until the following April. 'This idea is still in its infancy and there is so much more that can be done,' says Marlene. Similar projects called Abundance already exist in Manchester and Sheffield, and enquiries have come from Woodbridge in Suffolk and from Brighton. There cannot be a parish or borough in Britain that does not have surplus fruit. This innovative idea has massive potential and could be adopted virtually anywhere in the UK.

# Reconnecting our Food, Culture and Community

ROSIE BOYCOTT, JANUARY 2009

On a warm, sunny day in mid-October I found myself spending the day in convivial company at Julian Temperley's apple festival in Somerset. Julian is a hero in the cider world, for he has done much to restore its fashionability and boost not only his own sales but also those of cider makers across the West Country, Herefordshire and Kent. The day was a celebration to mark the moment in the year when the cider apples have been gathered, their smell filling the air with a tangy sweetness, so it was a perfect excuse for a large and noisy party. As I looked around the 200 or more guests, I was struck by the fact that there were people there in ages ranging from six weeks (two of Julian's daughters had given birth to sons within 10 days of each other) to 90: there were landowners and cidermakers, painters and plumbers, locals and those who had driven up to 100 miles to join the fun. And all because of apples; because of food.

Over the ages, gatherings that celebrate occasions such as harvest have been one of Britain's great traditions. But you don't need a special occasion to celebrate food: just the simple act of shopping in a local store, swapping recipes, sharing your crops on an allotment, exchanging tips over the garden fence or visiting your local farmers' market all form a social binding glue that helps hold a community together. I don't think I have ever met anyone I know when I venture (which I occasionally do) into a supermarket, but when I go shopping, either in our local market town of Ilminster or on the Portobello Road near my London home, then I almost invariably meet a familiar face doing his or her weekly food shopping.

> "We lose touch with our food culture at our peril"

However, like many similar spaces in our towns and cities, Portobello Road is under threat from developers wanting yet another street filled with shops selling overpriced clothes and ornaments, the fate of many local markets in our headlong rush to believe that the answer to all life's problems can be found in cheaper chicken and imported, out-of-season fruit and vegetables. In the process, we have lost touch with the most fundamental of human needs – food – surrendering its production, distribution and retailing to an increasingly small number of large companies whose only interest is in lining shareholders' pockets.

Further undermining the basic value of food, we have become a nation of snackers, responsible for consuming more than half of all the ready meals sold in Europe. While Monty Don was running his project to help rehabilitate drug addicts in Herefordshire, he told me what depressed him most was that many of the young people had never eaten a single meal around a table in their lives. Instead, it was instant noodles in front of the television or take-away pizza eaten cross-legged on a bed. Even within the family, the sense of community and belonging that the simple act of sitting down and eating a meal together can engender is under threat.

In my role with London Food (a board established in 2004 by the London Mayor to lead on food matters) I hope to reverse some of these trends. We will create 2,000 new growing spaces in the city – these will be as varied as gardens on reservoir and canal banks to bits of land that would otherwise end up as derelict spaces.

Yet, up in Tower Hamlets, where steely-grey blocks of flats hover over previously no-go areas, that is precisely what groups such as the Women's Environmental Network are doing. I was stunned the day I went to visit. There were 30 small, neat growing spaces, allocated on an annual basis to interested tenants. There were herbs and vegetables growing in profusion, fortified by a central compost system to which all the flat dwellers contributed. In the centre of the once-empty space were benches and a barbecue. At the far end, a children's playground. All was neat, tidy and, above all, loved. The community, which once sat indoors in frightened isolation, now had a focal point around which to gather and, like us on apple day in Somerset, a good excuse for parties when the vegetables were flourishing and ready for cropping.

We lose touch with our food culture at our peril. Already this has led to issues such as ill-health and obesity, but it has also destroyed something that is maybe less easy to articulate but no less important. And that is the socially binding effect that food – its growing, harvesting, buying, cooking and eating – brings both to families and neighbourhoods. Luckily, I don't think it's too late to reverse the process.

# The Kelsae Onion Festival

JOY LARKCOM, FEBRUARY 1982

If nothing else of note happens in my lifetime, at least I'll be able to tell my grandchildren that I was present at the 7th National Kelsae Onion Festival, held at the Harlow Carr Gardens, Harrogate on September 26, 1981, when the World Record for the heaviest Kelsae onion was broken by Mr Bob Rodger of Crail, Fife, with an onion weighing 6lb 7oz (2.93kg), so breaking the record he had established the previous year! I might add that the century's record for cold and wet September Saturdays was probably set the same afternoon; mercifully such unspeakably foul weather is as rare as 6 lb. onions, but it must have deterred some of the 300 entrants who had been nurturing onions all summer. Absolutely nothing, however, would deter the enthusiastic hard core, who were there in force – albeit in wellington boots!

I should make it clear at the outset that I'm very ignorant of the showman's work and have never so much as displayed a peapod in a village show. But knowing only too well the numerous hazards which beset the production of ordinary vegetables grown for the kitchen, I have nothing but admiration for the patience and skill required to produce perfect show specimens – those unblemished sticks of celery, beetroot 2ft long (60cm) with full 12in (30cm) of what can only be called 'rat's tail', smooth skilled show onions neatly bound at the necks, parsnips and carrots which could have been moulded in a potter's studio rather than exposed to nature in garden soil, and in this case, these enormous, heavyweight, Kelsae onions.

"Apart from its remarkable capacity to grow to an enormous size, it is a handsome, good quality onion with very high neck and shoulders..."

Weight competitions, I learnt, are a relatively new development. Indeed the rules are not yet fully established. There is controversy over the trimming of the neck: a political hot potato, which must be grasped by the heavyweight establishment.

What is so special about the Kelsae onion? Apart from its remarkable capacity to grow to an enormous size, it is a handsome, good quality onion with very high neck and shoulders, giving it a flask-like appearance; it is very popular as an exhibition onion.

It originated over 40 years ago in a old Scottish country estate, and was introduced to the public by the Kelso nurserymen Laing and Mather, who maintained it for many years. A few years ago their business was taken over by the seedsmen Sinclair McGill, who are now guardians of the Kelsae, the sole producers of the seed and the sponsors of the annual Kelsae Onion Festival.

But back to the Festival itself. Just before 2.30pm the assembled throng were allowed to walk the plank (almost literally), between the general marquee and the exhibition marquee, to witness the public weigh-in. On the benches down the side and centre of the marquee were the mannequin-like vegetables in the show classes, while on a long table across the far end, lined up beside the scales, were the hopeful Kelsae heavies. Notable for 'their high shoulders and distinctive shape' (I quote from one of the organisers), some rough skinned, some smooth, most about 9in high with a girth of 4–6in, each was mounted on a little plastic stand and bore a label round its neck – a label with all but the most vital of its various statistics. They had been well protected overnight. As I was told later 'it can get a bit cut-throat when there's big money at stake'.

At the appointed hour the solemn weigh-in began. Each onion in turn was picked up, gently turned over, and checked for the last time, presumably for any signs of cracking or rot. They must 'be sound and true to type'. Surplus dirt was rubbed off the trimmed roots. Were they also, I wondered, looking for secret slugs, which might tip the scales? Inspection completed they were passed smoothly to a second man, who put them on the scales. The weight lit up on the illuminated register; the judge behind the scales wrote the weight on the label and hung it back around the onion's neck; the name of the grower, his area, and the weight were announced over the microphone, and the onion journeyed further down the human conveyor belt, either to be placed on the stand in the 1st, 2nd or 3rd position – or to join the dejected group of 'also rans' at the far end of the table.

It took time; interest flagged and conversation mounted, but when only a few remained tension mounted until master of ceremonies Philip Swindells, Superintendent of Harlow Carr Gardens, cracked the inescapable joke – 'It looks as if someone here knows their onions' – and the winner topped the scales.

In no time a Miss World scene had broken out – cameras flashing, reporters jostling around the ebullient, £500 the richer Scottish farm worker, Bob Rodger – who with infinite patience and good humour answered the first of countless questions on how he'd done it.

Some vegetable champions are very unwilling to discuss their methods. They'd 'rather not say'. But Bob Rodger and his clan of relations and friends, who between them walked off with most of the Festival prizes, were not at all secretive. Bob Rodger himself is a relative newcomer to showing, only starting six years ago. He was taught the basics by his brother. Then perhaps, as often happens, he applied a fresh outsider's view to the received wisdom of generations and started beating the old hands at their own game.

For example, the traditional method of preparing the beds in autumn is to build up sandwich-like layers of soil and manure, adding fresh manure each year. But Bob decided this created too rich a mixture, so this year omitted the manure – and got healthier onions and far better results.

It's the early stages that matter in producing the champs, along with attention to detail and a good strain of seed. (Many of the best growers save their own seed.) The seed is sown at Christmas in a greenhouse or frame in 3in pots and the seedlings moved in stages into 5in and finally 9in pots, the greenhouse being kept at a temperature of between 13 and 15.5°C (55–60°F). They are planted out in the open ground in April or early May with polythene protection, and during the summer measures are taken to keep them free of pests and disease. But it's all a question of good husbandry, the winners I talked to agreed, helped along in the north, which seems to produce all the winners, by the long hours of daylight in summer.

Bob Rodgers goes to about nine shows a year, and selects his winners from about 135 onions planted out in his garden. He'd grow more if he had the space, but it's only a small council house garden and, as he says, you've got to have them on your doorstep. You can't keep your eye on them if they're on an allotment a couple of miles away.

# Cherries on Top

TOM LA DELL, JUNE 2010

For many people, cherries are the perfect summer fruit: bite-sized spheres of glistening red, black or yellow on delicate stalks, with skin firm enough to keep your hands clean and hold a burst of sweet and tangy flesh and juice.

> "...in the Tamar Valley, with Cornwall to the west and Devon to the east, you could take a paddle steamer to view the spectacular cherry blossom on the valley sides"

The stone is not too big to break your teeth on, or too small to swallow. Fresh, they are the great taste of midsummer; sour cherries make wonderful wines, tangy tarts and luscious liqueurs. They are rich in vitamins C and A, with anti-oxidants and anthocyanins – terms that tell you that they are good for you, too.

Cherries have long been part of British culture: from Chaucer ('many a one is fond of them') and Shakespeare ('thy lips – those kissing cherries – tempting grow'), to lovers playing cherry-chop (trying to bite them while still hanging on the tree).

In Europe (including the UK) and western Asia, two cherry species have been important in the development of selections grown for fruit. Sweet cherries are derived from *Prunus avium* (wild cherry or gean), found wild across Britain and Europe; sour cherries are from *P. cerasus*, a shrub or small tree native to much of Europe.

Native cherries were part of our prehistoric ancestors' diet, but it was the Romans who probably introduced some of the first cultivars; cherry stones are found at many Roman sites. They were also popular in early medieval times, so perhaps some selections survived the Dark Ages. In the

14th-century poem *Piers Plowman* by William Langland, the lead character has cherries brought to him when he is hungry.

Henry VIII was obviously dissatisfied with the quality of fruit at his table (like so much else), so in 1533 he sent his royal fruiterer Richard Harris to the Continent to obtain better selections. How did Henry know they were better? Had he been offered other cherries by Francis I at the Field of the Cloth of Gold in June 1520? The trip changed British fruit growing. Harris established an orchard at Teynham in Kent, with cherries, apples, pears and other fruit, located just to the west of today's National Fruit Collection at Brogdale Farm, Faversham.

## Cherry heyday

Over the centuries, cherry growing expanded rapidly in Kent, helped by the excellent transport links via the Medway and Thames rivers to London. By 1950, 5,200ha (12,850 acres) were producing cherries. Traditional orchards of magnificent standard trees with sheep grazing beneath were an unforgettable picture of rural beauty. Each spring the 'blossom route' was signposted in the lanes of Kent for day trippers and coaches to enjoy. Also, in the Tamar Valley, with Cornwall to the west and Devon to the east, you could take a paddle steamer to view the spectacular cherry blossom on the valley sides.

Research work by the John Innes Institute (now Centre) in the early 20th century produced fine cherry selections such as 'Merton Glory', 'Merton Bigarreau' and 'Merton Heart'. 'Merchant', which was selected in the 1970s, is still a top cultivar. These are big, juicy, usually red cherries with a high flesh-to-stone ratio.

The other big breakthrough came when this attribute was combined with self-fertility in the cultivar 'Stella', from Summerland in British Columbia. In the spirit of free plant exchange from these growers and researchers, the self-fertile seedling that led to 'Stella' came from John Innes. Other cultivars such as 'Van', 'Sunburst' and 'Lapins' followed. At Brogdale, these cultivars provide high-quality fruit for at least six weeks.

From 1945 cherry production declined for half a century as pickers disappeared; the lovely trees were too high for inexperienced workers and imports started to arrive from the Continent. By 1994, there were just 550ha (1,360 acres) left.

Thankfully, in recent years, a renaissance has come about both for home gardeners and commercial growers, with the advent of self-fertile cultivars and dwarfing rootstocks such as 'Gisela 5' and 'Gisela 6', developed in Germany in the 1960s. Other dwarfing stocks may be available soon. Growers can now plant dwarf trees that are easily picked and can be covered against birds and the late rain that causes splitting when the fruit swells too quickly. Such orchards are being planted across the northern and central Kent fruit belts (and elsewhere); slowly, cherry orchards are returning.

With their cloud of white blossom in spring, autumn colour and fruit that attracts birds, cherry trees can be a delight in domestic gardens. However, until recently, they could be cultivated only as big trees and needed a pollinator to set fruit. Thomas Rivers struggled with this in his 1866 book, *The Miniature Fruit Garden*, without a reliable dwarfing rootstock. Cultivars grafted onto wild cherry rootstock were root pruned to control their size for pyramids and fans.

"With self-fertile cultivars, only one tree is needed for an excellent crop"

With today's dwarfing stocks, however, fans, cordons and pyramids are now easy to grow in small gardens. If a small standard tree is required, 'Colt' is still the best rootstock. With self-fertile cultivars, only one tree is needed for an excellent crop. 'Stella' is popular, together with 'Lapins' and 'Sunburst'. Some other cultivars need a pollinator from the same group, which flowers at the same time. When planting historic cherry cultivars for a garden or new orchard, they need to be carefully selected for compatibility as pollinators.

Cherries need a deep, well-drained fertile soil to do well, but older, local selections do well in less favourable conditions. They can be pruned just after fruiting, as this reduces the risk of silver leaf and bacterial canker diseases. Winter pruning will unfortunately lead to gum production (it was once a popular, early chewing gum) in spring – consequently bacterial and fungal infections like canker or silver leaf can develop.

Recent advances in cherry growing means producing these fruits is simpler than ever – good news both for amateur and commercial growers, not to mention those of us who enjoy simply eating this delicious summer fruit.

## The origins of cultivated cherries

The Greek historian Herodotus, in the 5th century BC, mentions a type of cherry he calls 'ponticum' from the coast of the Black Sea. In 74BC these cherries reached Italy and 120 years later arrived in Britain. Some of these old cultivars still seem to be grown in Georgia, east of the Black Sea.

We can assume that these arose from plants of *Prunus avium* growing in the great fruiting forests that stretched to east Kazakhstan, from where the eating apple originated. These Asian cultivars probably brought the requirements for a deep well-drained soil and near-continental climate, both of which occur in Kent.

It is unclear exactly which cultivars royal fruiterer Richard Harris brought back from the Continent. These may have included 'Lukeward', 'Cluster' and 'Naples' cherries illustrated in *Tradescant's Orchard* of around 1620. It is reported that he planted in the quincunx form – one tree at each corner of a square or rectangle, and one in the middle. This is both practical and decorative, and gives complex views of patterns across the orchard. By 1639, in the Wimbledon garden of Queen Henrietta Maria (widow of Charles I), there were avenues of fruiting cherry trees with a fountain in the middle. Orchards continued to be a feature of gardens until the time of the wonderful Kip illustrations of the great houses of Britain around 1700.

Advanced breeding of new cherry cultivars began with plant physiologist and fruit enthusiast, Thomas Andrew Knight, who also became the second President of the RHS. He introduced 'Knight's Early Black', 'Elton Heart' and 'Waterloo' from 1805 onwards, while his daughter, Elizabeth, continued the work and introduced 'Black Eagle'. RHS records show 'Bigarreau Napoléon' was introduced from Germany in 1832. In 1864, 'Frogmore Early' was introduced and became another popular cultivar. 'Governor Wood' arrived about the same time from America. Thomas Rivers, the great nurseryman and fruit breeder, produced 'Early Rivers' and many others around 1870.

# A Novelist in the Garden

BRENT ELLIOTT, OCTOBER 1992

Unlike plant hunters, and the designers of gardens, growers of fruit do not linger in the public consciousness. The RHS Fruit Committee is the oldest of its standing committees, founded in 1858, but how many of its members' names would mean anything today? [But] one past member has come close to being a household name: not for his 40 years as a fruit grower at Teddington, however, nor for his work on the Fruit Committee. He is remembered as a novelist, or at least as the author of one novel: *Lorna Doone*.

Richard Doddridge Blackmore was born in 1825 in Longworth, Berkshire. A clergyman's son, he studied at Oxford and the Middle Temple, and was called to the Bar in 1852; but his career in the law did not last long. In 1857 he inherited a legacy, on the strength of which he bought a house in Teddington with 16 acres of land, and settled down to grow fruit and translate Virgil in his spare time.

By the 1880s he had become an authority, especially on pears; he was on the organising committee for three RHS conferences and he delivered a paper on vine pests to the Grape Conference of 1890.

"John Ridd, in *Lorna Doone*, was a 17th-century horticultural progressive, growing potatoes and hyacinths, and looking forward to the day when science would explain the phenomenon of trees bending during frost"

His first novel, *Clara Vaughan*, was published in 1864; his second, *Cradock Nowell*, in 1866. Both novels received a mixed reception, and both were heavily revised in the following decade.

Blackmore followed these with *Lorna Doone* (1869), which established his reputation permanently, and created an Exmoor cult, with attempt after futile attempt to identify the real Valley of the Doones. In one sense, it can hardly be called a neglected novel, since it is still in print almost a century and a quarter after its publication; but it is not taken seriously in the literary-critical world. As far as the reading public is concerned, he has remained a one-book writer; but he went on to write 11 further novels, some of them as good or better than *Lorna Doone*.

In these novels, Blackmore revealed a conservative nostalgia for Old England, but carried to greater extremes than with most of his contemporaries. But if it is difficult to think of another novelist of the period who was quite so blatantly reactionary in his politics, it is almost without parallel to find a gardener so reactionary in his horticulture.

The gardening press was, broadly speaking, liberal and progressive, championing new methods and setting principle above tradition. A comparison between political and horticultural progress lurked barely under the surface of some garden writing, to appear explicitly in Donald Beaton's remark that 'only four years before the first Reform Bill [i.e. 1828], some of the best gardeners in the country did not know or understand the principle of potting plants'. Blackmore resisted this rhetoric, sceptically mocked the claims to scientific understanding in the gardening magazines, and defended the abilities of pre-Victorian gardeners.

John Ridd, in *Lorna Doone,* was a 17th-century horticultural progressive, growing potatoes and hyacinths, and looking forward to the day when science would explain the phenomenon of trees bending during frost. A changed emphasis appeared in this satirical comment in *Alice Lorraine* (1875): 'For the growers did not understand the pruning of trees as we do now. They were a benighted lot altogether, never lopping the roots of a tree, nor summer pinching, nor wiring it, nor dislocating its joints; and yet they grew as good fruit as we do! They had not right to do so; but the thing is beyond denial.'

More than any other novelist, Blackmore made the practical operations of gardening into an important theme. In *Cradock Nowell* horticulture emerges as a principal interest. Indeed, the action of the novel can be dated precisely by a horticultural reference, for at one point two characters discuss the merits of *Spergula pilifera* [now *Sagina pilifera*] as a substitute for grass in lawns; this was a short-lived fashion, begun by the nurseryman E G Henderson in 1859, and largely abandoned after 1860, when the plant had proved unable to cope with the English weather. *Cradock Nowell* contains the best portrait of a gardener in Victorian fiction: Dr Rufus Hutton, the toast of the *Gardeners' Chronicle* for his experimental garden, but who is also (a touch of realism) self-righteous, short-tempered, and inquisitive.

Professional gardeners appear as important characters in *Alice Lorraine, Christowell,* and *Kit and Kitty,* the last two particularly rich in horticultural activity. Here is the gardener's daughter in *Christowell* meditating on her family craft: 'I am sure, there is nothing in the world half so beautiful as gardener's work. What are jewellers, or watchmakers, or ivory-carvers, or even painters, to compare with a genuine gardener? The things that they handle are dead, and artificial, and cannot know the meaning of the treatment they receive. But our work is living, and natural, and knows us, and adapts itself to follow our desires, and pleases us; and has its own tempers, and moods, and feelings, exactly the same as we have.'

Blackmore's obituaries in 1900 were uniformly critical of his views on fruit, attributing his lack of financial success not to climate but to management. The *Journal of Horticulture* made the point most succinctly: 'Mr Blackmore was a connoisseur in Pears, and grew an enormous number of varieties. Many of these were quite useless for commercial purposes; and yet because they did not "pay" he was apt to write letters to *The Times* against fruit culture generally as a profitable industry. He did not perceive that the most successful growers proceeded on exactly opposite lines to himself, namely, in planting many trees of a few wisely selected varieties, instead of one or two trees of as many varieties as he could obtain or find room for. He had quite a museum of Pears, interesting but unprofitable, and could happily afford to indulge in the luxury.'

# High-Rise Vegetables

NEWS, NOVEMBER 2012

The previously unsightly and underused rooftop of the private bank, Coutts, on The Strand in London, has been transformed into a productive and attractive garden. Containers with a total length of 350m (1,150ft) contain three tonnes of compost to grow vegetables and fruit for use in the company's restaurant. Coutts Executive Chef Peter Fiori created the garden with gardening consultant Richard Vine. All recipes now contain an element of The Coutts Skyline Garden, which also has ornamentals such as lavender to attract pollinators.

# Wartime Baby

JOY LARKCOM, MARCH 1992

I started working on the 1991 revision of *The Vegetable Garden Displayed* while on a train. Not far short of Edinburgh a fellow passenger leant across and declared, 'I've got the first edition of that'. Our subsequent conversation brought home to me that 'VGD' was heading for its 50th anniversary, and spanning as it did the era from World War II in the 1940s to the threat of global warming in the 1990s, it was something of a social document.

"The battle on the Kitchen Front cannot be won without help from the Kitchen Garden"

*The Vegetable Garden Displayed* was a wartime baby. Within a month of the outbreak of war the Royal Horticultural Society Council was doing its bit by publishing an inexpensive pamphlet on *Simple Vegetable Cooking*. It sold like hot cakes. Quick on its heels was a broadsheet chart for allotment holders, varnished on one side so it could be pinned on outdoor noticeboards. By late 1940 plans were afoot to support the 'Dig for Victory' campaign with an 'illustrated vegetable gardening book'.

The eminent scientist Sir Daniel Hall, then in his early seventies, was responsible for all these publications. By the time of his death [in 1942] the year-old *Vegetable Garden Displayed* was already well launched on its long and successful career: three impressions, totalling 75,000 copies, were printed and sold in 1941.

Nothing captures the mood of the times better than the advertisements and exhortations in the first edition. 'Your Gardens is part of the National Defences. Don't arm it with poor weapons.' (Suttons Seeds, illustrated with a bunch of carrots bearing a remarkable resemblance to a cluster of falling bombs.) 'When buying sprayers insist on buying British. Don't grow your fruit with foreign-made machines.' (Four Oaks Sprayers.) 'Speed up the Nation's Food Supply by sowing Fogwills' Best Result Seed.' The Ministry Collection for a 10-rod allotment cost 12s 6d. Chase Continuous Cloches advertised a booklet impertinently called *Cloches versus Hitler* by Mr Charles Wyse-Gardner.

The exhortations were most evident in the Ministerial forewords. Lord Woolton [Minister of Food] was strongest on the military implications. 'This is a Food War. Every extra row of vegetables in allotments saves shipping. If we grow more potatoes we need not import so much wheat.' Stored carrots and swedes could replace imported fruit in winter. We should grow our own onions instead of importing 90 percent. He saw the vegetable gardens as 'our National Vegetable Chest yielding a large proportion of the vitamins which protect us against infection' and concluded with the stirring words, 'The battle on the Kitchen Front cannot be won without help from the Kitchen Garden'.

The Minister of Agriculture and Fisheries [Robert Hudson], after commending the hundreds of practical men (no women?) from the Society who were enlisted as volunteers advising 'Dig for Victory' projects, stressed the need for 'orderly planning'. The challenge, he said, was to provide vegetables all year round, not just in summer but 'in the dark days of winter when the food problem reaches its most acute phase'. This was indeed a preoccupation: contemporary articles on continuity planning, late sowings in autumn, the used of cloches, frames and greenhouse, were all directed to this end.

The book was a success from the start. By February 1942, a quarter of a million had been printed and it was making a profit of over £1,000, 'Entirely due to the advertisement revenue'. The limiting factor on production was the paper shortage, both during the war years and as late as 1947, when the severe weather of that year precipitated the fuel crisis and a 10 percent cut in paper quotas.

Shortly after the war, *The Vegetable Garden Displayed* was translated into German. Lt Col M Wilson, commanding 617 Detachment, Military government, BAOR requested permission to translate it 'for the sake of encouraging and helping food production in Germany'.

# New Potatoes

ALAN ROMANS, FEBRUARY 2010

In these health-conscious times, UK gardeners are increasingly growing vegetables, including our favourite: potatoes. Over the last few years there have been major developments in potato breeding and cultivation, providing a widening range of cultivars. Some of the newer ones offer enhanced resistance to pests and diseases over traditional cultivars, making them a much more attractive proposition for gardeners to grow at home or on an allotment.

"The most resistant potato cultivars come from Hungary, selected by the Sárvári family. They began decades ago, crossing wild potatoes gathered by Soviet Union expeditions to South America..."

Potatoes are native to the Americas, and were one of the earliest crops domesticated in South America, around 7,000 years ago. The first tubers reached Europe in ships returning from the New World in the 16th century. More productive and nutritious than grain, and easier to grow and to process, potatoes can be said to have changed history, feeding a burgeoning European population as industrialisation developed.

It was not plain sailing, however. The few selections that had reached Europe had no defence to a strain of late blight (*Phytophthora* fungus) that hit in the 19th century. During the resultant Irish potato famine, at least 1 million people died of starvation and more than twice as many migrated.

Plant breeders gradually developed blight-resistant potato cultivars and more productive methods of agriculture, work that continues to this day. Potatoes are the fourth most important global crop after wheat, maize and rice, with annual production of some 320 million tonnes.

About 15 to 25 years ago, only a dozen or so potato cultivars were available to British gardeners. Declining interest in home vegetable growing, horticultural suppliers' concentration on only the most popular selections, and increased postal charges on mail order seed potatoes had conspired to reduce the choice. Today, some 150 to 200 cultivars are available from different suppliers, including plenty of older, 'heritage' cultivars. There are also some excellent recent introductions, with much-improved resistance to pests and diseases, giving ever-widening choices to adventurous home gardeners increasingly interested in 'growing their own'.

In the UK, blight and eelworm are the two biggest problems that can destroy potato yields in gardens and allotments. The best way British gardeners can avoid several other pests and diseases – including viruses and bacterial blackleg; brown rot and ring rot (two serious bacterial diseases); and at least two new bacterial wilts now found in Europe – is to only buy seed potatoes certified as disease-free from producers registered with the UK Safe Haven Certification Scheme.

## Blight advice

Late blight fungus (*Phytophthora infestans*) is widespread. Infecting potatoes and tomatoes, it is likely to become more prevalent if our summers get wetter and warmer. For 150 years only a single strain, called Type A1 blight, existed in Europe, proving challenging enough. A second breeding type, A2, reached Europe from Mexico in the 1970s, raising the spectre of yet more virulent strains arising from the genetic variation produced by the two reproducing. This already seems to be occurring, as in just two years, Blue 13 (A2 type) blight has become the most common strain across the UK and now Ireland. It infects early in the year and, most worryingly, nearly all cultivars resistant to earlier blight strains are susceptible.

There is an easy way to avoid problems with blight: plant only quicker-maturing first and second early potato cultivars rather than traditional maincrops, as their crops are harvested before blight hits in mid- to late summer. Modern second earlies are capable of growing uniform crops of mid-sized, multipurpose tubers akin to maincrop potatoes; 'Kestrel', 'Saxon', 'Bonnie', 'Osprey' and 'Smile' are good examples.

The most resistant potato cultivars come from Hungary, selected by the Sárvári family. They began decades ago, crossing wild potatoes gathered by Soviet Union expeditions to South America, part of a programme to develop low-input, disease-resistant crops that the next generation of the family continues. The Sárvári Research Trust at Bangor University in North Wales trials and assesses Hungarian selections, identifies worthwhile cultivars and registers them. This long-term hybridisation by traditional selection methods has achieved something genetic-modification techniques as yet only promise.

The Trust's introductions, some of which have Sarpo (from Sárvári and potato) as a prefix, could be a source of cheap, low-carbon-footprint potatoes (they require less pesticide and irrigation). So far the most interesting cultivar is 'Sarpo Mira', a vigorous red-skinned maincrop with high nutritional value, weed-suppressing foliage, a long season, long tuber dormancy (for good storage) and the highest virus and blight resistance recorded in trials. It even shows resistance to frost and drought.

"I am not a fan of phurejas, as similar flavours and textures can be found in standard potatoes..."

'Sarpo Mira' tubers grow continuously, whatever the day length, and are good for everything from early-season light salad potatoes to large, floury, late-season tubers ideal for baking. Remove foliage in August to arrest tuber development and before they become too starchy to eat.

Blight resistance is extraordinary – plants show symptoms, but just keep growing. A plant infected in July will still be growing in autumn and tuber blight resistance means few of these will be infected. Refrigerated storage is unnecessary. Chitted tubers can be left until July and planted after first earlies as a second crop. Taste, I think, is quite good, like 'Kerr's Pink' or 'Rooster'. Other Sarpo cultivars with different characteristics such as 'Axona', 'Sarpo Extra' and blue-skinned 'Blue Danube' are being introduced, all much more blight resistant than competitors.

Also recently introduced, Phureja Group cultivars are potatoes derived from what was called *Solanum phureja*, and have gained attention in recent years with the release of the Inca and Mayan series (bred from material kept at the Commonwealth Potato Collection at the Scottish Crop Research Institute). 'Phurejas' are descended from the ancestral, 'pre-tuberosum' potato, previously called *Solanum stenotomum*, which has only half the chromosomes of *S. tuberosum*. They were selected for yellow flesh and good flavour and texture, and have a wide range of skin colours but little dormancy so do not store well.

I am not a fan of phurejas, as similar flavours and textures can be found in standard potatoes such as 'Golden Wonder', 'Arran Victory' and 'Kerr's Pink', with which they cannot compete in yield, and they show little disease resistance. Publicity claims these were the potatoes presented to Queen

Elizabeth I, but *S. tuberosum* tubers travel better and have the same number of chromosomes, 48, as our oldest cultivars.

Hybrids between phurejas and *S. tuberosum*, however, have the sought-after flesh colour, quality and flavour but with fewer drawbacks: well-established 'Yukon Gold' and soon-to-be-released 'Apache' are among the best.

The choice of potatoes available to home gardeners is burgeoning. Choosing the right ones, and growing them at the right time, means pest and disease problems are less of an issue, with great strides in resistance to both. Allied to new propagation techniques, the humble spud seems set fair for a real home-gardening revival.

# Asian Vegetables

NIGEL SLATER, DECEMBER 2009

Of all the plants that have eluded me in the vegetable patch, it is fleshy-stemmed pak choi (*Brassica rapa* Chinensis Group) that hurts most. I know others who grow this with ease. But then, it has the juiciest stems of any of the Oriental greens, making it exceptionally tempting to garden herbivores. I think of it as the canna lily of the vegetable patch. Luckily, other Oriental greens – mizuna, mibuna and hot mustard greens (*Brassica juncea*) – have all been successful somewhere in my garden or cold frame.

"Mizuna is often up within a couple of weeks of sowing and their serrated leaves are ready to pick for a salad in a further two or three"

From March onwards I start mizuna, 'green in snow' and mibuna, the leaves of which I use mostly for salad, in shallow trays of potting compost, then transfer them to the garden only once they are showing two pairs of leaves. I protect them with an open-ended cloche. They appreciate good air circulation and will rot if kept in too humid a situation. I would also advise any potential grower to pull out all the stops when it comes to slug control, the average garden gastropod being apparently quite partial to a Chinese takeaway. I use both copper rings and organic slug pellets.

The brassicas we associate with Chinese or Southeast Asian cooking are among my favourite in the kitchen, and not always easy to find in the shops – a sound reason to grow our own. The sorts that appeal to me are: fleshy-stemmed pak choi with its spoon-shaped leaves and those such as choy sum with its tight yellow buds; the blue-green-leaved gai lan; and the hot leafy mustard greens. They have much similarity to many of our own leafy green vegetables but with the bonus of hot or mustard notes and tender stems.

Oriental greens such as young mustards germinate easily. A seed tray of mizuna is often up within a couple of weeks of sowing and their serrated leaves are ready to pick for a salad in a further two or three. If you leave them growing for four to six weeks longer you will have leaves sturdy enough for a stir-fry. The same goes for purple-leaved mustards such as red giant, which are extraordinary in both flavour and colour, being mottled and veined with deep purple and having a cabbage flavour with notes of hot mustard.

In the kitchen these greens are split into two: those best for use in a salad and those steamed or fried. A leaf's suitability for one or the other has as much to do with its maturity as its cultivar. Young pak choi and mustard greens, for instance, will almost dissolve in the searing heat of a stir-fry and are more suitable in the salad bowl. As mustards age, larger leaves can become too hot to eat raw in large quantities so they are better used as a cooked vegetable, when heating seems to temper their pungent notes.

When used in a salad, young mustard leaves add a lively note. Most of these peppery leaves are best mixed in with other, milder leaves, including some that are sweeter or cooling to offer some sort of contrast. I like to use approximately one part young hot leaves to three parts milder ones such as lettuce 'Little Gem' or Batavia types.

Chinese broccoli, like choy sum and pak choi, is mildly flavoured and requires rich, water-retentive soil and plenty of sun, but it is fairly quick to grow and plants can produce several crops, branching once the lead stem is cut out. I have found these to be rather greedy and thirsty, too – they grow best when pampered by a gardener who is generous with the hosepipe. In many ways they are similar to calabrese or headed broccoli, but they have fleshier, more tender stems which are eaten in their entirety. In the kitchen they are usually steamed. I serve them with ginger, garlic and soy sauce.

All these greens are good with the ingredients we most associate with Chinese or Thai cooking: garlic, ginger, spring onion, soy sauce, nam pla (Thai fish sauce), chillies and oyster sauce. The leafier greens with particularly juicy stems such as gai lan and pak choi can be quite mild in flavour and often need the contrast of rather salty or hot seasonings. Fleshy greens and pungent flavourings – it is as if they were made for one another.

# Hosta Sushi

STEPHEN BARSTOW, APRIL 2009

Young hosta shoots are a good mild-tasting spinach alternative in spring. *Hostakopita* is a Greek spinach pie made with hosta shoots; in Japan, *nori maki sushi* is filled with parboiled hosta shoots marinated in soy sauce, salt and sugar. Young shoots can be gathered, skinned and boiled or steamed like asparagus. Larger species and cultivars, such as *Hosta sieboldiana*, are best. In Japan, hosta petioles or *urui* are enjoyed but become increasingly bitter as they mature. The shoots of *Typha* (reed mace) are also edible, tasting similar to water chestnuts.

> "Young shoots can be gathered, skinned and boiled or steamed like asparagus"

# Making the Most of Allotment Space

LIA LEENDERTZ, JUNE 2012

I have run out of space; it happens every year. That tray of lettuce seems so compact in the glasshouse but planted out it takes up half a raised bed. Seedlings will insist on growing – and how the space disappears when they do. I look at the allotment with a sharply assessing eye, not for weeds and diseases but for indispensability: does anyone eat all those runner beans? And who on earth decided to put that row of cabbages in?

> "Increasingly I find myself thinking rather as a balcony gardener might – how can I get the most flavour out of this small patch of earth?"

More and more I want flavour over bulk. Increasingly I find myself thinking rather as a balcony gardener might – how can I get the most flavour out of this small patch of earth? What can I fit in alongside something else? What can I do without? And so I find my gaze falling upon my potatoes with their shocking, plot-engulfing tendencies. That bag of seed potatoes seemed modest before they were chitted and planted, but now, properly spaced out, they luxuriate across the front of the plot, impossible to partner with anything else. They are lucky they go into the ground early, when allotment space seems infinite, and I am grateful to have something, anything, to plant.

If they went out at the same time that everything else was jostling for space, I doubt I'd be so lenient. They are an allotment stalwart, sure, and I can't quite imagine doing without the soft, sweet, yielding bite of a new potato, boiled minutes after being pulled from the earth. But on the other hand, just how much citric sorrel, peppery watercress, bitter endive or soft, mild, pillowy lettuce could that same potato patch yield?

For similar reasons, onions were shown the allotment gate long ago, to be replaced by garlic and shallots. Cabbages – but for their unsanctioned incursion – have been long ousted. I make sure I grow nothing out of habit, or simply because I have seed hanging about. Question everything and ensure that each crop makes a good case for its space, even the sweetest little new potato.

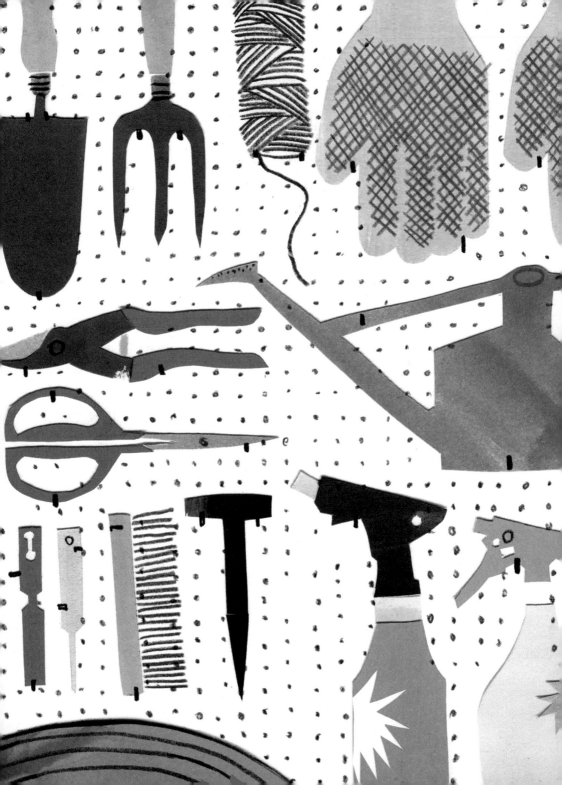

# PRACTICALITIES

*Note from the editor*

The craft of gardening is, at bottom,
the same as it has always been. However,
many practices have of necessity changed,
as the numbers of affordable professional
gardeners have declined, while technology
and engineering have provided us with many
machines to take the place of human strength
and finesse. Most of us thank our stars that we
were not gardening 50 or 100 years ago, when
we read of, for example, the primitive (and
unsafe) weedkillers that were commonplace.
And we take pleasure when experts tell us of
new techniques for doing old tasks or even,
as in the case of using straw bales to grow
cucumbers outside, and of grafting tomatoes,
when they remind us of old techniques that
still have a place.

The RHS has always had an interest in invention and has given publicity to ideas whose time has come, such as the treating of lawns more as meadows than bowling greens. But there is also plenty of space given to the eternal practical preoccupations of gardeners: weeding, composting, protecting, salvaging, watering and trying to keep difficult plants alive. (I suspect few gardeners have the confidence to be as frank about this as Helen Dillon!) Lest we get too bogged down in the minutiae, however, Chris Beardshaw tells us what it is all for, why we became professional or amateur gardeners in the first place and why it is so important that the rest of the world understands the value of what we do.

**URSULA BUCHAN**, editor

# On Your Own Turf

MATTHEW WILSON, APRIL 2009

There is something so terribly British about a well-tended lawn that it borders on a national caricature: a tightly clipped, emerald-green sward, the grass napped with precision into parallel lines of regimental straightness, bowed into submission by a puttering mower. And, without pushing gender stereotyping too far, it is an undeniably masculine affair by and large – something to do with power mowers I suspect: in many ways a grown-up boy's toy.

> "A major benefit of a more relaxed approach to the lawn is that you can make it much more wildlife friendly"

There are, however, many more options than such monocultures to using grass creatively in the garden. Grasses rarely grow in isolation in the wild – they are found, rather, in a range of plant communities with other herbaceous and often bulbous species. The 'grasslands' available to the gardener vary, therefore, from high-input, grass-only bowling green to no-input wilderness where native grasses and the wrong kind of coarse wildflowers – vigorous weeds – are left entirely to their own devices.

Between the two extremes are some highly attractive, much less formal, easier and quicker-to-manage planting styles that are less demanding of resources than the standard lawn. A major benefit of a more relaxed approach to the lawn is that you can make it much more wildlife friendly. Achieving a completely different look may be simply a matter of introducing a few bulbs or wild flowers into an existing lawn, or changing the way it is managed, for example by allowing some areas to grow long and mowing paths through them. After all, who said turf must be mown once a week, and always to the same height?

There is no denying the visual impact of a really great lawn. It can set up dramatic vistas, especially when mower lines accentuate the view. And it can also set off the surrounding plants, providing a neutral green foil for flowers and other foliage.

An immaculately cut lawn has always been something of a status symbol, a means of showing that humans, not nature, were in charge. In times past, the time and costs associated with maintaining such a feature were huge:

skilled scythesmen would be required to shear the grass, and later horse-drawn cutters. After Edwin Budding patented the mechanical lawnmower in 1830, a wider public could enjoy the glories of a manicured sward, but it was many years before the majority could justify, or have use for, a mower.

Today lawns are still regarded as status symbols, in terms of size and/or quality (a large, ride-on beast of a mower being the gardening equivalent of a sports car). Alongside the development of the ornamental lawn came the other great promoter of turf science – sport. While many sports require a similar hard-wearing mix of creeping fescue, dwarf perennial ryegrass and meadow grass to most domestic lawns, golf and bowling greens in particular need fine grasses that creep less aggressively. Such fine grasses are often found at the seaside, as an occasional covering by the tide or salt spray kills off coarser grasses and weeds. These seaside swards were the main source of bowling-green turf until the science of growing suitable turf was perfected.

While some of us may want to go to the extreme lengths required to create a bowling-green finish, the pursuit of even the average great British lawn still comes at a price. Crucially, to create a really good lawn, a monoculture of grasses must be established, and all other plants – particularly mosses and wild flowers – excluded. The only way to do this is through regular intervention: annual scarifying to remove thatch; the application of feeds, weedkiller and top-dressing; aeration; irrigation – and, of course, constant mowing.

All these interventions have an environmental price tag attached to them. Fertilisers and weedkillers are resource-and energy-demanding to produce, creating pollution in the process. The extraction and processing of such bulky products as lawn sand and topdressing uses fossil fuels, as does delivering them to your local garden centre. Even without hosepipe bans, watering a lawn is hard to justify given water shortages, despite two miserably wet summers.

There are also ecological reasons to question high-intensity lawn management. More life exists below ground than in all the above-ground ecosystems on Earth, so any intervention into the soil disturbs the balance of life. Applying chemicals to target earthworms, because their casts are unwelcome on golf and bowling greens, affects other soil-dwellers. It may be imperative for the sport, but is not at all sound ecologically.

So should we all be mothballing our mowers, hanging up our spring-tine rakes and saying farewell to the lawn? I think that would be unrealistic. Most lawns are there as open spaces for children's play, to entertain friends or to exercise the dog and are not that intensively-managed. But surely it is time to reassess exactly what, why and how we do what we do to lawns; there are alternatives to cutting each blade of grass in our gardens weekly.

Perhaps the first step is to understand what we want the lawn for, which will help decide the area it needs to cover. If your only requirement is an open space for a table and a few chairs, then perhaps you only need a small lawn? What then happens with the rest of the space that was once lawn is up to you.

There are plenty of opportunities to enhance the garden through different approaches to grassland. Leave some areas to grow longer and mow paths through, add some bulbs or perennials, or try an area of wildflower meadow. Traditional hay meadows are only cut in late summer as this is the best time for agriculture. In a garden situation, meadows can be left until late autumn or early winter – and removing and composting the 'hay' helps reduce the soil fertility, which makes for more diversity. Better still, you can swap the weekly grass cut for an annual one.

Relaxing our approach to lawns can not only give us more time for the rest of the garden, it produces a more natural, informal feel, and undoubtedly attracts more wildlife. At the same time, and without changing the garden too much, you can reduce the time, resources and energy a lawn consumes, making it far more sustainable long-term.

# Gosling Scrotch

HUGH JOHNSON (WRITING AS TRADESCANT), JULY 1995

As goosegrass years go, this is proving a relatively light one. Goosegrass (you can call it cleavers, cleggers, hayriff, burweed or even gosling-scrotch – I doubt whether anyone likes it enough to call it *Galium aparine*) is one of the weeds I class as more irritating than infuriating. Its speed and spread can be astonishing, especially as the whole sprawl of nature's

"...the whole sprawl of nature's Velcro arises from one stem not thicker than 15-amp fuse wire"

Velcro arises from one stem not thicker than 15-amp fuse wire. It can overtop shrubs before you notice it has started. It regularly clogs hedge-bottoms, and insinuates itself into beds and borders just enough to blur the focus without really drawing attention to itself. But even a hefty infestation is not heavy work to remove. In spring before it flowers you can usually roll most of it up into an inconsiderable ball, which you can hide (I get scolded for this) in any out-of-the-way corner. Teasing it out of plants is rather soothing work, I find.

It is a different matter when it reaches the seeding stage, covering everything it touches with little green pellet-like burrs. It is particularly fond of socks, and soon gets into your shoes as maddeningly as gravel.

# Popular Weedkillers

DR M A H TINCKER, FEBRUARY 1935

The perfect chemical weedkiller should possess these attributes:

1 It should be thoroughly effective throughout the various seasons of the year and should be independent of climate and weather.

2 It should be easily handled by operators unskilled in dealing with chemicals; it should be safe. A weedkiller which is relatively non-poisonous to live stock, including birds, is preferable to a virulent poison, for it is exceedingly difficult to prevent small quantities of chemicals from entering the body either by the skin or mouth if operators are handling them all day.

3 The chemical should be cheap, so that large areas may be treated economically.

Salt has been used for long as a weedkiller on paths. A strong solution prevents the osmotic uptake of water by the roots of adjacent plants. Heavy rain at once destroys the efficiency of such weedkillers, which are dependent upon high concentrations and are not toxic at great dilutions. The after-effect left in the soil is for all practical purposes negligible unless repeated applications are used.

The toxic reactions of arsenical compounds is well known. Small quantities taken up by either plant or animal may prove fatal. As so small a quantity as 0.125 to 0.25 gram. (that is, less than one hundredth part of an oz.) may prove fatal, except perhaps to some Styrian addicts to the habit of arsenic-eating and to other workers in arsenic works, it is therefore obvious that the greatest care is required in handling arsenical sprays and solutions, and that such compounds do not meet all our requirements. The modern use of arsenic as a weedkiller tends to be restricted to particularly troublesome weeds.

[If mixed with sulphuric acid] the acid injures the leaves, killing the outer tissues; plants sprayed in the late afternoon readily take up the arsenical solution into their tissues, owing to the existing demand for water exhibited by these tissues after a period of active transpiration during the heat of the day. The arsenical compounds may reach the deep roots, passing downwards in the plant and slowly spreading from the vessels into the tissues. It will readily be appreciated that success is closely related to the physiological condition and water requirements of the plants; it might be limited by the presence of a high degree of saturation of soil and air.

Chlorates are exceedingly toxic to plants: sodium chlorate is particularly destructive. The danger of poisoning from chlorates is a very small one if elementary precautions are observed: quite large quantities must be taken up to prove toxic.

The relatively transient nature of these compounds in the soil permits of their use on open or cultivated ground; after early autumnal application of the weedkiller it is safe to sow most garden crops in spring; certain seeds may be sown even earlier. Were it not for the danger of fire, sodium chlorate would meet all demands.

# Straw Bales Revisited

PHILIP CLAYTON, APRIL 2010

As with other industries, horticulture is always changing, but modern concerns about sustainability as well as the environment may increasingly force us to look back to find the most appropriate ways forward.

Five years ago, an article in *The Garden* by Martin Fish outlined a technique from the past that is still effective today. Growing crops commercially (such as cucumbers) in straw bales was experimented with in the 1960s, although the idea dates back further. However, once modern nutrient-film growing systems were introduced, the procedure was all but forgotten. As the 2005 article outlined however, straw bale culture is worth trying. Rather than it being solely the preserve of commercial glasshouse crops, current ideas show it is adaptable enough to succeed outdoors, and can be used to grow ornamental plants seasonally.

Straw bales are like growing bags once plants are established in them, but they have special properties that make them suitable for certain plants. Straw bales absorb and store large quantities of water – acting rather like a sponge – although excess water quickly drains from them, preventing plant roots from rotting. During the growing season plants need to be watered and fed regularly, as with a growing bag, but bales do not seem to dry out as quickly.

> "...ideally, get your bale in place in early spring and allow it to absorb rainwater"

The addition of water begins decomposition of the bale. As it slowly rots it releases nitrates (which help promote plant growth) and also substantial amounts of heat, directly at the roots. While some plants dislike hot roots and high levels of nitrogen, others such as cucurbits and many ornamental plants with fleshy roots (such as cannas and gingers) grow well in such conditions. Push your hand into the bale and you may be surprised at the heat generated by the rotting straw. Bales are self-supporting – you do not need to buy a container or construct a bed to hold them in, and being heavy (and large) they will not blow over. Using them even allows plants to be grown where there is no soil, perhaps on hard standing.

Provided straw bales can be found, little else is required save a sheltered position and access to water. At the season's end the remains of the bale are surprisingly well rotted and can be composted or dug into the soil.

The most difficult part of growing in straw bales is the start – obtaining and then preparing them for planting. Bales are not always easy to find, especially for town dwellers and even in the countryside the huge round ones are now more commonplace. Bales of hay, while more easily obtained, are not suitable as they become soggy and rot down too fast. Once you have found your bale, a problem may be transporting it – they are heavy, awkward objects, so you will probably need help.

Preparation of the bale should be done in mid-to-late May and consists of ensuring it is saturated with water. This is critical, but no simple task. Leaving a hose to run on it is wasteful so, ideally, get your bale in place in early spring and allow it to absorb rainwater. After soaking (for a couple of days at least), the bale is heavier still; if possible, do this in its final position. Plastic sheeting can be put under the bale to help retain moisture.

Adding water begins the decomposition of the bale, but young plants will need pampering to get established. Planting holes should be cut carefully with a knife, pulling away straw by hand as you go. Before planting, spread the bale with high-nitrate feed, or put plenty of a granular equivalent (such as Growmore) into planting holes. Peat-free compost can be added to help establish plants as they send out feeder roots into the straw.

Plant up after the last frosts. Each bale can support around three big plants, although underplanting with smaller subjects is possible, and with ornamentals more can be added. If cold nights are forecast, covering plants with fleece will help prevent failures.

While plants establish they will not need too much water, but once they begin to grow they need daily watering, especially in hot weather. Feed plants once they are growing actively. Any fungi that appear are part of the decomposition process and will not affect the plants.

By autumn the bale will start to disintegrate; it and the plants, if not required, can be composted or dug into the ground where they will rot down over winter.

Provided suitable plants are chosen, this technique has great potential in many situations. The growth plants achieve is impressive and the bulk of the bales means they support large, greedy plants better than a pot or growing bag. For home growers it is a fairly sustainable technique: once the bales are soaked they do not need more water than containers, and at the end of the year the waste feeds your garden.

# Plants I've Killed

HELEN DILLON, JUNE 2009

As an antiques dealer in a former life I had a table in stock with a prominent warp on top. The only chance of selling it was on a Monday, as the warp would sink a bit while the heating was off on Sundays. This reminds me of my first sight of *Sisyrinchium striatum* 'Aunt May', on a sunny morning in June, when

"It's no good waking up in December thinking 'O-my-God – the ixias!'"

it was looking dreamy, with beautifully striped leaves and spires of creamy flowers. Nobody mentioned that its foliage rapidly clogs up with dead black leaves. Tolerate their ugliness, or sit down with scissors and snip them out. I reckon Shirley Conran and her 'Life's too short to stuff a mushroom' would feel much the same about such fidgety work. So 'Aunt May' went off to the compost heap (and the table eventually sold – on a Monday).

I've killed an embarrassment of plants over the years. I moved a 24-flowered clump of lady's slipper orchid (*Cypripedium reginae*) in midsummer and replanted it deeply to stop it toppling over. It resented such treatment – beautiful orchid, bye-bye.

You could describe some of my losses as wilful destruction: I decided that the variegated crown imperial (*Fritillaria imperialis* 'Argenteovariegata') was just too glitzy, the variegated *Abutilon megapotamicum* too blotchy, and why did I ever need a two-tone blackberry (*Rubus fruticosus* 'Variegatus')? My reasons for demolishing that sumptuous, orange-red climbing South American relation of alstroemeria, *Bomarea multiflora* (syn. *B. caldasii*)? My argument was that two flowers every few years isn't enough. It didn't survive the downgrade from south to west border. And what about remembering about bulbs dried off in summer that need watering come September, such as ravishing turquoise-green *Ixia viridiflora* or winter-flowering *Tropaeolum tricolor*? It's no good waking up in December thinking 'O-my-God – the ixias!'

As for Olympic-style runners, such as startling orange Oriental poppy *Papaver orientale* 'May Queen', and the white form of willowherb *Chamaenerion angustifolium*, I had to find out for myself that they want to annex the garden at the drop of a petal. (I've since restored the willowherb; it's too good to be without.)

Many plants are victim to a one-night strike of a passing slug, others would have preferred to stay in the glasshouse all year, but my main reason for losing plants is that they get squashed because I forget all about them. Just like at parties, when I'm so busy running around after new arrivals that people who come first get stuck in corners with an empty glass and nothing to eat.

# Let it Snow

URSULA BUCHAN, FEBRUARY 2010

February, it is general agreed, is the most testing time of the year. But until 2009, many British gardeners had, for 18 years, no experience of what deep snow was like, or what it could do to the garden. As a result it was brought home to us how valuable an asset good 'bone structure' can be.

I discovered last year that I was a really committed gardener – if I had ever doubted the fact. Despite acquiring two cracked elbows and a damaged wrist in an accident on New Year's Day, I shuffled on my coat, hat and gloves and (much against my better judgement, it must be said) ventured out the day it snowed, broom in hand, to shift the snow from the fruit-cage netting. This was because the netting will readily bow and break, once the snow freezes. Having achieved that, I brushed the worst of the snow from box and yew hedges, although I left the Leyland cypress boundary hedge (not planted by me) to its fate. By this time, I was covered in snow from head to foot and nursing two painfully aching arms. But I was cheerful, even triumphant.

> "…I brushed the worst of the snow from box and yew hedges, although I left the Leyland cypress boundary hedge (not planted by me) to its fate"

It seemed to me a pleasant irony that I had long since stopped advising people in print to knock the snow off fruit-cage netting and evergreen shrubs, since winter after winter had passed without any snow to speak of. Just as motorists had forgotten that high gear and low revs are better in these conditions than low gear and high revs, so gardeners like me had forgotten what terrible damage can be done by the weight of frozen snow. But will the same thing happen this February? I have no idea but, now that my arms are knitted, I shan't mind much if it does.

# All Kitted Out

HELEN YEMM, MARCH 2010

The pressure is on. For the past year or more, the growing army of grow-your-own newcomers has been ceaselessly bombarded with advice to equip itself with expensive, snazzy accoutrements. What price a few rows of posh lettuce, a couple of kilos of tomatoes and an almost inevitable surfeit of runner beans?

Of all the much-hyped 'essentials' it is, I suspect, the proliferation of costly raised-bed kits that has caused the most elevated eyebrows among the old guard, the dedicated row hoers who have been at it for longer than they care to remember.

To be fair, growing vegetables in raised beds is not new. Championed by 'no-dig' organicos, it has also been a solution for those (like me) with boot-sticking clay soil. I improve soil in beds (separated by coarse bark paths) with gritty sand, adding muck or compost each year. The soil level inevitably rises, hence the need for raised wooden edges, and as long as I keep up the summer watering, it does mean that I can plant more closely, and thus potentially get more produce from a pretty meagre-sized plot.

"...it is, I suspect, the proliferation of costly raised-bed kits that has caused the most elevated eyebrows among the old guard..."

Why does it *have* to be a raised bed? I'm sure many busy householders are quite simply experimenting in their (increasingly small) back gardens, perhaps by plonking a raised bed or two in former lawn. This way there is minimal digging and disruption to the garden layout and (maybe the reasoning goes) if it all goes pear-shaped, they can always plant petunias or re-turf the next year – and forget the whole episode.

Traditionalists should hold fire a bit: realistically, this is not about self-sufficiency or 'free' food; and the sort of ingenious, no-cost, Heath Robinson improvisation that goes on in most allotments – and indeed in spacious vegetable gardens that are tucked out of sight – is not particularly pleasing to the eye.

Are there no alternatives to extravagant use of commercial composts, smart new timber kits and all the rest of the raised-bed-in-a-box paraphernalia? As someone remarked to me recently, if we all viewed the building of really large, simple compost bins as a priority, bagged compost would be largely unnecessary. Dark coloured, plastic plumbing pipes from DIY stores, bent into arches, make cheap, discreet supports for protective fleece and mesh. And what about using recycled scaffolding boards, treated to prolong their life and if necessary stained to spruce them up, for making those compost bins and raised beds? Or (it has given me wicked pleasure to have done this myself) what about using second-hand decking? Come to think of it, when people finally get sick of skidding around in slime for half the year on their TV-makeover-style decking, there should be quite a lot of that going begging.

# Lawn Lesson

KEN FOX (LETTERS PAGE), AUGUST 2012

Matthew Biggs' column on ways to increase the drought tolerance of lawns reminded me of an old lawnsman's trick: to walk along the lawn on cool dewy mornings, dragging behind him an opened-out hessian sack attached to two lengths of garden twine. Dew droplets would be brushed from the grass and fall into the sward to be absorbed by the soil. Moreover, as the grass blades were now wet, any further dew would also run down to reach the soil. Thus, rather than leaving droplets of dew on the grass to evaporate wastefully by the rising sun, the dew provided a welcome drink to the lawn.

# How Watering Regimes can Affect Vegetable Flavour

RHS ADVICE, SEPTEMBER 2011

Vegetables consist mostly of water, with a relatively small amount of solid material that gives their texture and flavour. Withholding water might be thought to lead to more solids and stronger flavour and this is sometimes the case – but not always.

Tomatoes, for example, can be watery and tasteless if grown 'soft' (lavish irrigation and feeding), but sweeter and with more tomato flavour and texture if grown 'hard' (subjected to a certain amount of water stress). Overdo it though, and blossom end rot will quickly damage fruits, as calcium flow through the plant needs a steady supply of water. The same goes for other fruiting plants such as peppers and aubergines.

More watery vegetables such as lettuces, courgettes and cucumbers do best grown soft with plenty of fertiliser and water. There are also differences between cultivars – Batavian lettuces reputedly taste better than icebergs.

Some vegetables require ample water to give the right flavour and texture. Radishes and turnips become woody and develop a fiery flavour if grown too hard; water-stressed calabrese becomes coarse and stringy; cauliflowers produce small rubbery heads; while beetroots and baby carrots lack the desired delicate sweetness if kept too dry.

# Joined at the Hip

CLAIRE SHADDICK, MARCH 2011

Grafting is an ancient propagation method, dating back to at least classical Greece and Rome that fuses different plants to unite specific characteristics from each. Usually carried out on woody plants, grafting combines the ornamental or productive features of a cultivar – especially fruit trees – with the vigour of a different rootstock. Although less commonly applied to non-woody plants, grafting has also been used in tomato growing since the 1950s to produce plants for commercial growers. At that time, tomato selections were specially bred from wild relatives with natural resistance to fungal root diseases including fusarium and verticillium wilt, and to the pest, root-knot nematode, all of which had built up in soils in growers' glasshouses because of continuous production. These specially-resistant selections, raised from seed, had poor fruit quality but could act as rootstocks. Onto these, seedlings of cultivars (scions) chosen for their fruit quality and yields, but susceptible to pests and diseases, could be grafted. Nurseries were then able to continue growing commercial crops without the expense of steaming soil or using chemical fumigants to control the soil-borne problems.

*"...recently the range has been extended to grafted aubergines, cucumbers, sweet and chilli peppers, squashes, melons and watermelons"*

Within the tomato-growing industry, grafted plants fell out of favour when growers moved crops out of soil, first into peat, later investing in hydroponic systems, where grafted plants' resistance to soil-borne root diseases was no longer an advantage. But they have recently made a comeback as a way of instilling vigour into weaker-growing but popular cultivars, and also because commercial organic tomato crops, which have to be grown in soil, are being planted more extensively.

Gardeners can now buy young grafted tomato plants, pot-ready for growing on by mail order or, from some garden centres, for planting straight away. Grafted cultivars include cherry, beefsteak, mini-plum, orange, yellow and striped types. You can also buy organically raised grafted tomato plants, and recently the range has been extended to grafted aubergines, cucumbers, sweet and chilli peppers, squashes, melons and watermelons. The benefit is not just resistance to soil-borne diseases, but also the extra vigour lent by the rootstocks, which is claimed to produce larger plants and heavier yields as well as to bring plants into flower and fruit earlier – and for a longer period.

Grafting has to be done by hand, which is why buying a grafted plant will cost you more than one raised from seed. Do its advantages outweigh the extra costs?

The resistance that rootstocks have to a range of root diseases could be attractive for gardeners planting the same crops in soil in a glasshouse year after year, with limited room for rotation. This is especially true for tomatoes as they are susceptible to several soil-borne diseases. But some modern cultivars have been bred to carry some of the same resistance as the rootstocks. If you are using new growing bags or growing media each year, the disease protection provided by a rootstock is likely to be of little value, anyway.

Any extra vigour that the rootstock of a grafted plant can confer is another matter. One of the widest selections of grafted vegetable plants is offered by Suttons and its sister company, Dobies. 'Grafted plants make a bigger root system and take a much firmer hold than a cultivar grown on its own roots,' says Suttons Senior Horticultural Manager, Tom Sharples.

Grafted plants are also said to tolerate colder soils (which means they should fruit earlier in a cold glasshouse or polytunnel), crop for longer and generally perform better in more difficult conditions outdoors than seed-raised plants, particularly in a less-than-ideal summer. Tom estimates that grafted tomatoes can be three to four weeks earlier to fruit, depending on the cultivar.

Just a handful of rootstocks have been specifically bred for grafted vegetable plants. Several tomato rootstocks with different levels of vigour are used for tomato, and can also be used for aubergine, a member of the same plant family, *Solanaceae*. One rootstock used for cucumber is its wild relative, *Cucurbita ficifolia* (fig-leaf or Malabar gourd), but cucumber rootstocks have also been specially bred. Not all fruiting cultivars are suited to being grafted, however – a breeding aim for tomatoes for garden use, for instance has been a thin skin, but the extra vigour from grafted rootstocks in some cases will cause fruit to split, which rules out some cultivars for grafting.

Because of the grafted plants' extra vigour, their roots need plenty of room. Suttons advises a deep pot (at least 30cm/12in) if plants are to be pot-grown in the glasshouse. Most growing bags are unlikely to give their roots enough space for the best results. Grown outdoors, plants should be 60cm (2ft) apart. Tom Sharples recommends a proprietary high-potash feed twice a week once fruits start to set (cucumbers, once a week). 'You don't want to give too much nitrogen because you don't want to encourage more leaf and stem growth,' he says.

"The disease resistance or early harvest some grafted plants offer could make it worthwhile paying the extra..."

The disease resistance or early harvest some grafted plants offer could make it worthwhile paying the extra if: your tomato or cucumber crops have suffered soil-borne disease; you struggle to find the time to replace border soil in the glasshouse; space is tight to rotate crops outdoors; you have missed the window for raising your own plants; or you just want to hedge your bets on a poor summer.

With a limited number of cultivars available, you may have to settle for one you have not tried before, or with which you are unfamiliar. But more suppliers are beginning to market grafted plants, and in pots as large as 1 litre. From this year, Suttons will offer grafted tomato plants that have been pinched to produce two main stems or where two different cultivars have been grafted onto one rootstock, both making better use of a small growing area.

❧

# Skills to Save our Heritage

CHRIS BEARDSHAW, MARCH 2009

If you think for a moment about the breadth of knowledge and skills needed to perform even the most basic horticultural tasks, well, it soon becomes clear just how complicated an activity gardening can be.

The harmonious and mesmeric clip of shears on topiary; the tenderness with which seedlings are reared; and the process of creating a fine tilth are all multifaceted processes that, while often assumed to be instinctive or innate, demand an understanding of science, botany, practical expertise, experience, emotional connections, artistic vision and passion, to name but a few.

Perhaps it is because gardening originated as a subsistence activity, or that it is easily accessible to so many people and appears simple when executed by the experienced, but it is indisputable: gardening has never been accepted as a skilled, high-profile profession.

## Roots of a passion

Not so long ago, when I was 15 or so, I told my careers tutor I wanted to study horticulture. I explained how my fascination in the subject began as a toddler, watching grandparents tend and cultivate, and that my interest had developed to the point where I was rearing an eclectic collection of trees from seed in my parents' garden, and that I had worked part time for two years at a nursery.

I supplemented my pitch with the information that a dedicated horticultural institution existed only a dozen miles away, and it was here I wished to further my education. The response was a startling demonstration of how gardening is widely perceived. My tutor exclaimed in amazement that, with good predicted grades at O level, I would be wasting my talents in farming. Apparently my interests and passions would be best utilised by following a career in the Royal Navy, specifically as a submariner.

I recount this tale as an example of how a clear passion to follow a path could have been irrevocably pruned. Inherent in this tale is also a clear indication of the role of third parties – grandparents, parents and friends whose gardening enthusiasm infects and inspires those at a tender age. Perhaps a few snatched moments with your grandchild observing the frenetic activity of a pollinating bee, or sharing the harvesting of a sumptuous strawberry crop will be the catalyst required to inspire the next generation of professional gardeners and horticulturists.

Halcyon images these may be, but without such intimate engagement I fear for the tradition of professional gardening in Britain. In this generation our once world-admired horticultural education centres have all but disappeared. Some are wizened shadows of their former selves while others have been enticed into multifunctional academic centres. We also witness an unprecedented withering of student numbers entering the profession. The debate over cause, effect and blame continues under the canopies of botanical collections, in glasshouses and within the corridors of learning but the net result is a starvation of talent. This is talent that could so easily tread in the footsteps of Wilson, Tradescant, Jekyll, Robinson and Jellicoe et al, while driving innovation and pioneering work in the realms of design, conservation, botany and, of course, practical gardening.

There is perhaps no better time than now to state our case: when testing economic circumstances encourage reconsideration of priorities and opportunities, the traditionally modest gardening fraternity are required to shout loud our cause. Passing on clear information to a targeted audience is needed to highlight the range of professional opportunities on offer, and we should not be embarrassed to promote the personal and social benefits that may be reaped by those both within, and witnessing, the results of the profession.

> "...allowing the great gardening achievements evident across our country – botanic collections, heritage sites, parks and private gardens – to do anything less than prosper is something for which future generations will not thank us"

Educationalists should try to focus on long-term needs rather than training students for careers in which there are few sustainable jobs. Key to this would be establishing a culture where continuing mentoring and learning is achieved without the current 'bums on seats' mentality, which is stimulated by targets and financial pressures.

Why should gardeners concern themselves with these matters? Well, it could be argued that nothing denotes a dysfunctional society like the wasting of talent and opportunity. Coupled with this is a realisation that allowing the great gardening achievements evident across our country – botanic collections, heritage sites, parks and private gardens – to do anything less than prosper is something for which future generations will not thank us.

Then, of course, there are the individual, human justifications for pulling focus; in my case it is nothing more complex than the extraordinary excitement, stimulation and emotional rewards I gain, especially when plants are combined as a means of artistic expression. These were, I believe, catalysts for me at the age of four to decide gardening was my future, and as such are something I wish everyone could experience.

# SCIENCE & INNOVATION

*Note from the editor*

In 1900, William Bateson, later professor of biology at Cambridge University, gave a lecture to the RHS, which was then printed in the Society's journal. Its importance lay, at least in part, in the fact that this was the first time that the work of Brother Gregor Mendel, the so-called Father of Genetics (an Augustinian friar working in a monastery in Brno, Moravia, in the 1850s and 1860s), had been explained to Britons. Bateson himself was the originator of the term 'genetics', to mean the study of heredity, and he did much to further research into genetics in the early years of the 20th century. The Society is justifiably proud that such an important subject should have first seen the light of day under its auspices.

At the same time as Bateson was revealing all this, other horticulturists were reflecting on the many other advances that had occurred in the 19th century, in particular in the design and layout of glasshouses as well as the huge and permanent impact that the growing of tender plants reasonably cheaply had on British gardeners and gardens. It was a self-confident time for horticultural scientists and innovators, as is instanced by a very positive article reproduced here on the benefits of strong poisons such as nicotine used as insecticides. More recent articles on science, such as that by Mary Keen, strike a rather more timid note. Nevertheless, there continues to be some interesting scientific research done by the Society on plants, in particular. In *The Garden* can be found articles explaining aspects of science either useful to the home gardener or simply interesting in their own right – such as plants that have leaves of different shapes, as botanist Mike Grant reveals.

In this chapter you will also find pieces on the DNA of Welsh wildflowers, the prospects for biodegradable pots, the extraordinary benefits that can be bestowed by medicinal plants – and a possibly fruitful future topic for the scientists, namely does planting by the moon work?

**URSULA BUCHAN,** editor

# Problems of Heredity as a Subject for Horticultural Investigation

## W BATESON, FROM A LECTURE DELIVERED IN MAY 1900

An exact determination of the laws of heredity will probably work more change in man's outlook on the world, and in his power over nature, than any other advance in natural knowledge that can be foreseen.

"It is not a little remarkable that Mendel's work should have escaped notice, and been so long forgotten"

There is no doubt whatever that these laws can be determined. In comparison with the labour that has been needed for other great discoveries it is even likely that the necessary effort will be small. It is rather remarkable that while in other branches of physiology such great progress has of late been made, our knowledge of the phenomena of heredity has increased but little; though that these phenomena constitute the basis of all evolutionary science and the very central problem of natural history is admitted by all. Nor is this due to the special difficulty of such inquiries so much as to general neglect of the subject.

No one has better opportunities of pursuing such work than horticulturists. They are daily witnesses of the phenomena of heredity. Their success depends also largely on a knowledge of its laws, and obviously every increase in that knowledge is of direct and special importance to them.

The want of systematic study of heredity is due chiefly to misapprehension. It is supposed that such work requires a lifetime. But though for adequate study of the complex phenomena of inheritance long periods of time must be necessary, yet in our present state of deep ignorance almost the outline of the facts, observations carefully planned and faithfully carried out for even a few years may produce results of great value.

These experiments of [Gregor] Mendel's were carried out on a large scale, his account of them is excellent and complete, and the principles which he was able to deduce from them will certainly play a conspicuous part in all future discussions of evolutionary problems. It is not a little remarkable that Mendel's work [on crossing varieties of the garden pea,

*Pisum sativum*] should have escaped notice, and been so long forgotten. For the purposes of his experiments Mendel selected seven pairs of characters as follows:

1. Shape of ripe seed
2. Colour of 'endosperm' [the word Mendel used for cotyledons]
3. Colour of the seed-skin
4. Shape of seed-pod
5. Colour of unripe pod
6. Shape of inflorescence
7. Length of peduncle [flower-stalk]

Large numbers of crosses were made between Peas differing in respect of each of these pairs of characters. It was found that in each case the offspring of the cross exhibited the character of one of the parents in almost undiminished intensity, and intermediates which could not be at once referred to one or other of the parental forms were not found.

In the case of each pair of characters there is thus one which in the first cross prevails to the exclusion of the other. This prevailing character Mendel calls the *dominant* character, the other being the *recessive* character.

That the existence of such 'dominant' and 'recessive' characters is a frequent phenomenon in cross-breeding, is well known to all who have attended to these subjects.

By self-fertilising the cross-breds Mendel next raised another generation. In this generation were individuals which showed the dominant character, but also individuals which preserved the recessive character. This fact also is known in a good many instances. But Mendel discovered that in this generation the numerical proportion of dominants to recessives is approximately constant, being in fact *as three to one*. With very considerable regularity these numbers were approached in the case of each of his pairs of characters.

# Horticultural Progress during the 19th Century

JOHN CLAYTON, VOL XXV 1901 (PART III)

"What a revolution the greenhouse has wrought in our land!"

It is impossible at the close of this century to look back and review from quite the beginning the growth of our profession – the honourable calling of gardening. We have not the time. The work would be enormous. We must content ourselves with glancing back a hundred years, and noting the changes wrought in our profession during that time. I sometimes think we do not always sufficiently value our privileges and the ancient establishment of our craft. Gardening is undoubtedly the oldest existing profession. We are told that in the very earliest days 'God planted a garden', and placed our first forefather there as gardener. Truly it was only a single-handed place to begin with, but what a start was then made! It was the commencement of the most delightful and engrossing of the occupations ever given to man. Medicine and law, while being of ancient origin, cannot claim quite the same antiquity as gardening.

I shall not, however, attempt to do more than refer very briefly to some of the more important changes which have taken place in connection with horticulture during the century just come to a close, which has probably been the most progressive century from every point of view since the foundation of the world. And I think that in the enormous increase in recent years of the devotees of the Goddess 'Flora' we have an overwhelming evidence of the intellectual advancement of our times.

What a revolution the greenhouse has wrought in our land! When I read that one firm of renowned market growers possesses 130 acres of glasshouses! – why, if our grandfathers could see those enormous areas covered with glass they would hardly credit their senses that such a revolution could have taken place in a century. Beyond a doubt a great impetus in the erection of these miles of glass has been the adaptation of heating by means of hot-water pipes, a plan unknown to our grandfathers, which has worked a veritable revolution in many of our methods of gardening. We smile now when some dear old gardener tells us of the watchful care and terribly hard work expended on growing and forcing fruit or flowers when the only known means of heating the houses was by diverting the flue all round the house before it was allowed to enter the upright of the chimney. We wonder how it ever was done, and we hardly realise the transformation now when the merest amateur can have his tiny greenhouse heated by an up-to-date method of hot-water pipes, easily fixed, in a manner which fifty or sixty years ago the gardener of the king could not command.

A marked feature, attributable to the improvements in glasshouses, has been the great multiplication of the kinds of plants grown in them: Orchids, for instance. At the commencement of this century the places where these royal plants were cultivated could be counted on the fingers of one hand, and now every year millions are imported and sold. Market growers have houses full of each variety, and many of quite the most beautiful are to be had at a price paid by our fathers for bedding plants. The stimulus given to the growth of all choice exotics, as Crotons, Dracaenas, Palms, and the all the many beautiful tropical plants, can be traced to the same cause. Nor has the advantage of these improvements been only to the benefit of the wealthy, for the universal extension of glasshouses has had the supremely beneficial effect of bringing many real luxuries within the reach of the poorer classes; for example, Grapes, which years ago were sold at 10s. to 15s. a lb., and can now be had at a tenth of that price, and both early and late in the season.

We have in quite recent years called nature in to our aid in another very opposite form to hot water; I mean the refrigerating process, whereby the growth of vegetation is arrested; and the gardener has now only to pass the plant from the refrigerator to the forcing pit and 'Ah, presto!' it is in bloom; be it Lily of the Valley in summer, or *Lilium* in February, it is all the same.

# Nicotine: Its Use and Value in Horticulture

GEORGE EDWARD WILLIAMS, FROM A LECTURE DELIVERED IN FEBRUARY 1902

Nicotine is an alkaloid, which occurs in various parts of the Tobacco plant. The compound owes its name to one Jean Nicot, a Frenchman, who first introduced the seeds of the Tobacco plant into France in the year

1560. Nicotine when pure is a colourless compound of an oily nature, but readily soluble in water. It has rather a sickly smell, not at all like the odour we usually associate with Tobacco. It acts upon all animal life as an extremely powerful poison; it is the strongest insecticide known to the scientific world that can be used with safety in checking the ravages of blight and other insects that are injurious to vegetable life.

"Prejudice cannot stop scientific and economic progress; prejudice only recoils upon the people who indulge in it"

In studying the chemistry of insecticides and their relation to plant life one is bound to come to the conclusion that nicotine is the compound amongst all others that can be used by the horticulturist with perfect confidence and success. It is absolutely harmless to all forms of vegetable life if used under proper conditions, and if used under these conditions it will not injure or impair vegetable life, but will prolong and strengthen it.

There are three ways of using the compound.

First, by the application of heat, and so vaporising the nicotine, and bringing the vapour into contact with the plants requiring treatment.

Second, by direct application in a liquid form to the plant.

Third, by mixing the nicotine with a combustible fibrous medium and burning it or by burning dried Tobacco leaf, which is practically the same thing.

The first and second methods of using nicotine are reasonable and scientific, and are strongly recommended to give satisfactory results The third method is clumsy, unreliable, and by no means unlikely to cause injury to plant life.

I regret to say that even today in England there are many horticulturists prejudiced against the use of nicotine; but as time goes on, and they see the splendid results obtained by its use, their number is rapidly decreasing. Prejudice cannot stop scientific and economic progress; prejudice only recoils upon the people who indulge in it. In nicotine the horticulturist has a means ready to hand with which he can successfully fight against the ravages of blight in his glasshouses, only let him see to it that the compound is used properly. Abolish all rule-of-thumb methods. My own short experience has taught me that rule-of-thumb methods are useless in practical work. We must be in either an experimental stage or a practical stage, and we may be quite sure that the old truism still holds good – practice makes perfect. I am glad to say that strong efforts are being made to alter the law relating to the sale of poisons for horticultural purposes, and it is to be hoped that at no very distant date it will be possible to obtain nicotine from any respectable nurseryman or seedsman.

# Tidying Up our Science

MARY KEEN, MARCH 2012

Here we are in the age of science and, with the announcement of a push 'to create a world-class scientific research centre for the benefit of all gardeners and the environment', our own RHS is about to become a major player. And here I am, like (I suspect) many members of a certain age, grappling with 'why science matters'.

> "I am a completely unscientific gardener of the muck, mystery and ask-everyone-else school of gardening"

British writer C P Snow (1905–1980) spoke in the 1960s of 'the Two Cultures', that 'incomprehension tinged with hostility' towards science once attributed to intellectuals educated only in the humanities. These days, society may have moved on, but many of my generation remain puzzled by science. We just don't get it.

I am a completely unscientific gardener of the muck, mystery and ask-everyone-else school of gardening. So I went to RHS Garden Wisley to talk about my shortcomings with Roger Williams, [then] RHS Head of Science.

Roger was patient and I came away with a better idea of why the RHS needs to lead research for gardeners. In the wider world, Roger says, there is plenty of work being done into the genetic code and other important topics, but it leaves less time and money for horticultural research. Research at the Royal Botanic Gardens, Kew is more slanted towards wild plants than cultivated ones. Government cuts mean that many universities have had to reduce research budgets (some, like Reading, send several PhD students to work at Wisley).

Roger believes it is important for his team to engage in areas of biological science that can deliver the answers gardeners like us need. These include taxonomy, of course, even though non-scientists moan that plant names change too often. Roger says firmly that we would be 'in a big of a mess if we didn't know exactly what was what'. (Clearly scientists have tidier minds than most of us.)

Managing resources, particularly water, is increasingly vital. As water becomes scarcer, will we frown on neighbours who use it for hanging baskets rather than for crops? And can we be encouraged to find other ways of saving water? The new RHS science labs will teach everyone how to cope with the ever-shifting target that is climate change.

Scientists need to be a step ahead of what is happening to biodiversity and natural resources, so that they can help the rest of us to manage the problems that face us now. These are issues that were not around in C P Snow's time, let alone when the Wisley labs were built in 1907.

City gardens are high on Roger's research list. Gardens tend to be given over to extensions or offices for people to work from home, but keeping the city green matters more than ever. A quarter of London's land is occupied by gardens – which can support wildlife, help to cool the area or mitigate the flood risk that comes with freaky weather brought by climate change. I asked about green walls, but Roger says green roofs are probably a simpler way of delivering environmental benefits in built-up places.

The current flux in the natural world is worrying. After my trip to Wisley I felt more confident that, in the capable scientific hands of the RHS, all gardeners would be better prepared to cope with change.

# Plant Science Questions for the Curious

MIKE GRANT, JANUARY 2011

## WHO DISPERSES MY FRUIT?

Colourful, juicy, tasty fruits have evolved their colour, juiciness and flavour in order to appeal to creatures that eat them and hence naturally disperse the seeds.

"Avocado, native to Mexico, may have been naturally dispersed by giant ground sloths"

With cultivated fruits, humans have taken control to become the fruit thieves, and we try to fend off secondary thieves. Birds are our biggest competitor, taking small red fruits such as cherries and raspberries. Fortunately in Britain we don't have to contend with fiercer creatures, such as bears, that disperse larger fruits like apples in nature.

Some fruits no longer have living natural dispersing species, which has led to fascinating speculation as to what those creatures, now extinct, might have been.

Avocado, native to Mexico, may have been naturally dispersed by giant ground sloths. Osage orange (*Maclura pomifera*, inedible to humans) is native to Texas, USA and has no effective natural dispersers, not even deer. But the ease with which the seed germinates from domesticated horse dung suggests it was dispersed by Pleistocene horses, and possibly even mastodons and mammoths.

## PLANT CHILLING REQUIREMENTS

February is usually one of the coldest months. It is therefore an important time of year for plants that require winter chilling. Spring-flowering bulbs such as daffodils, hyacinths and some tulips typically require a period of winter cold in order to flower successfully.

"...even hops need specific amounts of winter chilling to flower and fruit productively"

Other plants for which winter chilling is important are fruit trees and bushes. In the UK, apples, pears, cherries, blackcurrant, plums and even hops need specific amounts of winter chilling to flower and fruit productively.

Growth inhibitors accumulate in flower and leaf buds when they are formed during the summer and autumn, and these prevent the buds opening during winter. The chilling is required to break down these growth inhibitors and ensure the buds open at the right time. Each cultivar needs a specific number of 'chill hours' below a certain temperature – usually given as 7.2°c (45°F) in the UK – to break dormancy, and the number of hours required can range from 200 to 1,500.

If plants get insufficient chilling they may suffer from delayed or uneven flowering and leafing, leading to poor crops. Inevitably, climate change has an impact, so warmer winters mean breeders are trying to select cultivars that have reduced chilling requirements.

## SHAPE SHIFTERS

H olly and ivy converge at Christmas in a decorative way. Apart from being evergreen, there is little to connect them – they are not related botanically.

"Dimorphism can be seen in many plants"

But they do have a biological feature in common, namely 'dimorphic leaves'. This is where the leaves of the same species exhibit two different shapes.

Ivy is one of the best-known examples: climbing stems have leaves that are lobed, while those on non-clinging, flower-bearing, aerial stems, produced when ivy reaches the top of its support, are barely lobed at all. The modified shape probably enables leaves to gather light more efficiently.

Holly performs a similar trick, but it is only noticeable on tree-sized specimens, tall enough to be out of the reach of grazing animals. And that is the clue; leaves from holly shrubs or lower tree branches are spiny to avoid being eaten, but those higher up can dispense with spines.

Dimorphism can be seen in many plants. Conifers such as juniper have needle-like juvenile leaves (again, for protection) and adult leaves that are scale shaped. Some water plants have linear submerged leaves to reduce drag in flowing water, but circular floating leaves to support flowers.

# Pots for the Future

SPENCE GUNN, FEBRUARY 2011

L ike death and taxes, plant pots are always with us. Who has not got a stack of once-used pots left over after their last planting or bedding-out session, perhaps even a tower or two at the back of the shed, just in case they come in handy?

But even plastic pots have a limited useful life, not least because they tend to become brittle over time. At some point they have to be disposed of but we are running out of landfill sites. An estimated 500 million plastic pots are in circulation in the EU (11 million a year are sold in the UK alone, according to one leading manufacturer). The polypropylene of which they are made takes thousands of years to degrade, so are there more environmentally responsible options?

The Garden Industry Manufacturers' Association points out that modern plastic pots can contain as much as 70 percent recycled plastic, and many are made in the UK, two factors that reduce both their carbon footprint and their impact as waste. Some local authorities will accept them for their plastics recycling schemes.

The alternative is a fully biodegradable pot – it will break down in the ground if it is left on the plant or it can be composted. But that is not a new idea. Paper, peat and 'whalehide' pots have been around for years, invented to protect young plants' roots at transplanting. But there is now an increasing drive to produce pots that behave like plastic on the nursery or in your glasshouse at home, but which will degrade quickly when you want to throw them away.

> "Biological materials now used for pots include rice husk and miscanthus waste that has been compressed and bonded..."

The balance between keeping the material stable during its useful life and fast degradation after disposal is a huge challenge. So, too, is making a degradable pot that performs as well as plastic when it is being handled on the nursery. Biological materials now used for pots include rice husk and miscanthus waste that has been compressed and bonded, and plastics derived from vegetable starches. One supplier has introduced what looks like the best of both worlds – a plastic pot that contains an additive that makes it break down to water and organic matter within five years (but only under controlled composting conditions).

It is not only gardeners who want choice in the type of pots they can buy. Many nurseries are looking at using biodegradable pots of various kinds. Unfortunately the additional cost, either of the pots (which can be four times that of plastic) or having to change their handling systems, can be a barrier.

For one Hampshire nursery though, their changeover to a biodegradable pot has opened up a new niche market. After initial tests in 2006, Kirton Farm Nurseries' half-a-million plant output is now grown in Hairy Pots, despite the extra production and handling costs. The nursery finds its customers, at least, are happy to pay the extra 30p or so for a 'greener' product.

# DNA First for Welsh Scientists

NEWS, JUNE 2011

W ales has become the first country in the world to map the DNA of all its native plants, using technology known as barcoding. Plant barcodes are useful in a number of fields, from biodiversity surveys to forensic science.

> "...all plants native to Wales can be identified from fragments as tiny as a single grain of pollen"

The team of scientists, led by the National Botanic Garden of Wales, spent three years collecting samples of all 1,143 species of native flowering plants before sequencing a section of DNA code from each one.

The barcodes create a catalogue of unique gene sequences, precisely identifying each species and allowing unknown genetic material to be compared for possible matches.

This means that all plants native to Wales can be identified from fragments as tiny as a single grain of pollen.

'It's a new take on identifying and classifying plants,' says project leader Natasha de Vere.

The team's next step is to liaise with other botanic gardens to barcode the remaining 364 native UK species.

# The Hidden Power of Plants

SARAH JANE GURR & JOSEPHINE PEACH, MAY 1996

M ankind has used extracts of poisonous plants for millennia, for hunting, hallucination and homicide. However, while we should appreciate the dangers of poisonous plants, we must also be aware that their powerful physiological effects make them important in the development of new drugs. An example is the arrow-tip poison, curare, which is a potent paralysing agent that can lead to rapid death by asphyxiation. The Southern American Indians prepared this poison from dried extracts of *Chondrodendron tomentosum* mixed with *Strychnos toxifera*. The active constituent of curare –

tubocurarine – is still sometimes used as a muscle relaxant under anaesthetic.

New and exciting times in the treatment of human disease have dawned with recent discoveries of novel pharmaceuticals from plants. Scientists have begun to realise that this invaluable source of potential drugs, when coupled with an intimate knowledge of the workings of the cell, august well for the rational design of new therapies. This article concentrates on four very different plants, linked only by the fact that each makes a 'spindle-poison'.

"*Catharanthus roseus* (Madagascar periwinkle) was once just thought of as an insignificant tropical weed"

All living organisms are built from cells – the smallest units of life. Cell structure varies between plants and animals but all cells are essentially chemical factories that import raw materials, and manufacture materials for export. In plant and animal cells chromosomes within the nucleus contain all the genetic information, within DNA, needed to produce a new individual. During cell division the orderly partitioning of this DNA gives two identical daughter cells, each with a complete set of chromosomes, and the process is called mitosis. The formation and degeneration of the spindle – strands of protein which stretch from the poles to the equator of the cell during mitosis and which push the poles apart so letting the cells divide – are both crucial stages. Cell division can be stopped by interfering with either event.

## Anti-cancer drugs

Cell growth is exquisitely controlled in a healthy person. When control is lost, rapid and unrestrained cell growth occurs, so many cancer treatments aim to destroy these rapidly dividing cells. Plants can provide drugs either to prevent spindle formation or to stop the spindle dividing into the daughter chromosomes. Some spindle-poisons are too toxic for clinical use but they can provide a basis for the design of new drugs.

Further possibilities arise from the chemical elaboration of any of these substances. So which plants make spindle-poisons and how can they be employed to combat cancer?

*Catharanthus roseus* (Madagascar periwinkle) was once just thought of as an insignificant tropical weed. Yet in the 1950s it was discovered that this plant produces two of the most valuable and effective drugs in the fight against childhood cancer. *C. roseus* produces the potent spindle-poisons vincristine and vinblastine. These drugs are especially effective against lymphoblastic leukaemia, a major childhood cancer, and are used in the treatment of Hodgkin's disease and to treat testicular cancer.

*C. roseus* is farmed in Texas, USA, and 8,000kg (17,600lb) of flowers are processed every year. Total chemical synthesis of the drugs in the laboratory is possible but it is protracted and difficult, and tissue-culture has met with only limited success.

The useful but poisonous nature of yew [*Taxus baccata*] has long been known. Caesar records that the Gaelic chieftain Cativolcus committed suicide by drinking an infusion of yew bark after the defeat of his armies by the Romans. Indigenous North American tribes used *T. brevifolia* (Pacific yew) bark to treat skin cancer and as an abortifacient and disinfectant.

In 1979 biological tests on Pacific yew bark revealed the presence of a potent spindle-poison, taxol, which stops cell division by preventing the spindle from dividing into the daughter chromosomes. Taxol is now invaluable in the treatment of ovarian cancer, but yew bark yields only small quantities of taxol; a 60-year-old tree gives enough taxol to treat just one patient. Pacific yew plantations have been established in the USA, but this is a long-term project.

The chemical structure of taxol is very complex; its laboratory synthesis is too complicated to be used commercially. However, it was noticed that although clippings of *T. baccata* contain only minute amounts of taxol, they also contain a considerable amount of a related substance called baccatin III. This can be elaborated in the laboratory to make either either taxol itself or the closely related unnatural drug taxotere.

The therapeutic value of taxol has led to considerable effort being put into making the active ingredient using yew grown in tissue-culture; the process should be commercially viable in the next few years.

*Colchicum autumnale*, although often called autumn crocus, is not, in fact, related to true crocus, despite its appearance. Its powerful effects have long been known; it was employed by Arab and Byzantine physicians, and the Romans to treat gout. It was administered widely in the 18th century in Europe, although the main effective agent, colchicine, was not isolated until 1820. Colchicine is used in plant breeding, for example to double the usual two sets of chromosomes (diploid) to give four sets (tetraploid), which can lead to plants with larger flowers.

Colchicine is too toxic for widespread clinical use, but it is an invaluable research tool. It is a spindle-poison which prevents the splitting of the spindle to form the nuclei of the two daughter cells.

Extracts of leaves, seeds, roots and flowers have been prepared for medicinal use for millennia but the move to identify the 'active principle' of individual plants and use specific drugs came only in the 19th century. With the advent of effective purification methods and an appreciation of chemical synthesis we have moved from plant extracts to clinical pills.

Whether a drug is extracted from the whole plant or synthesised in a laboratory depends on the plant's availability, and the comparative costs of extraction versus synthesis. Sometimes a 'semi-synthetic' process is more efficient – when a plant product is further elaborated in the laboratory, as in the preparation of taxol and taxotere from yew. Such semi-synthetic routes can be used to develop new drugs, which are even better than the original.

Two exciting areas of research in the use of plants as pharmaceutical factories have recently become important: tissue-culture, and plant gene engineering or 'molecular' farming.

Plant tissue-culture and micropropagation are terms used to describe a range of sterile methods used to grow whole plants from individual cells or from pieces of tissue, such as apical meristems.

Tissue-culture can produce many types of useful compounds but not necessarily the same compounds as the adult plant. Tissue-culture of *Catharanthus roseus* has not produced any of the valuable vincristine or vinblastine. Intriguingly, although ginseng can be produced by root tissue-culture of *Panax ginseng*, commercial ginseng dealers do not want the laboratory product; the appeal of whole ginseng roots lies in the desirable shapes! So, the large-scale production of pharmaceutical products by cell culture looks promising, though there are few examples of commercial production yet.

Plant gene engineering gives us the ability to endow a new trait into certain plants by the insertion of a foreign gene. This means that, in the future, we could harvest and purify drugs from easily grown plants, which would not normally produce the compounds.

Most of the world's population depends on plants as a primary source of health care. Even in the most developed countries many new and modern drugs come directly or indirectly from plant extracts. Indeed, about a quarter of prescription drugs contain compounds either directly derived or modelled from natural plant products. Yet few of the world's well-known 250,000 plant species have been fully screened for their medicinal effects; in 1988 only about 20 pure chemical compounds from plants were used in clinical practice and these came from just 90 plant species. Much remains to be discovered and it is therefore of paramount importance to maintain the diversity of the world's flora as well as protecting and recording the wealth of knowledge of different cultures regarding the use of medicinal plants.

# Does Planting by the Moon Work?

MATTHEW BIGGS, SEPTEMBER 2011

Since the ancients peered from their caves at the constellations to mark the passage of time, man has believed that the moon exerts a profound influence on the earth. In the 4th century BC, Pytheas, a Greek geographer and explorer, was the first to record that tides were influenced by the moon.

In the 1920s, Austrian philosopher Rudolf Steiner proposed his theories on biodynamic agriculture, including the idea that the moon, just as it affects tides, has an effect on water in people, plants or wherever it may be. This was developed in a series of sowing and harvesting experiments by Maria Thun in the 1950s and further summarised in a paper by Nicholas Kollerstrom and Gerhard Staudenmaier in 2001.

Devotees, such as HRH The Prince of Wales and John Harris, Head Gardener at Tresillian House, Cornwall, claim that sowing vegetables that crop above ground during a waxing moon, and root crops as the moon wanes, produces better, healthier crops and is part of an environmentally friendly treatment of the earth. For others, however, this is lunacy. In the 21st century we demand hard evidence. Yet statistical analysis suggests that the moon is also responsible for such diverse events as starting fights in pubs and successful depilatory waxing. So why not sowing by the moon?

"Those who believe in planting by the moon have a gut feeling that it just might be true. Yet the science is lacking to support their claim"

Things instinctive or spiritual cannot always be explained – as anyone who has seen a ghost or has fallen in love will tell you. Those who believe in planting by the moon have a gut feeling that it just might be true. Yet the science is lacking to support their claim. Those gardeners who need facts to support their practice simply argue, 'How can the world be influenced by a ball of cheese?'

# PESTS & DISEASES

*Note from the editor*

Like death and taxes, pests and diseases
are about the only things in the garden
that are absolutely certain. The result is
that they often bulk rather too largely
in our imaginations, preventing us from
enjoying our gardens to the full. The RHS, for
example, receives thousands of enquiries
every year about them so we can assume
there are a great many more discontented
gardeners out there. But at least the Society
can provide its members with accurate
information to ensure that no more time than
is necessary is expended on identifying the
problem, and doing something about it – if
possible. If not, we will be told just to accept
it, which is probably better than nothing.

Pests come in all shapes and sizes it seems:
wasps (perhaps), rabbits, roe deer, even
exotic parakeets, to name just a few.
They are not even confined to lower
mammals – humans play their part as well,
as Vanessa Berridge has discovered about

her neighbours. Many diseases are always with us. Dutch elm disease, for example, was devastating in the 1970s and is still a threat, while rose replant disease and grey mould can be controlled or circumvented, but never eradicated.

Of course, the list and virulence of pests and diseases change over the years: some are solved or neutralised, while others continue to arrive (often from warmer climes) to plague us. Nowadays, we should think ourselves really lucky if we *were* plagued by house sparrows or skylarks in our gardens, as earlier generations have apparently been, but at least those before 1940 were saved from the cursed lily beetle which makes lily cultivation so difficult these days, the citrus longhorn beetle that threatens trees, not to mention pathogenic horrors like *Cylindrocladium buxicola* (box blight), *Phytophthora ramorum* (sudden oak death) and *Chalara fraxinea* (ash dieback). Sometimes it seems a miracle that we can make thriving gardens at all.

**URSULA BUCHAN**, editor

# Birds versus Gardening

CHARLES E PEARSON, FROM A LECTURE GIVEN IN MARCH 1902

Some gardeners speak as though horticulture would benefit by the extermination of *all* birds, whilst others would strive to whitewash the sparrow and endeavour to prove that the sooty suburban raider is a very slightly disguised angel. Being myself fond of both birds and garden, I have tried to speak without prejudice and judge each of our feathered visitors to the garden on its merits.

> "...the majority of the sparrow's iniquities in the garden are ascribable to sheer love of mischief rather than stealing to satisfy his hunger"

Taking our foes first, the sparrow heads the list. The most annoying part of it is that the majority of the sparrow's iniquities in the garden are ascribable to sheer love of mischief rather than stealing to satisfy his hunger. In the early spring, when even a few Crocuses are a joy to the amateur gardener as an earnest of summer glories to come, the sparrow makes that joy extremely brief by rending the flowers in pieces and strewing them about the border. Curiously enough, he seems to have a strongly developed colour sense, and attacks the yellows more persistently than any other shades. A 'Primrose by a river's brim' is a subject of indifference to a sparrow, but he seems to take a fiendish pleasure in pulling out all the flowers from those which have been the objects of the gardener's solicitude. The cultivation of the Gooseberry is almost a hopeless labour where these pests abound, as they pull out all the buds from the twigs as soon as swelling commences. Something may be done by dusting the trees with lime, soot, etc., and by threading the branches with cotton. It is also wise under these circumstances not to go in for hard pruning, as birds seem to find more difficulty in abstracting *all* the buds from slender whippy shoots than from shortened stumps, and by leaving a sufficient number of whiplike shoots on lightly pruned trees you ensure at least a partial crop. I have seen beds of Carnations absolutely ruined by being pecked to pieces by this destructive nuisance.

I was reminded this afternoon not to forget the lark in my list of feathered enemies, and I regret to say that there is some reason for its inclusion [because] it also visits the garden and completely skeletonises all the Spring Cabbage. No one would be Philistine enough to wish to lose the 'fine careless rapture' of the skylark's song, but at the same time one is led to regard the slight annual thinning of its numbers for table purposes as so far beneficial as not to call for discouragement.

Turning now to the brighter side of the picture, one is glad to be able to chronicle a small army of friends whose manner of life causes the gardener to regard them with unmixed benevolence. These are the purely insectivorous birds, including, among residents, the modest hedge sparrow, the graceful wagtail, the lively wren, and the robin. This last, though sanctified by common sentiment in this country, is a pugnacious little rascal, fighting to the death intruders on the small domain he has marked out as his own; he has also one blot on his character, his principles failing to keep him in the path of honesty when ripe Cherries are about.

Among the migratory hosts all the warblers, the chiff-chaff, willow-wren, white-throat, fly-catchers, etc., are without reproach and ought to be carefully protected. The cuckoo, too, though needing a kindly veil over its domestic affairs, is a gardener's friend, being a destroyer of caterpillars, and is the only bird I know of which will tackle the long-haired section of them.

# Parakeet Protection Reduced

NEWS, JANUARY 2010

Non-native parakeets colonising parts of southern England and causing problems in many private and public gardens can now be controlled more easily. From the beginning of the year, rules obliging landowners to apply for a special licence to cull the species have been lifted (they must apply for a general licence to control them legally).

> "Their exotic, bright green plumage is a common sight at RHS Garden Wisley..."

Populations of naturalised ringnecked parakeet (*Psittacula krameri*) have exploded in the last decade and now number tens of thousands. Their exotic, bright green plumage is a common sight at RHS Garden Wisley, where they cause considerable damage to apples. 'Parakeets hang on the branches and peck at the more brightly coloured fruits,' says Fruit Supervisor Alessandra Valsecchi.

The Wisley vineyard, which began producing wine in 2006, has yet to be affected but at nearby Painshill Park, grapes that could make thousands of bottles of wine are eaten by flocks of parakeets each year.

# Why Welcome Wasps?

STUART LOGAN, JULY 2011

Wasps have entered the rich pantheon of English simile. The phrase 'as welcome as a wasp at a picnic' has joined other ironic adages such as 'as passive as Japanese knotweed' or 'as organic as DDT'. Certainly wasps are slightly scary, given their propensity to sting humans without any apparent provocation. That only females inflict this injury makes wasps a tricky subject for a politically correct male writer. Worse still, the male wasps (most evident around August Bank Holiday), being completely unable to multi-task, spend their short lives feeding on plums and trying to mate with newly emergent queens – albeit not stinging anybody.

> "All a freshly fertilised queen wasp wants to do is to hide in the dining-room curtains until next spring"

Believe it or not, for much of their lives common wasps (*Vespula vulgaris*) are beneficial to gardeners. All a freshly fertilised queen wasp wants to do is to hide in the dining-room curtains until next spring. When she emerges from the Laura Ashley she starts a new colony. She finds a suitable nesting site such as a disused mouse burrow, your loft or the rafters of a shed and creates a small structure using a type of papier-mâché made from chewed-up wood. You may already have had the pleasure of watching wasps gnaw away at your favourite garden furniture or sheds.

The young queen builds several cells in her new nest and lays an egg in each. These fertilised eggs hatch into grubs which the queen feeds with captured insects. (Wasp larvae are carnivorous, unlike bees, which feed only on pollen and nectar-points, if they remember their card.) Wasp larvae secrete sweet saliva, which serves as a food for the queen.

Infertile female workers hatch out from the first few eggs and fly off to munch up more garden sheds in an effort to enlarge the nest. As the colony increases in size, worker wasps will use their stings to paralyse caterpillars and other garden pests before carrying them off as fodder for their grubs. The queen concentrates on laying fertilised eggs until mid-August when she lays a few unfertilised eggs in some slightly larger cells. These hatch into males that will mate with females from other nests.

At this point the colony's work is finished and it begins to disintegrate. Unfortunately for us gardeners, the unemployed worker wasps then change from being largely beneficial caterpillar and aphid killers to predators of our plums, pears and apples.

Undoubtedly there will be times when a persistent wasp needs to be shown a rolled-up copy of *The Garden*, but these insects do have a useful place within the fauna of our gardens. So if any wasps are reading this as it descends towards them at high speed, take note: my plums are off limits.

# Asian Beetle Import Alert

NEWS, APRIL 2010

UK import regulations have been stepped up in a bid to prevent citrus longhorn beetle (*Anoplophora chinensis*), recently found in parks and gardens in the Netherlands, from entering and establishing in this country.

The Dutch Plant Protection Service has now destroyed all deciduous trees within 100m (330ft) of a find in Boskoop. All plant nurseries within a 1.2-mile radius (said to be more than 550) had to cease trading while inspections were carried out. Boskoop is a major horticultural production area for Europe.

The beetle could be potentially devastating in gardens. Adults eat foliage and young bark, but the larvae do more damage, feeding inside trunks on the pith and vascular system of a wide range of deciduous trees and shrubs. Each female beetle can lay 200 eggs.

The discovery has had (and may still cause) serious repercussions for British gardeners, including increased prices and restrictions on the availability of some plants. Andrew Halstead, RHS Principal Entomologist, says there is no treatment. 'The only thing you can do is destroy infested plants, which is serious if they are important specimens or have historic significance.'

The Food and Environment Research Agency (FERA) estimates it would cost around £300m to deal with a substantial outbreak of citrus longhorn in the UK – yet this would not guarantee eradication. It is asking gardeners and those in the horticultural industry to be extra vigilant for signs of the pest, particularly on its favourite host, Japanese maple (*Acer palmatum*).

The agency speculates the pest could have arrived in the Netherlands as early as 2001, given the numbers of plants affected in the Boskoop area. Larvae are difficult to spot as they can live within plant stems for up to three years. Breeding populations have been found in Lombardy, Italy and France as well as the Netherlands since 2000.

> "...be extra vigilant for signs of the pest, particularly on its favourite host, Japanese maple..."

In the UK, the Plant Health and Seeds Inspectorate is targeting inspections of large shipments from Boskoop and the Far East (the main source of the beetle), and some British nurseries and garden centres. The only way to detect larvae is by 'destructive testing' of a sample of plants in a shipment. Seventeen hosts including *Cotoneaster* and *Betula* have been identified, but acers imported to the UK from China have been the plants most commonly infested.

Adult beetles are 21–37mm (¾–1½in) long, with antennae up to twice the length of the body. The most obvious visual sign of the beetle's presence are 6–11mm (¼–½in) diameter exit holes at the base of trunks. More difficult to detect is bleeding sap (where eggs have been laid) and bulges in the trunk (indicating a pupal chamber).

Anyone who suspects seeing symptoms should contact their local Plant Health and Seeds Inspector.

# Book-Bugs

HUGH JOHNSON (WRITING AS TRADESCANT), SEPTEMBER 2004

How do insects learn botany? It has been another sad season of elm attacks by *Scolytus scolytus* and his little cousin *Scolytus multistriatus*, with their fungus-infected feet, leaving young trees burnt or bare in the hedge. I am hardened to that, 30 years after their brutal arrival destroyed all but one of our elms in, or close to, the immemorial class. But this year, to my horror, they have been at the botany books and discovered that the graceful zelkovas, cousins to the elm in the niceties of botany but in appearance quite different, are fair game too.

We have three: two of the comparatively common *Zelkova carpinifolia* from the Caucasus and one of the rarer and even more elegant *Z. serrata* from Japan. Our *Z. carpinifolia* turned limp and jaundice-yellow almost overnight in early July. *Z. serrata* is seemingly following, with brown sprays in the canopy and, worse, brown stains appearing on the bark of the lower trunk. One of the last of the East Anglian breed once known as *Ulmus nitens*, the shining elm, for its gleaming dark leaves (most elm leaves are rough and dull), is under branch-by-branch attack, to which we respond laboriously with a saw. How soon will the scholarly scolytus cotton on to *Celtis australis*, the so-called hackberry, another elm relation and one of the best Mediterranean street trees? Ours looks fine now, but how do I tell it not to breathe?

> "Our *Zelkova carpinifolia* turned limp and jaundice-yellow almost overnight in early July"

# Autumn Precautions

GEOFFREY DUTTON, OCTOBER 1992

In fully-fenced hill pasture voles swarm beneath tussock or snow, gnawing young trees' stems (hazel and birch excepted). We baffle them by tube guards of old 2-pint milk cartons or double storeys of cat-food tins (800g size – years of them, all Natural Rust Brown). These are easily renewable and if not attractive, neither are 200 girdled oaklings. (*How* many cat-food tins? Well, after all, don't we keep *Felis catus* to protect our plants?)

> "...roe deer – unlike the execrable goat – don't seem to push down trees..."

Trees that I plant outside the fence proper require individual protection against rabbits and roe deer as well. Small oaks and such like begin there in tall (420cm) plastic tree-shelters (expensive and non-durable) but are weaned into cans and rabbit-netting rolls (420 x 10cm diam.) that ease apart as the boles expand; taller saplings start off in the rolls. A temporary post prevents weak stems bending invitingly under snow-load. These rolls prevent the lethal fraying of young stems by bucks' horns, and as roe –

unlike the execrable goat – don't seem to push down trees and posts, they prevent nibbling of branches as well. They also keep off rabbit teeth in hard two to three-foot deep snow, when rabbits are really hungry and low guards useless.

# Secateur-Happy Neighbours

VANESSA BERRIDGE, JUNE 2010

The old Victorian adage 'Growth follows the knife' may be true – but within limits. It's those limits, sadly, that my neighbours just do not recognise. Good friends all, they will unhesitatingly run you and your child to A&E, lend a cup of sugar, or feed the cat. But let them loose with a pair of secateurs – and problems begin.

*"...rambling roses, a foaming Acacia and scented jasmine have all fallen to that deadly snip, snip"*

'She's in the garden,' I shriek. My husband sighs wearily, knowing I'll shoot out like Dickens' Betsey Trotwood shooing away donkeys. Experience has shown that my neighbour will be busily clipping away at stems that have unwisely poked their way through to her side and I'll find my *Clematis* 'Perle d'Azur', previously a mass of vibrant blue blooms, hanging lifeless from the fence. The initial warning was an assault on her cooking apple tree, which once provided us with welcome borrowed landscape and its creamy-pink blossom in spring. 'Why do you think it's died?' she wondered, apparently unaware that July is not a key month for savage orchard pruning. Her lofty *Cupressus*, which removes light from our garden by 2pm for much of the year, would have been a better victim.

On the other side, a Victorian pear once soared to 18m (60ft), its blossom an avalanche of snow in April. It died some years back, but its cadaver still haunts our skyline – partly because our other secateur-happy neighbour is too busy trimming back my carefully interwoven *Clematis armandii* and white *Solanum* to reveal an uninterrupted view of his drain pipe and a Stalag 17-like shed in the garden beyond.

London gardens have enough challenges, such as slugs, snails and the squirrels that rip through my tulip bulbs unless I cover the pots and beds in winter with unsightly chicken wire. Then there's my soil – cold London

clay. To put that into context: a 1930s lease on a house a few streets away had a restrictive covenant forbidding brick-making in the back garden. So I've added sand, humus and helpings of our own compost to the soil, and planted damp shade-lovers. I've divided the 9m x 18m (30 x 60ft) space into four, using clipped box and arches covered with roses and evergreen *Muehlenbeckia* to draw in the eye and hint at further delights. But I can't rely on my boundaries, as rambling roses, a foaming *Acacia* and scented jasmine have all fallen to that deadly snip, snip. Would it seem unfriendly to build walls?

# Hopes for Ash Come Back

NEWS, DECEMBER 2013

To date there have been more than 600 reported cases of ash dieback (*Chalara fraxinea*) in the UK. However, good news has emerged from the National Trust's Holnicote Estate, Somerset, home to a 2001 plantation of 6,000 ash trees. The disease was identified there in September [2013], but only 10 percent of the population is infected and some trees are thought to display signs of resistance. Because of their location, the Trust's Natural Environment Director Simon Pryor believes that the trees were not infected by wind-borne spores but already had the disease when they were planted more than 12 years ago. 'Even the trees affected have not suffered as much as we'd have expected, and few have died, despite apparently having had the disease for nearly a decade,' he said.

> "...good news has emerged from the National Trust's Holnicote Estate, Somerset..."

# Phytophthora

JOHN SCRACE, MARCH 2011

In recent months there have been many reports about the spread of *Phytophthora ramorum*, its threat to oaks and Japanese larch as well as its ability to infect *Rhododendron* and other shrubs. But what is this disease, and what does it mean to gardeners?

*Phytophthora ramorum* has been responsible for the widespread death of oak (*Quercus*) species and tanbark oak (*Lithocarpus densiflorus*) in parts of the USA, where the disease was dubbed 'sudden oak death'.

It was soon detected in Europe, and there have now been hundreds of findings in the UK. However, our native oak species (*Q. robur* and *Q. petraea*) are much more resistant to infection. In the UK, the majority of cases have been in the nursery trade, affecting container-grown ornamentals such as *Camellia*, *Rhododendron* and *Viburnum*. There have, however, been significant outbreaks in gardens, amenity areas and woodland. In the UK and Europe the disease tends to be referred to as 'ramorum dieback'.

"Plants that are susceptible should be pruned only in dry weather and the tools used cleaned and disinfected"

*Phytophthora ramorum* (and a closely related organism, *P. kernoviae*) are known as 'notifiable pathogens', which means that suspected cases must be reported to the appropriate plant health authority. Until recently, common beech (*Fagus sylvatica*) appeared to be the most susceptible tree under UK conditions. There have also been significant findings on a common heathland plant, bilberry (*Vaccinium myrtillus*). A major epidemic could thus have far-reaching consequences for woodland and heathland habitats, as well as for the horticultural industry, gardens and amenity plantings.

Infected Japanese larch trees *(Larix kaempferi)* were first found in August 2009 in southwest England. There since have been outbreaks on larch in Wales, Northern Ireland, the Republic of Ireland and, most recently, in Scotland. Larch has added a new dimension to the problem: this is the first time that the disease has been found affecting a commercially important conifer species; it is also the first time that large numbers of any tree species have been infected in the UK; numerous spores are produced on infected larch needles, which have the potential to spread the disease widely.

Thousands of hectares of affected Japanese larch plantations are currently subject to statutory control measures. Affected trees are being felled, although the timber can still be used.

Gardeners can help prevent the spread of the disease mainly by following good garden practice. Plants that are susceptible should be pruned only in dry weather and the tools used cleaned and disinfected. It is better to water these plants in the morning than at night and, to help prevent the disease spreading, allow good air movement by keeping plants well spaced. Damaged leaves can be more liable to infection, especially in wetter weather.

All gardeners should familiarise themselves with the symptoms of *P. ramorum* and *P. kernoviae* and keep an eye on plants and trees known to be hosts. The diseases do not kill shrubs such as *Rhododendron* and *Camellia* but will weaken the plants, and their infected leaves can generate spores that can pass to susceptible trees.

By being able to recognise the symptoms, by reporting suspected cases, and by following sensible cultivation techniques, gardeners can help prevent the spread of these diseases.

# False Alarm

HUGH JOHNSON (WRITING AS TRADESCANT), AUGUST 2001

There was an unnerving article in last September's journal about a new box fungus of such potency that it threatens all the box hedges, the parterres, the dinky little pompons, the cloud hedges – all the pretty horticultural contrivances from nature's most malleable plant.

> "There was a pause while the scientific staff went to work. The spores of *Cylindrocladium* take a while to incubate"

This spring a yelp of fright went up from Saling. Our most-photographed feature is the bank of what are fashionably called clouds clipped over the past 25 years by Eric Kirby with ever-growing ingenuity.

In March they started to die. In part, that is, but enough to scare us silly. I noticed that the dead leaves and shoots were principally on hollows and crevices where fallen leaves had lain, sodden, winter-long. Hoping that this, rather than an imported fungus, was the proximate cause, I sent samples of dead wood to Wisley. As I cut it, though, my spirits rose. Down at the base the old bushes were sprouting new growth. These were not exactly at death's door.

There was a pause while the scientific staff went to work. The spores of *Cylindrocladium* take a while to incubate. *Volutella*, a relatively benign fungus, was found. Three weeks later came the all-clear: no *Cylindrocladium*. Meanwhile with fingers crossed we had cut the infected bushes back to good new shoots, sprayed them with copper fungicide, fed and mulched them heavily and given them a foliar feed for good measure.

I see now how the bushes were weakened. A quarter-century of clipping, on a gravelly bank, with feeding neglected, leaves a plant with few reserves. Accretions of wet leaves gave fungi an open door. It won't happen again..

# Rose Replant Disease

RHS ADVICE, NOVEMBER 2010

Replant 'disease', or soil sickness, is a problem that can occur when re-establishing plants on sites where the same species has been grown previously. It affects many different plant species, but may be most common with roses.

> "Some gardeners line the hole with a cardboard box with its bottom removed; by the time the cardboard rots, the plant should have established"

Symptoms are variable, but above ground are characterised by stunting of growth and a general lack of vigour, often with yellowing of the foliage and poor flowering. If the plant is lifted, on inspection the roots are usually small, dark and compact. Some of the fine roots may be rotten. A healthy plant put into affected soil will deteriorate and may die. More often it survives the decline and slowly improves, but is unlikely to catch up with unaffected plants, even those in close proximity. Moving a stunted plant to fresh soil often aids in its recovery.

The exact causes of replant diseases are not completely understood. In most cases they are thought to be due to microbial agents in the soil, as soil sterilisation prevents the disease. Causes probably vary with different plant species, and in some instances it is possible that other factors – such as exhaustion of certain nutrients or impoverished soil structure – are more important than microbes.

For small areas, changing the soil may be effective (it either removes the microbes or overcomes soil impoverishment). A planting hole should be excavated wider than the full spread of the roots – at least 60cm (2ft) in diameter and 30cm (12in) deep. Fill the hole with soil from another part of the garden or buy in topsoil. Some gardeners line the hole with a cardboard box with its bottom removed; by the time the cardboard rots, the plant should have established. There is some evidence that boosting plant growth by applying high nitrogen fertiliser can help to counteract replant disease (follow the manufacturer's application rate: too much can do more harm than good).

Choosing plants with resistant rootstocks may help avoid the problem, if the grower indicates which they use – some *Rosa canina* rootstocks are prone to replant disease. *Rosa* x *dumetorum* 'Laxa' shows some resistance. Some rose nurseries recommend mycorrhizal fungi – there is some evidence that these can be effective in preventing replant diseases, but the results are not conclusive. They can be applied as granules or dips for bare-root plants. No chemical soil sterilants are available to home gardeners to control replant disease.

# Bees Help Counter Strawberry Grey Mould

NEWS, AUGUST 2013

Spraying strawberries against fungal infections could become a thing of the past, as researchers have found that bumblebees can do the job just as well. Commercial growers often use bumblebee hives for good pollination.

Scientists at East Malling Research in Kent, with agricultural consultant ADAS, have designed

> "As they forage through strawberry plants, the bees transfer some powder into each bloom..."

a dispenser to fit into the hives that bees must move through on their way out to forage for nectar. As they do so, a tiny quantity of a biofungicide, *Gliocladium catenulatum* (a fungus that suppresses the growth of grey mould), sticks to their bodies and legs. As they forage through strawberry plants, the bees transfer some powder into each bloom, preventing grey mould being carried onto developing fruit. The bees' control was just as good as on plants that were sprayed, and fungicide residue on fruit decreased.

# THE INTERNATIONAL DIMENSION

*Note from the editor*

An impressive feature of the Society's journal over the years has been the emphasis placed on what was happening beyond the seas. The fact that so many plants in British gardens come from other countries was probably at least part of the reason why the journal allowed plant hunters, such as William Lobb, George Forrest, Reginald Farrer and Frank Kingdon-Ward, so much space to describe their romantic and sometimes harrowing journeys, together with their remarkable finds. (When reading Forrest, it's as well to remember that many of his finds have changed their names over the years and also that, in his day, species named after a person, such as *Pleione Forrestii*, would have a capital letter.)

These days, there is less plant hunting abroad, but *The Garden* continues to carry accounts of modern botanists following in the footsteps of earlier plant explorers. Not everyone who wrote about foreign expeditions was a plant hunter. Some were just inveterate travellers, with a keen eye for the remarkable, like Viscountess Byng, widow of the great British Field Marshal, Julian Byng, who described her trip to California in 1935.

Important foreign gardens, especially in countries like Holland that RHS members might be tempted to visit, are also described and illustrated. And recently, there even appeared an article on gardens that have survived in places such as Afghanistan and Gaza, which are rather less tempting to garden visitors, but show very clearly the deep human urge to make something beautiful even in the most difficult of circumstances.

The fact that the RHS is the most visible of horticultural organisations in the United Kingdom means that a number of distinguished foreign societies or individuals have links with it; evidence of this is the support given by eminent horticulturists such as Dr Kiat Tan and the Vicomte Philippe de Spoelberch as honorary vice presidents of the Society. As far as Stephen Lacey is concerned, Britain should be very proud of its extraordinarily rich and colourful gardening heritage, but not forget that there is, and always has been, much of value and interest happening elsewhere.

**URSULA BUCHAN**, editor

# Good Will Hunting

ROY LANCASTER, JUNE 2009

This year marks the bicentenary of the birth [in 1809] of one of gardening's most famous Cornishmen, William Lobb, who successfully introduced to Britain some of the most notable conifers, and many other plants such as *Berberis darwinii* and evergreen climber *Lapageria rosea*, from the Americas. Some of these had already been described by others and introduced as seed, but only in limited amounts.

"It was the opportunity of a lifetime. Lobb gathered foliage and cones, two living seedlings and packed his saddlebags with seed, before returning at once to San Francisco and booking a place on the first available ship home"

To William Lobb, however, goes the credit for introducing seed in such quantity that many of these plants became well-established in British cultivation. The most spectacular of these is the 'big tree' – in Britain named *Wellingtonia* by John Lindley in 1853 in memory of the Duke of Wellington, who had died the previous year. Giant redwood was to undergo several name changes before finally settling down to *Sequoiadendron giganteum* in 1939.

This famous conifer, a popular landmark in botanic gardens, country estates, churchyards and pinetums, was first discovered accidentally in California by an American hunter-cum-prospector named Augustus T Dowd in 1852. The following year, details of this major find were being discussed at a meeting of the then-fledgling California Academy of Sciences in San Francisco.

Attending as a guest was William Lobb who, on hearing the news and realising its significance, lost no time in heading for the area. In a place now known as the Calaveras Grove, he first set eyes on '80 to 90 trees all within the circuit of a mile, and these varying from 250 to 320 feet in height and from 10 to 20 feet in diameter'. (This equates to 76–97m in height and 3–6m in diameter.) It was the opportunity of a lifetime.

Lobb gathered foliage and cones, two living seedlings and packed his saddlebags with seed, before returning at once to San Francisco and booking a place on the first available ship home. The seeds were immediately sown by his employers, the Veitch Nursery of Exeter, germinated quickly and were being offered in the summer of the following year, 1854, at two guineas each or 12 guineas a dozen. Less than two years after Lobb's return, young trees of this amazing conifer were being planted throughout the country by wealthy landowners, many of whom saw this noble exotic as a living, growing status symbol.

William Lobb was born in a village in Cornwall, Perranarworthal, and was first employed as a gardener by John Williams of Scorrier House near Falmouth in 1837. William's younger brother Thomas was employed by the Veitch Nursery. In 1840, its owner James Veitch was looking for a collector to send to South America in search of new ornamental plants. Having heard encouraging comments from Thomas of his brother's abilities, Veitch hired William and booked him on HM Packet Ship *Seagull* to Rio de Janeiro, where he arrived in November.

## Over the Andes

During the next four years Lobb travelled extensively, beginning in the Organ Mountains near Rio where orchids, salvias and alstroemerias were among plants collected and despatched to Veitch by ship. Unfortunately, Lobb kept no written records of his adventures so few details are known of his activities. We do know he subsequently sailed south to Buenos Aires before travelling through the Argentine pampas and crossing the Andes into Chile. It was in the latter country that Lobb made some of his most notable collections, principal among which was *Araucaria araucana* (Chile pine or monkey puzzle).

This curious conifer had been introduced in a limited quantity as seed by Archibald Menzies who accompanied Captain George Vancouver's voyage along the Pacific coast in 1795, but it was Lobb's introduction of some 3,000 seeds that helped establish this tree as a must-have feature both in Victorian country estates and urban villa gardens.

Other conifers that Lobb introduced from Chile included mighty *Fitzroya cupressoides* (alerce), South America's largest tree, now endangered because of its valuable timber, *Podocarpus nubigenus* and *Austrocedrus chilensis*, the last two collected during his second stint in Chile in 1845. In contrast to the monkey puzzle, the others have never caught the fancy of the gardening public; they remain collectors' items in botanic gardens and arboreta.

It was a different story with some of Lobb's other collections, especially those made in the temperate rainforests of the southern Andes. Anyone who has visited gardens in wetter western and southwestern regions of Britain and Ireland will have seen and admired *Crinodendron hookerianum* (Chilean lantern tree), a large shrub with pendent, bell-shaped crimson flowers in May, introduced by Lobb in 1848.

*Desfontainia spinosa* has waxy, tubular, scarlet flowers with yellow mouths in summer and was a Lobb introduction in 1843, but perhaps the most colourful of 'his' plants is famous *Embothrium coccineum* (Chilean fire bush). The spectacular crowded, fiery, orange-scarlet blossoms of this member of the *Proteaceae* are magnificent and each year from late May into June a fine example in a neighbour's garden blooms like a column of lava from a volcano. There are similar examples elsewhere in the south and sheltered gardens in the maritime west of Britain, where they thrive with their head in the sun and their roots in cool, moist, well-drained, lime-free soils.

> "...Lobb was re-engaged by the Veitch Nursery and instructed to head for Oregon and California..."

In 1849, having returned to Devon, Lobb was re-engaged by the Veitch Nursery and instructed to head for Oregon and California, including the Sierra Nevada, from whence came large seed collections of several notable conifers including *Abies grandis*, *Pinus radiata*, *Thuja plicata* (Western red cedar) and *Xanthocyparis nootkatensis*, all of which became well established in Britain thanks to Lobb.

He also collected seed of *Sequoia sempervirens* (coastal redwood) and, according to some sources, bristlecone pines (then *Pinus aristata*, now probably *P. longaeva*, the species having been split into two). If so, then together with giant redwood, this would mean that Lobb sent to Britain respectively seeds of the world's tallest, oldest and most massive trees (though the great age of bristlecones only emerged in the 1960s).

Lobb's last three-year contract was a disappointment to the Veitch Nursery; apparently quite ill, he sent no new discoveries but only seed of plants he had already collected. When it ran out in 1858, the contract was not renewed. Rather than return home, Lobb continued living, ill, in San Francisco. His family heard from him last in 1860; he died a sad and lonely death in 1863. The cause of death is recorded as 'paralysis' but it was probably syphilis, then a progressive, largely incurable disease.

Lobb was survived by his brother Thomas who, having himself travelled as a plant hunter for James Veitch in India, Indonesia and the Philippines (losing a leg while orchid hunting), eventually retired to the village of Devoran in the county of his youth, where he died in obscurity in 1894.

# Notes on the Flora of North-Western Yunnan

GEORGE FORREST, 1916 (PART I)

The flora of North-West Yunnan is so rich and varied, the area so extensive, the mountain and river systems so complicated, that it is a matter of no small difficulty to select one portion in illustration of the whole. The region includes the watersheds of the mid-Salwin, Mekong, and Yangtze; these watersheds are broken into an indescribable chaos of subsidiary ranges and spurs, many of them bearing species which are purely local. Much of the area is still unknown or at least unmapped.

"Many fine herbaceous plants were secured; in the shady gorges the damp moss-covered boulders and cliffs bore many terrestrial Orchids, such as *Pleione Delavayi* with purplish-rose flowers marked a deep crimson..."

It is a marvellous country, planned on Nature's grandest scale, prodigal in flora and fauna, rich in minerals. Numerous tribes, nearly all of Tibetan origin, people it – the diversity of whose customs, languages, and religions is truly remarkable.

All of the principal ranges, which fall away from the Tibetan plateau and enclose those three great rivers, run due south as far as mid-Yunnan, at which point the divergence eastwards of the Yangtze causes a break in the regular contour of the country.

As is now generally known, the formation of those ranges is purely limestone, a hard grey magnesian limestone, and that possibly accounts in great measure for the exceptional richness and high development of the vegetation.

The Tali range, in the Mekong basin is one of the most prolific of the west. For forty miles it forms the western bulwark of the Tali valley, enclosing the beautiful lake called Erh-hai. Owing to its great bulk acting as a rain-screen, the rainfall on the western flank is greatly in excess of that on the eastern side. As a result the vegetation on the west is much more luxuriant and of quite a different character. Though on both flanks there is a decided pine belt from about 10,000 to 12,000 feet, the spurs and ridges on the east, from their bases to the higher alps, are mostly of a pastoral character, with the arborescent vegetation confined to the gullies and lateral valleys. On the west the vegetation is principally arborescent, so dense in places as to be almost impenetrable; it attains a much greater altitude, and is carried right to the base. That part of the range has never been explored to any extent, and, judging by the results of two short and hasty journeys in 1906, and one in recent years, it carries many interesting and new species. During these journeys were found the following: *Buddleia myriantha*, a shrub of 10 feet, allied to *B. variabilis* [*B. davidii*] but with deeper-coloured blooms; a new *Berberis*, named *B. centifolia*, an excellent rock shrub of 2–5 feet, with charming yellow blooms, and an interesting new species of *Diapensia*, *D. Bulleyana*, also a rock shrub, and peculiar in having bright yellow flowers instead of the normal purple-red. There also, in moist open situations amongst scrub, was found the beautiful *Pieris Forrestii* [now considered a variant of *Pieris formosa*] with its waxy-white fragrant blooms. On the cliffs the dominant shrub was *Rhododendron crassum* [*R. maddenii* subsp. *crassum*], its large white fragrant blossoms showing most freely. Many fine herbaceous plants were secured; in the shady gorges the damp moss-covered boulders and cliffs bore many terrestrial Orchids, such as *Pleione Delavayi* [*P. bulbocodiodes*] with purplish-rose flowers marked a deep crimson, *P. grandiflora*, with snow-white blooms blotched a deep crimson-lake; and a remarkably fine new species, *P. Forrestii*, having orange-yellow blooms laced and marked deep brown. The colouring of the last is unique, the precocious flowers arising from the deep green moss having all the appearance of our yellow Crocus at first sight.

# Plant Hunting in Yunnan

TOBY MUSGRAVE, JANUARY 2009

The beautiful landscape and flora of Yunnan Province in western China, described in the pages of *National Geographic* magazine by plant-hunter and ethnographer Joseph Rock, provided James Hilton with the inspiration for the fictional Shangri-La of his novel *Lost Horizon* (1933).

"A significant proportion of our widely grown garden plants originated here..."

Covering 404,687sq km, Yunnan is the most topographically diverse of China's 22 provinces, boasting climatic zones ranging from tropical and sub-tropical through temperate to alpine. These diverse habitats are home to more than 60 percent of China's native biodiversity, including more than 15,000 species of higher plants (more than half the national total). In recognition, Yunnan has been designated, by the WWF among others, as a Centre of Plant Diversity, a Global 200 List Priority Ecoregion for Biodiversity Conservation, and a Global Biodiversity Hotspot. A significant proportion of our widely grown garden plants originated here, and were introduced into cultivation in the early part of the 20th century by several intrepid plant collectors, who endured real hardships.

## Three trailblazers

It was to the remarkable and florally-rich northwest of Yunnan that plant hunters George Forrest (1873–1932), Frank Kingdon-Ward (1885–1958) and Joseph Rock (1884–1962) ventured. Between 1904 and 1932 they made a total of 14 separate expeditions (seven, three and four respectively). The deep valleys and snowy peaks were 'virgin territory' for plant hunting, and the numbers of new ornamental species introduced by the three men are legendary. Even today, hundreds of familiar garden plants, including *Buddleja davidii*, *Iris bulleyana*, *Paeonia delavayi*, blue poppies (*Meconopsis*) and many primulas came from (or can trace their ancestry to) Yunnan.

Forrest, a resourceful Scot, was the first, arriving in China in 1904. Notwithstanding the many beautiful orchids, herbaceous, bulbous and alpine species from the valleys, it was the high ridges and valley flanks of Yunnan that yielded Forrest his major speciality: rhododendrons. Forrest's tally of more than 300 new *Rhododendron* species alone required taxonomists to re-evaluate and reclassify the entire genus. He was also the first to observe that rhododendrons will grow on limestone where the overlying soil is heavily leached by rain.

Forrest described working in Yunnan as 'like living on a volcano', but developed excellent relationships with the indigenous peoples, whom he used as guides and collectors. Less good were his relationships with Kingdon-Ward and Rock, whom he considered intruders on 'his' turf.

It was to this region, in order to seek out 'their' plants in the wild and to get a feel of the conditions under which these three men operated, that I journeyed in June 2007 (to coincide with the peak flowering period). The planned route included as many different locations and habitats as possible.

A four-man team assembled in Lijiang on the evening of 5 June. It comprised myself; Nongbu, driver of a four-wheel-drive Landcruiser; Ashou, translator, guide and cook; and my old friend, horticulturist Chris

Gardner. An hour's drive the following morning took us into the mountains of Yulongxue Shan (which translates as Jade Dragon Snow Mountain) National Park. Once at the desired location, the *modus operandi* throughout the expedition was to drive slowly and spot either plants or likely-looking habitats which were then scoured. Our activities were obviously considered rather quirky, but Nongbu entered into the spirit and soon began to point out plants.

> "Rock was a real eccentric, and always travelled in the field with a complete set of silverware..."

Abutting Yulongxue Shan, the village of Yuhu (then called Nguluko) contains Rock's residence for much of his 27 years in Yunnan (1922–49). Born in Austria in 1884, he became a US citizen in 1913. As well as plant hunting for the Arnold Arboretum (part of Harvard University in the United States), he photographed for the US Department of Agriculture and the Smithsonian Institute.

Rock's lengthy stays in Yunnan also exercised his other talents as a geographer, a cartographer and, above all, an ethnographer and linguist. He was as fascinated by the people as the plants, particularly the indigenous Nakhi or Naxi people, an ethnic group living in the foothills of northwest Yunnan. He studied extensively their unique pictographic language (more akin to ancient Egyptian hieroglyphs than any modern language). His dictionary of this, a thorough labour of love that he continued right into retirement, was eventually not published until two months after his death, on Hawaii, in 1962.

Rock was a real eccentric, and always travelled in the field with a complete set of silverware and china, and a collapsible rubber bathtub. The dark-wooden, two-storey buildings in which he lived, now a museum, enclose a quiet, square courtyard and I could envisage him relaxing and ruminating here. But on entering the rooms that ambience vanished, for the grubby glass cases of mouldering relics emanated an air of wanton neglect. Sadly, too, the picturesque village is metamorphosing into a caricature of 'old China' for tourists. This attitude of 'tourism equals exploitation opportunity' was symptomatic of many of the 'developments' we encountered.

Thankfully, once off the beaten track we were made welcome, albeit occasionally as curiosities. And as we headed north we could already chalk up some notable finds, including pink-flowered *Incarvillea mairei*, the purple-spotted yellow trumpets of *Lilium bakerianum*, scarlet-flowered tree peony *Paeonia delavayi*, nodding, golden-yellow *Primula forrestii* and the first of several blue poppies, delicate and variable *Meconopsis racemosa* var. *racemosa*.

Our route next took us up the spectacular valleys of two rivers. In this area the landscape is dominated by three mighty rivers, the Mekong, Yangtze and Nu Jiang (Salween). All rise in central Tibet and have cut precipitous parallel courses through the plateau before diverging to empty into three different seas. Their gorges and those of their tributaries have created geographically isolated areas and a huge range of habitats, the major reason for the diversity of plant life in the region.

Crossing from the Yangtze's watershed into that of the Mekong, our destination was Dêquên (Dechen) – as close as we could get to the Tibetan border – the aim being to find where Forrest had his greatest adventure. During his first plant-hunting season (1905) he was staying at a French Catholic mission station when it was attacked by murderous Tibetan warrior monks (lamas), enraged by the British invasion of their holy city, Lhasa. Of the 80 who fled, only 14 escaped and of Forrest's 17 collectors only one survived. Forrest himself dived into a tributary valley and spent nine days without food evading the lamas before being guided to safety over peaks reaching 4,300m.

The Mekong valley was most atmospheric in the mist and rain, and we found the monastery in the small village of Cizhong. The original buildings were burned in the attack, but reconstructed on the same site. Standing there in the teeming rain, my emotions were a mix of sadness for the poor, terrified souls who fled in vain, and admiration of Forrest for his stamina, bravery and ingenuity in escaping.

It was outside Dêquên in 1913 that Kingdon-Ward discovered the lovely, yellow-flowered *Rhododendron* that now bears his name, *R. wardii*, but we arrived too late to go in search of the actual plant he found – which apparently still survives. It had been quite a nervous afternoon driving up the ever-more precipitous valley with sides of saturated, unstable-looking shales.

It was no surprise the next morning to find a landslide temporarily blocking the road. After an impromptu lunch we scrambled up to the scree and cliffs, reaching 4,465m. Highlights were yellow-flowered *Meconopsis pseudointegrifolia* and, later, as we descended to camp, a vast drift of mixed candelabra primulas: yellow-flowered *Primula sikkimensis* and purple *P. secundiflora* nodding gently in the breeze beside a babbling brook. My tent leaked, leaving me wishing for camping à la Forrest, who travelled with a drinks table, bottle of Johnny Walker and soda siphon.

On to 'civilisation' and the city formerly known as Zhongdian (now renamed 'Shangri-La' to appeal to tourists), our base for a few days. Day trips to Napa Hai, a range of hills about 10km away, yielded more blue poppies and five terrestrial orchids: yellow-flowered *Cypripedium flavum* and pink *C. guttatum* (both slipper orchids), orange-flowered *Oreorchis erythrochrysea* and two species also found in Europe, green-flowered frog orchid (*Dactylorhiza viridis*) and sword-leaved helleborine (*Cephalanthera longifolia*), with white spikes.

Yet these triumphs were tinged with melancholy: only a few years earlier the Alpine Garden Society had visited this area, but their glowing report bore no resemblance to what we saw. We knew exploitation was accelerating, but it was still shocking to see 'on the ground' such extensive habitat destruction caused by clear felling for timber and overgrazing. Next day, however, our excursion to Shika Shan revived depressed spirits. We took a cable car to its 4,400m summit, cloaked purple by shimmering drifts of small *Primula amethystina*, then walked through a forest of Chinese hemlock (*Tsuga chinensis*) and rhododendrons, including the previously elusive *R. wardii*.

> "Bleak, sawtoothed peaks wreathed in mist gave way to dark, mixed forest as we descended"

Yading was the next objective, a mountainous nature reserve explored by Forrest and Rock and renowned for its beauty. However, a dispute between locals and the government, intent on building a cable car and hotel complex, had resulted in the authorities closing all roads in. We set off northeast nonetheless, along a dirt road and across rolling moorland smothered in a mix of dwarf rhododendrons including lilac-flowered *Rhododendron russatum* (parent to many compact hybrids) and pink-blooming *R. racemosum*. In the overcast afternoon, just short of a windswept pass at 4,616m, we encountered colonies of yellow, monocarpic *Meconopsis pseudointegrifolia*, photographed by Rock in the wild in the 1920s.

We were stopped at a roadblock into Yading, so plan B was a four-day loop, via Daocheng, Xiancheng and Haizi Shan (or King of the Mountains, first climbed only in 2006) that offered a succession of varied and dramatic landscapes. Bleak, sawtoothed peaks wreathed in mist gave way to dark, mixed forest as we descended. We then drove up a narrow gorge, over a pass in blazing sunshine and down into a wide, precipitous valley dotted with verdant fields and well peppered with massive, four-square Tibetan farmhouses.

The vertiginous scenery of river-cut valleys suddenly gave way to a high plateau studded with huge granite boulders and lakes. There was a strong sense of being on top of the world. That is, until the last morning mists cleared, when on the horizon appeared majestic, snow-capped Kawa Karpo, sacred to Tibetan Buddhists. Lying between the Nu Jiang and Mekong valleys, at 6,740m Kawa Karpo is Yunnan's highest peak and remains unclimbed.

That afternoon another pass gave us our trip high-point of 4,760m. The next morning, as we scrambled up the steep, slippery limestone crags above Daxue Shan pass, the thick mist, as if in celebration, parted to reveal a truly spectacular view of limestone peaks above us, their great sweeps of scree descending to wooded valleys below. The slopes looked good plant-hunting grounds, and it was there that I saw our last blue poppy, *Meconopsis lancifolia*, with its exquisite purple-blue, tissue-thin petals and hairy stems holding silvery drops of dew.

The topography of northwest Yunnan is truly beautiful, and no doubt our three plant-hunting pioneers of yesteryear would recognise the landscapes today. There is still a huge diversity of plants growing there – our tally was 242 species identified from 116 genera in the 18 days. But no doubt all three would be shocked by the habitat destruction and floral losses the region has suffered – plants now cling on in small numbers where once they were massed. By comparison, my previous expedition to northern Sikkim found it relatively pristine.

We may not have followed in the exact footsteps of Forrest, Kingdon-Ward and Rock, but we did experience the excitement of finding 'their' plants. We also gleaned an insight into how difficult it must have been to operate here, pre-four-wheel-drive, and how resourceful and determined these men were. I was able to gain an understanding of how this beautiful area became something of an addiction for all three. Yet my abiding emotion is one of sadness – sadness at what has been lost from 'Shangri-La' in a mere century.

# Californian Jottings

**VISCOUNTESS BYNG OF VIMY, SEPTEMBER 1935**

Dr Goodspeed showed us the Botanical Garden of the University [of California at Berkeley] – now in the making – and the garden is his love and his despair. His love, because it should be so beautiful; his despair, because in these hard times money is scarce, and though he has a vast quantity of seeds collected in the Orient by Dr [Joseph] Rock, he lacks the funds to grow them on or to clear suitable places for their development, which is very hard, for

"...on the way we saw a signpost, 'To the Petrified Forest', and my itching curiosity made us turn aside"

I have never seen, except at Kirstenbosch, in South Africa, a more perfect site for a botanical garden. Here, as there, the ground is formed by a series of canyons running far back into the mountains above Berkeley, with astounding views over the harbour and the Golden Gate, and you can get any aspect you choose, any amount of shade or sun, and also any variation in soil that is required. Himalayan and Chinese Rhododendrons flourish at Berkeley, native trees and shrubs have been judiciously thinned and left in sheltering groups, for above San Francisco shelter is needed from cold as well as heat, and if any money is available and the government can become interested in Dr Goodspeed's dream, I am fully convinced that in a few years' time he will have a botanical garden second to none in beauty and interest.

We left the 'seat of learning' early next morning, setting our faces toward Ukiah, where we had planned to meet Mr Carl Purdy, but on the way we saw a signpost, 'To the Petrified Forest', and my itching curiosity made us turn aside. Well worth while it was, for the great petrified Sequoias are magnificent, and according to history, six million years ago, during the volcanic eruptions of Mount St Helena, the lava flowing down uprooted and buried the forest of giant Redwood, and by the infiltration of silica turned them into stone, which preserved their exact form. The 'queen of the Forest' is 80 feet long and 12 feet in its mean diameter, and the 'Monarch' 126 feet in length by 8 feet in diameter. There they lie amid many great blocks of petrified wood, exactly like their living brethren, and one cannot believe they are no long alive till one touches the ice-cold surface of these dead giants lying full length in a lovely grove of Madrones, Manzanitas and other native shrubs and trees.

# Intricate Tapestry

NICOLA STOCKEN TOMKINS, JUNE 2010

At first glance, Lumine Swagerman's garden resembles an intricate tapestry in which individual leaves and flowers are expertly interwoven, lying dormant until the sun filters through the trees behind. 'The evening light brings my garden alive, and the flowers seem to glow against the sombre background of the forest,' says Lumine of her little garden on the outskirts of a small village towards the centre of the Netherlands. It is an ever-changing picture, but this variable nature is essential to its charm – she sees her garden as an unfinished canvas on which she is continually working and changing.

With its narrow pathways, packed beds and carefully graded planting, this is a garden for lingering in lest some rarity be inadvertently overlooked through undue haste. Its creator loves seeing plants close-up, as well as standing back to enjoy the textures and colours of particular combinations. And with some 250 different perennials packed among shrubs and bulbs in a plot measuring just 180sq m (less than 2,000sq ft), there is always something special that amply repays closer inspection.

"...hers is a high maintenance garden, and certainly not to be imitated for any of her clients, but she enjoys her personal rebellion against the trends for restricted planting and easy-care plants"

It was not always so. When Lumine and her partner Henk Sinnema moved to the village of Laag-Soeren, not far from Arnhem, in 2003, the garden was a rectangle of lawn and unimaginative borders, the whole of it visible in a single glance. Some back-breaking labour followed, not only to remove several gigantic tree stumps, but also to dig volumes of compost into the poor, sandy soil. Henk nobly laid the paved paths according to Lumine's simple, even sober, design, which dispensed with a lawn to turn all the space into borders within the paths' strong framework: the garden's 'bones', these allow it to be enjoyed from the house and appreciated from many angles.

There are two terraces, one beside the house, the other sunken at the far end of the garden, hidden behind tall plants. A yew hedge marks the furthest boundary, parting at a pergola, which allows a path to continue beside a sunken parking bay, between narrow borders, for another 10m (33ft). This additional strip of land gives the impression the garden is far longer than it actually is. Its focal point is purple-leaved *Cotinus* 'Grace'. Lumine loves the way its leaves hold water droplets. 'And when the sunlight shines through, it looks as if it's on fire,' she says.

The garden also contains many rarities, mostly sourced from specialist nurseries such as De Hessenhof at nearby Ede. When she comes across something special, she finds it hard to resist, but it has to blend into her colour scheme. 'Lady gardeners tend to use a lot of pink, but it's too sweet for me: I prefer the palest yellows, almost white.' She especially loves hazes of soft violet-blue with accents of purple or dark red, so it is no surprise to find *Lobelia* x *speciosa* 'Hadspen Purple', *Salvia* x *sylvestris* 'Blauhügel' (often sold as *S. nemorosa* Blue Mound) and *Scutellaria incana* featuring strongly. It is not so much colour as proportion that is the overriding consideration – many

plants are simply too big for her tiny plot, so she is always on the lookout for smaller selections, such as a recent find, a miniature *Cotinus coggygria* called 'Young Lady', reaching no more than 1.8m (6ft). She is now searching for 'baby' *Philadelphus* (mock orange) and *Syringa* (lilac).

Lumine's English is excellent, in part due to the large number of gardening books she has read over the last two decades. 'When I first became interested in gardening, I bought and studied just about every English and Dutch gardening book I could lay my hands on,' she says. Starting with Russell Page's *The Education of a Gardener*, she has read Vita Sackville-West, Penelope Hobhouse and Beth Chatto, and re-reads books by Christopher Lloyd on plant behaviour and plant care. Following a course in garden design and visits to well-known gardens in Britain, Italy and the Netherlands, Lumine started working as a garden designer, enjoying the challenge of translating the wishes of clients into good design, with 'interesting' plants.

It is the plants that lie at the heart of Lumine's gardening philosophy, and she is painstaking in her research. This is how she came across a little-known white rambler rose, *Rosa* Guirlande d'Amour ('Lenalbi'), a *R. moschata* hybrid introduced in 1993. The name translates as 'garland of love'; trained on a freestanding wooden frame, it flowers for almost four weeks, repeating the display in September. It needed to be strong to cope with the poor, sandy soil, and to have small flowers to blend with the woodland backdrop.

With so little space, she has to avoid vigorous, invasive plants, so was delighted when she came across a neat, non-spreading *Lysimachia*, tidy *L. atropurpurea*. One of her best performers is *Geranium* Rozanne ('Gerwat'), a must-have perennial which flowers from the end of May until late November, its neat foliage and pretty flowers held aloft as if on an invisible frame. Inevitably, not every plant settles in so readily. *Eryngium giganteum* (Miss Willmott's ghost), for example, has taken several years to get established, but Lumine is unfazed: the longer she has to wait for a plant to develop, the more she appreciates it when it does.

One of her greatest challenges lies in creating interest all year round. 'It's the hardest thing to achieve in a small space, so I try to design each bed so that as one plant goes over, another nearby flowers,' she says, admitting she has to be incredibly careful when digging because her beds are so tightly packed.

Nevertheless, she prefers to plant in groups of three or more; it is not always possible in a small garden, so she compensates by contrasting flower sizes, or leaf colours and forms. As a background to perennials she has planted shrubs such as grey-leaved *Salvia officinalis* 'Berggarten' and *Physocarpus opulifolius* 'Diabolo', its dark purple foliage a wonderful foil for tall, airy plants such as *Thalictrum lucidum* or *Sanguisorba tenuifolia* var. *alba.*

No discussion of gardening in the Netherlands would be complete without mention of Dutch plantsman and designer Piet Oudolf; is he, I wondered, as highly regarded in his own country as overseas? 'Oh yes, Dutch gardeners are greatly influenced by his ideas, and the unusual perennials and grasses he has promoted,' says Lumine. 'He has dramatically changed the traditional style of a border to something far more naturalistic. I have huge respect for Oudolf; he is a genius, but his style needs space, and I just do not have a large enough garden to indulge myself.'

So every spring and autumn Lumine has to reconsider which plants need cutting back (*Cotinus* are always on the list), while others are divided. Still others are moved to more suitable places, or to produce new combinations. It's rather like reinventing a puzzle, she admits: hers is a high-maintenance garden, and certainly not to be imitated for any of her clients, but she enjoys her personal rebellion against the trends for restricted planting and easy-care plants. 'It has been a rare luxury to be able to follow my own ideas, without having to please others,' she says. 'My garden is a personal experiment, a chance to try out exciting plants, combining their forms and colours to create a beautiful picture year round. It has surpassed my expectations, but if you love plants and learn where to position them, they will perform for you.'

# Botanists Target War Zone

NEWS, FEBRUARY 2011

A group of botanists from Edinburgh has travelled to Afghanistan to train a new generation of plant scientists in conserving the region's unique plant species. The team from the Centre for Middle Eastern Plants, part of the Royal Botanic Gardens, Edinburgh, are working with Kabul University to teach students how to identify and conserve plants.

"Afghanistan has one of the richest populations of plants in the world..."

'I could do it myself, but that's not engaging the botanical community in Afghanistan,' said team member Dr Matthew Hall. 'This way we leave a lot more of a legacy than a list with a lot of Latin names on it.'

Afghanistan has one of the richest populations of plants in the world, nearly a fifth of which grow nowhere else. However, more than 30 years of war have devastated the environment and threatened the survival of many species.

The team hopes to travel into more stable areas to assess populations of wild tulips, irises and other monocots with the aim of drawing up a Red List of plants in need of protection.

# Gardening in Places of Conflict

LALAGE SNOW, DECEMBER 2013

While gardens symbolise permanence, longevity, triumph in adversity, hope, growth and paradise, they also provide food, shade, peace, fuel, protection, privacy and escape. Nurturing them is an integral part of survival, resistance and therapy in times of war.

"Green is happiness, green is peace"

Having lived in Kabul on and off since 2010, it became clear to me that behind the headlines and images of chaos and bloodshed exists a country most people never see – a country with a colourful culture and a stubborn dedication to horticulture.

Once regarded as a 'City of Gardens', Kabul is struggling to define itself as a developing city in a maelstrom of security checkpoints, insurgent attacks and ongoing instability. Yet behind the razor wire and walls of private homes are verdant serenities, worlds away from the bedlam outside as Afghans keep the garden tradition alive.

Through photographing these gardens and listening to the personal stories of the gardeners, a different narrative to the ongoing conflict can be built, a far cry from the usual stories of Talibs, soldiers and insurgency.

Mohammad Kabir has created a garden for soldiers stationed at the Darul Aman Palace, which translates as 'abode of peace'; zinnias and tagetes flourish among other plants. Built in the 1920s outside Kabul, the palace has been proposed for restoration and use as the future seat of the Afghan parliament. 'I'm a poor man, but can live without food as long as I am surrounded by greenery and flowers,' says Mohammad, aged 105. The young soldiers stationed at Darul Aman Palace seem to appreciate his efforts: 'Green is happiness, green is peace. Who doesn't like that?' they say.

The first Mughal emperor Babur built the Bagh-e-Babur gardens in Kabul in 1528, and is said to have enjoyed so many long afternoons with concubines and fountains of wine here that he chose it as his final resting place.

Time has taken its toll on Babur's original garden. By 2001, three decades of foreign occupation, unrest, a devastating civil war and the iron-fisted Taliban rule rendered them non-existent. Restoration of the site began in 2002 by the Aga Khan Foundation. The gardens attract more than 300,000 visitors per year who pay 20 afghanis (25p) to enjoy the open spaces and picnic beneath shady trees. Few Kabulis can afford the luxury of their own patch of land; for many the gardens are one of the few green, open places in the city. Seasonal planting includes displays of dahlias and cannas.

The Bagh-e-Babur gardens are overseen by Engineer Latif, chief horticulturist; there is a nursery on site where potted pelargoniums and oleanders grow protected from bitter Afghani winters – as well as from the searing summer sun.

Away from Afghanistan, land and water have been at the core of the struggles between Palestine and Israel from Israel's origins. Access to, and control of, these resources is critical. Palestinians face the confiscation and destruction of land, homes, and water services. The tradition of nurturing nature remains strong and a powerful reminder of the importance of the land for which Israeli settles and Palestinian farmers fight.

However, in spite of Israeli sanctions, Gaza is home to a huge array of private gardens, and their gardeners stand defiant in the face of adversity. Abu Ahmed gardens on his roof using hydroponics and is helped by his daughter, who still has nightmares from the last war. Naif Dubaidi lost his entire garden in the war in 2009 but immediately set about making a new one to forget the horror.

About 3km (2 miles) on the other side of the wall or separation barrier, kibbutzim communities live in the shadow of Hamas rockets yet, like their Gazan counterparts, their gardens have become a means of escaping the conflict. Shlomo in Kibbutz Nir Am makes sculptures out of spent rocket-propelled grenade shell cases for his garden. His daughter was murdered a few years ago but gardening keeps him 'sane', as it does for Mikhail Elimi, who lives in the border town of Sderodt which has been rocketed some 10,000 times since 2006.

# Gardening: Does Britain Lead the World?

STEPHEN LACEY, AUGUST 2010

We would be more consistent title winners if we played the world at gardening rather than football (or tennis, or numerous other sports). Shut your eyes and listen to the roar of the crowd as Beth Chatto outfoxes the German perennials team, Andy Sturgeon takes on American contemporary designers, and Jekka McVicar and Medwyn Williams effortlessly dribble past Cameroon with armfuls of perfect herbs and supersized carrots.

I won't pursue this analogy, as it is a bit shaky and I don't know anything about football; I only like penalty shootouts. But it seems to me that this outpouring of shared excitement, media coverage and (briefly) national pride that we witness on sporting occasions might be more rewardingly focused on things we are really good at. And is there anything we are better at in Britain than gardening?

We take our skill largely for granted, but we should not – it is pretty amazing. The richness and quality of our heritage alone is a marvel. Stick to one letter of the alphabet: Stowe, Stourhead, Sissinghurst, Studley Royal, Sheffield Park, Shute House. One county: Hidcote, Kiftsgate, Westonbirt, Snowshill Manor (Gloucestershire). One region: Bodnant, Portmeirion, Powis Castle (North Wales). Any visitor on a garden tour can still be enchanted and astounded.

This is because, fairly unusually among nations, we have sustained our fascination and creativity over centuries, encouraged by benign microclimates and deep soils, long periods of peace and prosperity, lots of foreign booty-collecting adventures, and a national delight in engaging with nature in a private idyll. In the hands of organisations such as the National Trust, this cornucopia of styles and planting is nurtured as nowhere else.

But we haven't sat on our laurels, spotted or otherwise. The brilliance is everywhere: village shows, the National Gardens Scheme, the John Innes Centre, Great Dixter, Tom Stuart-Smith, roundabouts in Telford, Avon Bulbs, Charles Jencks' Garden of Cosmic Speculation, David Austin Roses, Penelope Hobhouse, RHS Chelsea Flower Show, the parks in Leeds, blogging from Blackpitts, Chiltern Seeds, RHS Garden Wisley, Keith Wiley…

It is a glorious melting pot of Britishness in which amateurs and professionals, individuals and teams, hippies and bankers, prisoners and princes, all participate at the highest level, with a great exchange of knowledge and bonhomie.

But what of international competition? Heritage there can also take your breath away – look at Italy alone, with the newly restored Villa d'Este in Tivoli the jewel in its crown. The Dutch and German nurseries are leviathans. And surveying the contemporary creative scene – German garden festivals, Swedish garden design, French annual planting, Dutch perennial planting, American landscape architecture, the gardens of Steve Martino in Arizona and Fernando Caruncho in Spain. It is obvious that the British cannot spend too much time idly preening.

> "...as we emerge from our long infatuation with Arts and Crafts gardening into a new chapter of modern design, we ought to be able to find plenty of inspiration to keep us moving imaginatively forward"

Yet, worldwide, we are still viewed as the leading nation of garden-makers, and now, as we emerge from our long infatuation with Arts and Crafts gardening into a new chapter of modern design, we ought to find plenty of inspiration to keep moving imaginatively forward.

Raucous chanting is probably not the way to celebrate our achievements and spur on our practitioners. But neither should we bury our prowess in British reserve. Gardening is a deeply ingrained part of our national identity and we should sing about it a lot more at home and abroad as a sharing of our culture and affection for our planet – and, if we can make some financial gain from it in the process, well there is no harm in that.

So, let Downing Street fly the flag for our horticultural research, commercial and garden tourism industries. Let the BBC, which mysteriously but studiously eschews showing our great gardens and interviewing our great garden-makers in favour of surprise-surprise makeovers, make some proper programmes to market here and abroad. And let us gardeners spread the word quietly among the unenlightened – starting with any sports supporters in need of some patriotic feel-good therapy.

# INSIDE THE RHS

*Note from the editor*

The doings of the Royal Horticultural Society necessarily preoccupy the compilers of its house magazine, and nowhere more than in the matter of flower shows, which have always been such an important (some might say *too* important) aspect of the Society's work, and certainly its most visible manifestation to the outside world. Chelsea Flower Show is the most famous and prestigious (and in 2013 celebrated its centenary on the Royal Hospital site), but these days there are also shows held in the summer at Hampton Court Palace and Tatton Park. There are still (although they are a shadow of their former selves, sadly) the Westminster Shows at Vincent Square, where dedicated amateur growers such as Doug Palmer garner prizes for their exhibits. For many years – it seems hard to believe now – the Westminster Shows were held every fortnight. But of course that was in the days when the Society barely reached outside London and the Southeast of England. The welcome acquisition of regional gardens at Rosemoor, Harlow Carr and Hyde Hall has changed all that. Besides *The Garden* magazine's ample show reportage, the flower shows receive a great deal of coverage in the national and international media. In addition, it is often *The Garden* which primarily trumpets the sterling work done on other fronts, notably the Britain in Bloom campaign, the seed distribution scheme and the seal of excellence for a garden plant, the Award of Garden Merit.

Although much is made of the RHS' achievements in many spheres, some of the difficulties over the years – financial problems, members' revolts, criticisms over the judging of shows, how to remain solvent and relevant during two world wars – leak out, often in the dry accounts of the Annual General Meetings or Secretary's comments (as in 1940, below). They are always worth reading, since in a strange way they bring the RHS more to life.

**URSULA BUCHAN,** editor

# Wartime Apologies from the Secretary's Page

F R DURHAM, NOVEMBER 1940

It is very much regretted that the October number of the journal was late, and that many of the announcements in it on this page did not reach the Fellows and Associates in time, but circumstances are at present such that it is a little difficult to work to a time schedule, and this journal is [also] late.

> "...the high standards, which were attained prior to the outbreak of war, will be preserved"

The Birmingham Red Cross Sale was quite successful, the Lord Mayor of Birmingham opening the second day of the Sale. The thanks of the Society are due to the local Committee, who, with their enthusiasm, contributed greatly to the success of the Auction.

The year 1940 will soon be drawing to a close and Fellows and Associates will be considering the Society and its work. The Society's work in these days is of great importance; it does not appear in the spectacular form of Shows but in the constant pressure and assistance in the campaign of 'Dig for Victory' and 'Grow More Food'. The amount of advisory work the Society is doing has in no way fallen, and the importance of vegetable growing has been demonstrated in the Society's Gardens at Wisley.

The Panel of Lecturers has been hard at work and a complete collection of slides on the growing of vegetables has been compiled for the use of the lecturers during the present lecture season.

Besides the utility side of gardening at Wisley, the collections of flowering and other plants have been maintained. The importance of such collections need not be emphasised as it is by this means that the high standards, which were attained prior to the outbreak of war, will be preserved for horticulture.

The Council therefore appeals, with every confidence, to its Fellows and Associates, in spite of the loss of the Shows, to continue their Fellow- and Associate-ships and thus take their part in maintaining the Society as one of the essentials of National Life.

# Recollection in Tranquillity

## HUGH JOHNSON (WRITING AS TRADESCANT), AUGUST 2000

Everybody at the Chelsea Flower Show this year, whether in rain or sun, must have come away with thoughts about change and the passing of time. The old marquee, austere but redolent of John Major's England, village cricket and spinsters on bikes, used to cast its spell over the whole show. Exhibitors this year who found the new hard-edged backdrop [the new Great Pavilion] to their gardens less sympathetic than the mellow canvas will presumably be bringing taller trees next year. Certainly fastigiate oaks served Cartier and Clifton Nurseries well.

"...the two most memorable gardens, which tied for the elusive Trad Award, were the re-creations of a beach and an old mine"

There was clearly a buzz about where gardening is going. There has been time now to let it all sink in. In retrospect Chelsea was a wonderful performance, with a sense of renewal everyone seemed to share.

My own impression was that there is less consensus than ever about gardening fashion. On the one hand there is a powerful lobby for 'good taste', the colour green, symmetry and masses of clipped box. With some exhibitors it retreated into downright nostalgia, others had more original ways of playing the same cards. Certainly the hardware merchants bank on it. It is clear from all the purveyors of teak furniture, statues and faux-stone urns that we still miss garden architecture, with its historical references and connotations of status. (We apparently prefer a hard seat to a soft one, too: I counted one hammock and not one deckchair.)

The bold modernism of such as Christopher Bradley-Hole attempts to break this spell. It would be fascinating to know how many visitors feel they learn useful lessons from these non-traditional gardens. If *Ground Force* [the TV garden makeover series] is a guide, there should be a big constituency.

For me the two most memorable gardens, which tied for the elusive Trad Award, were the re-creations of a beach and an old mine. The sterility of a beach is a powerful image at Chelsea. A few sea-worn timbers, a hemp rope half-buried in sand and limpets, a whiff of brine and a hidden wave machine made from an old mower brilliantly evoked the sea; in nature the total antithesis of a garden. The result was to make the unexceptional planting round its little cottage strangely poignant.

A stream running towards you down the Rock Garden Bank is one of Chelsea's hoariest clichés. Yet somehow Her Majesty's guests at Leyhill used the idea of their abandoned industrial landscape so skilfully, with such fidelity to a vision that it seemed quite accidental. It might always have been there. Perhaps it still is.

Neither design nor horticulture were important elements in either garden. They were stage sets, evoking very specific moods, recalling hundreds of humdrum corners of our islands with discipline and almost passionate purity.

# Changes to Judging

NEWS, JANUARY 2010

A new points-based judging system is being introduced for floral exhibits across RHS flower shows, marking the end of a 100-year tradition of 'collective view' judging. Nigel Colborn, Show Judge and member of the RHS Council, said the change was part of the Society's effort to improve standards in all aspects of show judging. 'The points system results in greater objectivity, and in more consistency among the variable range of exhibits at our shows,' he said.

> "...panels of five will focus on specific groups of exhibits within their areas of expertise"

Previously, judging panels had 12–14 people, but from 2010 panels of five will focus on specific groups of exhibits within their areas of expertise. Already in place for judging show gardens, the system has been tested and modified at RHS shows over the past two years, and has proved to be a more accurate and effective way of judging.

'The system is fairer for exhibitors, better for show visitors, more satisfying for judges, and gives exhibitors better feedback and guidance,' said Nigel.

# Reflecting a Changing Society

JOHN BROOKES (CHELSEA CENTENARY SUPPLEMENT), MAY 2013

The visual pleasure of a visit to RHS Chelsea Flower Show and its gardens mirrors not only how fashions in garden style have changed, and continue to do so, but also how society has altered. The show has moved from an emphasis on gracious living and grand gardens to a more modest styling achievable by many more gardeners.

In the years between the two world wars, garden design (such as it was) was in the mood of the Arts and Crafts movement with formal layouts. Part of this ethos were the famous rock gardens built along the Embankment side of the Royal Hospital grounds.

Much was written at the time about the construction of these gardens – use of differing rock types, as well as the introduction of water through ponds and waterfalls.

I first visited Chelsea in the late 1950s, when the numbers of rock-garden displays had diminished. The show gardens were in the last gasp of the Arts and Crafts style, in what also became known as the 'Surrey garden tradition' of acid-loving plants. 'Surrey', I suspect, because of Gertrude Jekyll's influence on planting design from her home near RHS Garden Wisley in Surrey.

Coming from the north of England, the lush show gardens thriving on acid soil were a visual feast for me. But overlaying the whole event was the social superiority of the RHS itself. It used to be said that RHS committee members either had a head gardener or were one.

It was this whiff of privilege that provided the backdrop for my early interest in garden design and, I suppose, my potential clientele. At that time, one needed 'grounds' for such concerns and the staff to manage them.

The Festival of Britain in 1951 had been an amazing eye-opener in terms of garden design. It was not just the hugeness of the concept of the Festival itself, but also the external planting and construction detail of the Festival Pleasure Gardens and landscaping as well, not necessarily on a domestic scale, but different to my eye – and modern. This word has since become loaded, I fear, but only slowly did it start to penetrate the horticultural world.

When I was a student in the 1950s, some of us persuaded the RHS to show garden-design plans from members of the Institute of Landscape Architects (now the Landscape Institute) in a special design tent. Fairly well tucked away, it only became popular when it rained.

The concept of small-garden design was new. It started when domestic house construction and New Town building started to take off in the 1960s, and brought with it a need for small garden layouts for family use.

Old horticultural hands thought (I believe quite rightly) 'what do these youngsters know about growing?' I admit we knew little, but we were interested in putting plants together to make a composition and, moreover, how to use hard materials to create a working surround to buildings and provide the setting in which to plant them. We were interested in the design of the garden in its own right, and to consider not only formal symmetrical design, but think about an asymmetrical, even abstracted concept of a garden layout. Garden design is an art form after all. Various Scandinavian and North America designers (such as Thomas Church and Garrett Eckbo) gave evidence to this new concept. The ghosts of earlier garden designers – such as Ralph Hancock and Eleanour Sinclair Rohde – danced around the flower show at this time. I recall seeing an elderly Percy Cane exhibiting drawings, but earlier in his career he had built gardens as well.

> "The ghosts of earlier garden designers – such as Ralph Hancock and Eleanour Sinclair Rohde – danced around the flower show at this time"

However, gardens at Chelsea had nearly always been built and shown by nursery firms with a landscape constructional department. The first of these to excite my interest was a garden by Wallace & Barr of Tunbridge Wells in the 1950s, designed by their employee Anthony Pasley, in which a diagonal design was interspersed with fountains playing in concrete bowls in a small garden layout. It was an excitingly modern domestic concept at the time – and beautifully planted as well.

In the big, tented marquee at Chelsea I remember seeing amazing arrangements of plants, year after year, by Beth Chatto from 1976 onwards. These made me realise, after reading about it for so long, what planting design was all about. There is more to it than just colour: it is all about scale, texture and form – and yes, colour as well – though not just for the few days of Chelsea, but for the whole year round.

Constructional design and planting design were coming together in my mind. Where else, apart from Chelsea, could one experience small-garden layouts? At this time only grand gardens were open to visitors. And the designed small space was a new phenomenon.

My next challenge was to actually build a garden. The Institute of Landscape Architects, of which I was a student member, held a competition for a garden at Chelsea in 1961. Wow, I won it.

The competition was sponsored by the Cement and Concrete Association, so this comparatively little-used material needed to be included in the design. The public was generally hostile to concrete at that time (it had a wartime defence connotation, I think). So this was a challenge. My planting was mainly of *Rhododendron ponticum*, from which I removed many of the flowers, and the remaining greenery provided the setting for the structure. But the show is about plants and growing them, and this exhibit caused a bit of a flurry. The experience of working at RHS Chelsea Flower Show was exciting, however – not only seeing my plan come alive, but everyone else's as well.

In those early days sponsorship monies available for constructing a garden were only a fraction of what is now lavished upon them. I went on to design and build gardens for the *Financial Times* – a town, suburban and country garden in 1971 to 1973 – and for the Inchbald School of Design in the mid-1970s a Jekyll garden, a Middle Eastern garden and, I believe, the first vegetable garden.

The firm of Gavin Jones built most of my gardens – I recall dear old Mrs Gavin laboriously picking through my plantings to remove every dead leaf, and presenting an immaculate layout to the judges.

Each of my gardens needed a different styling in their layout, and required a choice of materials. But, most of all, the styling was in the planting. The use of plants has been the aspect of the show gardens, along with their increasing popularity, that has most changed over the years.

Those early 'Surrey gardens' were essentially spring-like and shrubby; shrub roses became popular, which then gave way to the great use of perennials, later stabilised with box balls of various sizes. It was only in the 1980s that the 'wild look' really took over, with an eco-sensibility pervading even the RHS. I bought into this vogue myself, but found that many of our native plants are too invasive for small gardens.

So the aspiration of the garden had now become not only a fine-weather place for family use but a mini sanctuary for wildlife as well. However, this is truly at odds with the latest passion for growing your own herbs and vegetables – and so it goes on. The way we think about and use our gardens reflects not only our status, but more importantly the way in which society is thinking, and what about.

# From Chelsea to the Wider World

WESLEY KERR (CHELSEA CENTENARY SUPPLEMENT), MAY 2013

M any claims are made for the RHS Chelsea Flower Show, but apart from the spectacle of one amazing week in May, what is the wider impact of this prodigious blossoming of horticultural excellence? For gardening enthusiasts it is a great annual fixture, but long ago Chelsea leapt over the fence beyond the horticultural community. It is the one week of the year when gardens and plants have the nation's attention. It also gives rhythm to the social season, enthuses the metropolis and boosts the economy.

> "For many people all over the world, Chelsea is irrevocably linked with the flower show"

Fewer than 200,000 people see the show in person, but the susurration spreads for miles. It generates themed street and shop displays, hotel bookings, special menus in restaurants, and busy tubes and taxis. The RHS estimates the annual spend of all visitors at £70–100 million, plus possibly as much again in orders taken at the show.

For the Royal Borough of Kensington and Chelsea, the visitor economy for 2009 was estimated at £3.1 billion; the show is central to their 'cultural placemaking'. The borough's Deputy Leader, Nick Paget-Brown says the show 'marks the beginning of summer, brings Chelsea alive with huge numbers of visitors to one of London's – and Sir Christopher Wren's – architectural gems. For many people all over the world, Chelsea is irrevocably linked with the flower show.'

Some residents grumble, but a 2009 report found 88 percent of those living near the site were positive about the show's benefits, almost as high as approval ratings for the borough's famous museums.

It is easy to forget that greater London has 3,000 public green spaces and dozens of named watercourses, 600 garden squares, almost as many trees as people and hundreds of pocket parks. Iain Edmonson, from tourism body London and Partners, says visitors from overseas are surprised at just how green London is. The lauded London 2012 Olympics, sited in beautifully landscaped parks, highlighted things visitors had not previously associated with London – such as wild flowers and sporting achievement.

The show, Iain says, also brings to the fore the unexpected and the excellent. 'It's a great example of leading the world in a specialist field.

One of the things London does is congregate world-class content and participation.' These sentiments are echoed by Colin Stanbridge, Chief Executive of the London Chamber of Commerce and Industry. Big events can garner tens of millions of pounds, tangibly and intangibly. Colin says, 'The RHS Chelsea Flower Show is one of the events that makes London a unique world city. There are the obvious economic benefits that come from such a world-class event attracting thousands of visitors from across Britain and the world. But to my mind there is a less-quantifiable benefit that may be even more important – the diversity of activity that events like Chelsea provide. That diversity is, I believe a key driver in attracting businesses from all over the globe to London.'

The show helps make London 'the events capital of the world' according to Baroness [Jo] Valentine of business lobbying organisation London First. 'Mixing the traditional and the cutting edge, Chelsea is the gardening equivalent of London Fashion Week, providing an international showcase for yet another element of London's world-class creative sector.'

The Horticultural Trades Association says that, especially if the weather is good, most retailers get an uplift in sales and link their marketing to the event. Horticulture is a big UK industry; £5 billion in sales, employing hundreds of thousands of people. For show stalwarts such as Hillier Nurseries, a Gold-medal exhibit is followed with promotions in its garden centres.

Apart from direct orders and purchases, Chelsea is a fabulous backdrop and marketplace for design ideas, new products and deals. Big guns from business and finance descend for the Charity Gala Dinner, which produces one of the biggest limo traffic jams of the year. Sponsors of show gardens may hand out 40,000 leaflets, or host 200 guests at an evening reception, enthused by a heady atmosphere of champagne and beautiful plants. For David Hesketh, Managing Director of Laurent-Perrier, sponsorship provides 'a unique entertaining opportunity for key clients'.

Some guests are willing to donate or be thanked for volunteering if it is a charity, or to invest if it is a finance company. Creating a show garden costs from £70,000 to several hundred thousand pounds, while an urban courtyard garden is estimated at £25–£50,000, but this brings many rewards for sponsors, the nurseries, garden designers and the contractors. It can keep 50 people busy for weeks. A designer might give 30 interviews over the week, while 1,300 media workers on site provide massive press and broadcasting coverage.

Celebrities are invaluable to the mix. Where else can you see the Royal Family, statesmen, crowned heads from overseas, stars of stage, screen and page, or remnants of the old Establishment? There *is* such a thing as 'society' – and you can see it at Chelsea. The show has intercontinental impact. I have interviewed plants people preparing for the event in Caribbean nurseries, a California vineyard, Antipodean forests, Asian and African botanic gardens, and Japanese orchid propagators. Chelsea is the world in a garden.

Acclaimed designer Cleve West has welcomed Dustin Hoffman and Michael Caine to his Chelsea exhibits, and regrets being too star-struck to impart to Sir Michael his admiration for the film *Zulu.* Cleve was 'flabbergasted' by Chelsea on his first visit in the 1980s. It honed his taste and inspired him into design.

> "...since 2012 there has also been an unofficial Chelsea Fringe, involving an estimated 45,000 people and 100 events across London..."

Not only has Chelsea influenced other shows (from San Francisco Flower and Garden Show in the USA to Ellerslie International Flower Show, New Zealand), since 2012 there has also been an unofficial Chelsea Fringe, involving an estimated 45,000 people and 100 events across London, street gardening and community-focused environmental action. Founder Tim Richardson says 'it's not a counterpoint' to the flower show, which he loves, 'but celebrates what's out there'.

The Garden Museum, just across the River Thames, marks show week with designer masterclasses and debates. Christopher Woodward, its Director, who is also an art historian, says, 'Having come from the art world to the garden world I see that there is no single event that is so pivotal as the RHS Chelsea Flower Show is to gardens – it is the watershed of the gardening year.'

Exclusive and accessible, excellent but attainable, at once traditional and innovative, Chelsea is part of the magical elixir of Englishness. It distils elements of tea parties, village shows and fetes. Ranelagh Gardens was, appropriately, a famous 18th-century pleasure garden. It is a great British institution. Her Majesty the Queen has attended most years since 1947, and on a recent visit she remarked, 'it was better than ever this year'. For her as for all Londoners, it is our local flower show. To mark its 75th anniversary in 1988, she planted a *Tilia tomentosa* 'Chelsea Sentinel' (silver lime) a cutting from a cultivar discovered onsite. I hope that the lime tree and RHS Chelsea Flower Show continue to flourish over the next 100 years.

# 45 Years in Bloom

LILA DAS GUPTA, MAY 2009

I have to admit that until a couple of years ago I was woefully ignorant about the Britain in Bloom competition, supposing that it was a scheme designed to fill city centres with garish petunias hanging off reproduction lamp posts. How wrong I was.

"...there is a real sense of competition and good-natured rivalry; these communities want to win"

It wasn't until a long car journey with Jon Weatley, one of the 14 national judges of 'Bloom' (as RHS Britain in Bloom is now popularly known) that I realised what a transformative and vital scheme this is. Of course, flowers are involved but, as Jon explained, the greatest benefit of both Bloom, and its sister initiative Neighbourhood Awards, lie in their ability to change communities. This could be anything from one woman in an ugly North London tower block getting support for her early morning, secret guerrilla-style plantings, to a Scottish project – in an area of high unemployment and plagued by vandalism – where the graffiti has been cleared and areas planted up.

The origins of Britain in Bloom, and perhaps the reason why some people still erroneously associate it with city-centre hanging baskets, lie with its first promoters: the British Tourist Authority (BTA). The idea for the scheme originally came from the distinguished horticulturist, broadcaster and RHS editor Roy Hay. While on holiday in France in the early 1960s, he was impressed by the 'Fleurissement de France' festival, started in 1959 at the prompting of General de Gaulle to promote civic pride and tourism. Hay persuaded the British Travel and Holidays Association (later BTA) to organise its own competition.

Britain in Bloom was launched in 1963. 'At first, it had the reputation of being a competition for municipal bedding and was accordingly dismissed contemptuously by those parts of the gardening community that also sneered at public parks,' says RHS Historian Brent Elliott. 'As the contest gathered strength, more local councils began to encourage civic decoration in the form of hanging baskets and tubbed floral displays, once again provoking contemptuous rejection.'

Nevertheless, the contest ran successfully for 20 years, but when the BTA had its budget reduced, the scheme was rescued by funding from Barratt Homes and run by the Keep Britain Tidy Group. In 2000, as part of its move to strengthen its presence in the regions, the RHS announced that it would help organise the scheme (taking part throughout the UK), and run the annual awards ceremony.

Bloom is now divided into 18 regions, from Jersey to Scotland. The competition takes place over two years, on a rolling programme of entrants. In the first year around 1,100 regional competitors take part. Of these, 70 will be selected to take part in the UK finals the following year. Competitors are divided into different categories: from 'small village' through to coastal town or 'large city'. Many of the entrants are directed by local authorities who view Bloom as a way to help regeneration in an area, and improve their environmental commitments.

All 14 national judges work on a volunteer basis and adhere to RHS judging guidelines. The award benchmarks are gold, silver-gilt, silver and bronze. With the new marking criteria [introduced in 2009], half of the marks are awarded for horticultural achievement, 25 percent for environmental responsibility and 25 percent for community participation. The judges are, understandably, on a tight schedule so tours of locations are kept to strict timing: for example, a small village tour would take one hour, whereas a large city (population of 200,001 and more) requires four hours-worth of judging. (All entrants must submit a written presentation to support their application, as well as give a verbal presentation lasting no longer than 15 minutes.) Funding – for planting, containers and so on – typically comes from local authorities, business partnerships and local fundraising.

For smaller groups, the Neighbourhood Awards (NA) scheme is a sister programme to Bloom, created by the RHS in 2006. It is not run as a competition, but awards certificates for achievement in a smaller setting. Sometimes this will be a group of neighbours who want to improve a handful of streets, or perhaps a local environmental group seeking to 'green up and clean up' small areas or maintain a local natural habitat. Instead of being formally judged (like Bloom), the awards scheme uses an expert 'mentor' to offer guidance and advice to the community, and help them achieve their objectives. The order of the day is encouragement and support rather than simply winning or losing.

For entrants to Britain in Bloom, there is a real sense of competition and good-natured rivalry; these communities want to win. They seem to work incredibly hard in striving to not only bring their community together, but also to make their environment more planterly and more cared for, all undertaken with a greater sense of ownership. Added to this is the excitement of the awards themselves; for many, the 'Champion of

Champions' award is possibly the most coveted, whereby a town or region is invited to be considered but only if they have achieved consistently high awards in the finals.

Competitiveness aside, the long-lasting effects of Bloom ripple out in many ways, says judge Jon Weatley. 'I believe that Bloom is the best country-wide horticulture scheme in the whole world,' he says. 'It's been a revelation to me as a judge when you see communities coming together, to see what they can achieve. There's nothing else like it.' He continues: 'I met some young mums in Torbay last year. They'd tidied up a churchyard, which was full of problems, people taking drugs there and that sort of thing. They produced a beautiful space from a sad situation and it brought tremendous joy and happiness to the people all around that area.'

In another case that he judged, Jon says a woman in her mid-60s got people around her involved in an 'adopt a street' scheme so that every street in the neighbourhood was looked after. 'Just imagine if you could get that adopted throughout every city and street in the UK. Imagine the impact,' he says.

Perhaps the biggest lesson of Britain in Bloom is that it teaches people that they are not powerless to change their environment. It also proves there is strength in numbers: get together with others in your local community and there are few things you cannot achieve. In a climate of economic uncertainty, where many people fear that serious rifts in society could occur, it is schemes like Bloom that show visible evidence of social glue.

# Meriting an Award

MATTHEW WILSON, JANUARY 2010

For many gardeners, some of our most popular and successful plants – blush pink *Rosa* 'New Dawn' perhaps or yellow-leaved *Choisya ternata* Sundance ('Lich') – are reliable performers. But how many people who bought them knew that they had received the RHS Award of Garden Merit (AGM)?

The AGM, the highest RHS accolade a plant can have, was instituted to help gardeners select the best plants for their garden. By choosing a plant with the award, gardeners can be sure that it is: 'of outstanding excellence for ordinary decoration or use; available; of good constitution; not requiring highly specialist growing conditions or care; not particularly susceptible to any pest or disease; and not subject to an unreasonable degree of reversion in its vegetative or floral characteristics'.

This is not an insubstantial list of aims, and one that most gardeners would no doubt be happy to know applied to the plant they were buying. But does the AGM deliver? Is it reasonable, given the wide range of growing conditions in British gardens, to expect a system based on trialling plants often (but not exclusively) at RHS Garden Wisley, Surrey, to provide a fair assessment? The AGM has managed to remain useful for gardeners, but ideas are now being shaped to make it even more relevant. The Award of Garden Merit has its roots in the very *raison d'être* of the Society's formation: the furtherance of the science and practice of horticulture. Trials of plant material began soon after the Society was established in 1804, with the systematic trialling of plants starting in the 1860s.

> "Is it reasonable, given the wide range of growing conditions in British gardens, to expect a system based on trialling plants often (but not exclusively) at RHS Garden Wisley, Surrey, to provide a fair assessment?"

But it was the move to Wisley at the turn of the last century that re-invigorated the trials programme, which since 1970 have been held on the trials field (known to many as the Portsmouth Field) and Deers Farm (a site in Wisley village, owned by the RHS but not part of the garden). In more recent years, AGMs have been awarded by assessing National Plant Collections from around the UK, trials within The Glasshouse, and also by 'round table' discussions at committee meetings. Hundreds of cultivars may be trialled at any time, and are judged by the members of the relevant committee.

The idea of enforcing consistency in the conferring of awards – different committees tended to have their own judging criteria – eventually took root in the form of the AGM, and the first award was made for *Hamamelis mollis* in 1922. Since then, several thousand plants have been awarded AGMs. But the award is not static, and new plants are constantly being looked at – many plants have their award rescinded as a consequence of better plants being bred, a plant's constitution proving questionable over time or falling out of favour with growers.

And therein lies the rub; how can the RHS ensure that AGM plants really are the best of the up-to-date bunch, whether you garden in Glasgow or Godalming? Kim and Stephen Rogers of Dove Cottage Nursery in Halifax, West Yorkshire have little doubt about the value of the AGM. 'RHS members will actively seek out an AGM plant over others,' says Kim, 'but novice gardeners tend to know little about it.'

For Michael Marriott of David Austin Roses, Wolverhampton (which does not quote AGM plants in its catalogue), there 'needs to be more notice of the opinions of gardeners. Trials are tricky things; they are so subjective – you can turn out roses that produce plenty of flower and are disease free but are as dull as hell. Trying to get independent thought on roses is difficult.'

Rogers and Marriott both see the opportunity for the horticultural trade, and the gardening public, to have a greater say in the assessment of potential and existing AGM plants, but is this realistic? According to Nigel Colborn, Chairman of the RHS Trials Advisory Committee, it is. 'The Award of Garden Merits are reassessed every 10 years,' he says, 'but the Society's new trials strategy will enable an even broader range of plants to be assessed under many different conditions.'

Kylie McKenna, RHS Head of Horticultural Relations, has the task of overseeing the reinvigoration of the AGM, which she feels will have an 'incredibly strong future'. 'The notion that anyone buying a plant can be reassured that they are choosing a plant that will perform, has to be good,' she says. 'But to keep the AGM up to date the Society recognises that it needs to actively get the support and opinion of other interested parties.'

In order to achieve this, she is looking to enlist the support of a quartet of allies: horticultural colleges, specialist societies, the gardening media and the horticultural trade – for whom the AGM can be a useful sales tool.

There is also the need to ensure that the Society's plant trials are timely and that judging criteria are standardised. 'We need to select the right plants to trial, ones that are relevant to UK gardeners,' says Kylie. 'For example, there are some plants on the trials field that have been there for a number of years without an award, and others that are no longer in cultivation so can't even be bought.' She sees one additional ally in the furtherance of the AGM: 'there's the potential for every RHS member to become a "trials person", feeding back their experience of plants'.

In our somewhat brand-obsessed world, the AGM has a strong heritage. But more importantly it has the potential to be the first thing a gardener looks for when buying plants; this would in turn place the RHS at the forefront of supporting and advising the choices of Britain's gardeners. Engaging a wider audience to keep the AGM list up to the minute, and a genuine reflection of plants that grow well in the broadest possible locations, would help ensure that AGM plants really are the pick of the pack.

# Special Collection

SIMON AKEROYD, NOVEMBER 2010

For more than a century the RHS Seed Distribution Scheme has benefited the Society and its members – the Seed Department, which has run the scheme from RHS Garden Wisley, Surrey since 1905, started life at the Society's former garden at Chiswick in the 19th century. Today, it receives every year between 5,000 and 6,000 orders from members (who pay a £12 administration charge), each able to choose up to 20 packets from the annual seed list.

"Some of the department's work requires caution. Seed pods such as those of *Euphorbia characias* explode if picked too late..."

As well as supplying seeds within the Society, the department also contributes to the Index Seminum, a seed-exchange programme between botanical institutions around the world. It also supports the Campaign for School Gardening and Britain in Bloom. More than 250,000 packets of seeds are distributed each year, undertaken by four staff, led by Horticultural Team Leader, Liz Blackler.

Looking back at past catalogues is interesting: of the 316 seed types in the 1911 list, 48 are still collected today (there are more than 400 species and cultivars this year). 'Herbaceous perennials are certainly the most popular,' says Liz. 'We generally get fewer requests for seed of trees, shrubs and bulbs – I suppose because people feel they take longer to grow. Yet, this year cyclamen seed has been popular.'

As seed is collected at all four RHS gardens, there is great diversity. Showy blue-flowered, thistle-like *Berkheya purpurea* at RHS Garden Hyde Hall, Essex thrives in the arid, warm conditions of the Dry Garden. The moist soil, early growing season and mild winters at RHS Garden Rosemoor, Devon, are perfect conditions for many plants – seeds seem to form better there than at the other gardens. RHS Garden Harlow Carr in North Yorkshire is well known for its drifts of *Primula* Harlow Carr Hybrids, and the shady, cool, moist atmosphere allows beautiful *Meconopsis* (Himalayan poppies) to grow better than in the Southeast. Wisley, however, grows the widest range, including tender plants from The Glasshouse, such as pink banana *Musa velutina*.

Timing is key in seed collection. Gathering when seeds have ripened but just before they naturally distribute themselves is vital. *Anemone blanda* and *A. nemorosa*, among the first each year to be harvested, are also among the hardest to judge, as their seed remains green. The year begins with bulbous spring plants; in midsummer, seed harvesting goes up a gear with *Iris*, *Primula* and *Kniphofia*. Late summer and autumn is the time for berries such as *Sarcococca*, *Ilex*, *Gaultheria* and *Myrtus*. The season ends in November with the compiling of the new catalogue, then attention shifts to cleaning seed and despatching orders to members from January to April.

Some of the department's work requires caution. Seed pods such as those of *Euphorbia characias* explode if picked too late, while gloves are worn when handling toxic plants such as *Aconitum* and *Helleborus*. The bloom or dust of some *Primula* can irritate lungs, so dust masks or extractor fans are used. The team are careful not to damage displays of ornamental seedheads when harvesting. Where plants in the gardens are deadheaded, some will be grown elsewhere for seed – sweet peas in Wisley village, for example, or climbers such as *Ipomoea lobata* on the Trials Field.

Much of the work is done by hand, just as when the scheme began. After collection, seeds are put into cardboard boxes (which date from 1905) and placed in a drying room with two dehumidifiers. Cleaning and sorting seed is a laborious task, mainly using tweezers. Berries are washed to remove the flesh while tough-skinned berries such as *Cotoneaster horizontalis* are briefly passed through a liquidiser with a blunt blade. Cosmetic exfoliating gloves work well on the hard seed casings of *Alchemilla mollis* or on papery casings such as *Hosta* and *Agapanthus*. Seeds are weighed, packaged and kept in the storage room at 10°c (37.5°F); seed of plants such as *Sarcococca*, roses, *Skimmia japonica* and *Mahonia* x *media* can germinate at this temperature, so are stored in refrigerators.

The list of plants available varies. 'Changeable weather may affect availability of some seed,' Liz says. 'Cold winters may reduce the number of pollinators, lowering seed set and viability, while hot, dry summers can dry out some seed prematurely or even prevent it forming.' This year's cold winter coupled with a hot dry spell in summer has caused problems with some plants. Even so, many RHS members will still be able to select seed and grow plants they have admired on visits to the Society's gardens.

# One Man Went to Show

JEAN VERNON, SEPTEMBER 2010

Growing fruit may be the latest gardening trend, but many people still assume that plenty of space is a prerequisite for good crops. However, Doug Palmer, an amateur grower from Devon, proves this to be a misapprehension. He grows an astounding range of fruit, admittedly in several small plots, but he maximises the yield by using methods and techniques that could be easily adopted by other gardeners with less space.

"Perfect ripe fruit is picked, labelled and boxed-up for the show. Any likely to go past their best are held back in a fridge while others ripen on windowsills..."

Doug is a showman. Not only can he claim to have the largest, most extensive amateur fruit collection in the UK but he also continually produces prizewinning fruit from five plots around Yealmpton, near Plymouth. He boasts 80 cultivars of apples, 40 pears, 40 or so plums and dozens of grapes, exhibiting the best at RHS shows at Vincent Square and elsewhere, winning many prizes. But his collection extends far beyond the commonplace. From figs to pomegranates, walnuts to pineapples, cape gooseberries, lemons and even avocados and mangoes, he has tried, tested (and sometimes abandoned) almost every fruit one can think of. Anything not destined for showing is used: some sold at a local market, much becoming juice, wine, cider or vinegar.

Now retired, Doug dedicates practically all his time to improving the quality of the produce he has been growing for 15 years. He keeps meticulous records, a trait from his career in microbiology; diaries and notebooks are filled with notes, diagrams and data – what he planted when, when it flowers and fruits, and all the growing and weather data – to compare yearly yields. He often adds new cultivars, unceremoniously digging up anything that does not perform well. Besides buying from specialist nurseries, he swaps or barters grafting material from his extensive contacts.

For gardeners with small gardens, Doug's methods are inspiring. Almost all his fruit trees have been trained or manipulated in some way to produce the best yield in the smallest space. Grown on dwarfing rootstocks to keep them compact, most are trained as cordons or espaliers. His walnuts are grown in special 35 litre (18in diameter) root-restricting bags, to induce them to fruit more quickly.

Doug has other tricks to maximise production. On one plot he grows apples on diagonal cordons, two rows facing each other forming a herringbone pattern. Dozens of trees, laden with fruit, are packed into an area only a few metres square. All were trained from one-year whips. 'I recommend growing them in trained forms,' he says. 'An upright cordon or espalier has enough fruit for a family and you can get four to six cordons in the space of one untrained tree.' Growing cordons at an angle reduces their vigour and encourages fruiting, and Doug also spirals the plants around their stakes to improve yield even further.

## New lease of life

He is always experimenting, trying out a technique, applying it widely, and replicating what works. In his back garden was a large 'Bramley's Seedling' apple tree. 'I cut it down as it was blocking the view, but then it threw up water shoots,' he says. 'I grafted these with different cultivars: now there are about eight different apples growing from the same stump. I think it all fruited this year – every bough. It's a good idea for an old apple tree: you don't have to dig out the roots. Just cut it off about 30cm (1ft) from ground level and the original rootstock will produce suckers. Once they are two years old they are ideal for grafting. You need to know a bit about taking grafts but I went to demonstrations and read up. Apples and pears are pretty easy.'

Doug has taken this technique further by making his new trees work harder. 'I put an extra graft on a tree fairly early: it doubles my chances. Grafts take best on younger trees. If the original grafted cultivar is no good, I cut that out and still have a fall-back,' he says. Some trees, for example the fan-trained cherry behind his house, show the scars of previous unsuccessful attempts, but this one now bears numerous successful grafts of 'Sunburst', 'Merton Glory' and 'Bradbourne Black'. It has been fruiting for 10 years – a single tree, yielding some 27kg (60lb) of fruit a year.

Doug's allotments sport glasshouses built from double-glazing units discarded by neighbours. Old carpet lines paths to keep weeds down; makeshift water-collection systems gather precious rain from gutters. Many of Doug's most interesting experiments are cheap and simple and yet have exotic results. He has made a name for himself growing pineapples. 'I cut a fresh head off one from the supermarket,' he says. 'If you peel away some of the shrivelled brown leaves from the crown you'll find little roots in the axils of the leaves. I dry the crown off for 24 hours, and then put it into compost, sometimes on a heated propagator bed.' The plants are often overwintered on the spare-bedroom windowsill and nurtured for three years until fruit is ready to form. Doug's dedication to each project – and his deaf ear to what he refers to as 'indoor management displeasure' – knows no bounds.

As the next fruit show approaches, the pressure on domestic space, and tolerance, increases. The fridge and every available surface in house and garage are requisitioned. Perfect ripe fruit is picked, labelled and boxed-up for the show. Any likely to go past their best are held back in a fridge while others ripen on windowsills around the house, a risky practice. Occasionally, Doug's wife Veronica has mistaken a potential prizewinner for kitchen ingredients; she once used his show onions in a casserole.

'I get a buzz out of showing,' says Doug. 'At the RHS Great Autumn Show [now the Autumn Harvest Show] in Westminster there are usually about 350 plates exhibited in the fruit categories, and I show more than 100 of them. I get a lot of first prizes; I think the best I've done is about 20 firsts, but 2008, for example, was a poor year: I only got five. You can't beat the weather.' But it is not just the winning that Doug is interested in. 'There's lots of friendly rivalry, and you can learn about other cultivars you may not have heard of and see others you may want to try.'

Any gardener starting out with fruit could learn much from Doug Palmer's approach. Not only do his methods of growing demonstrate what yields and quality can be achieved in a small space, but his enthusiasm is inspiring. Even a beginner can achieve great results from just a few trees. Who knows, you may even become a new competitor to Doug Palmer at one of the RHS shows?

# BIOGRAPHIES

Biographies are followed by page references to authors' contributions. Italics indicate the mention of one author by another.

Simon Akeroyd, horticulturist and garden writer, has worked at RHS Gardens Wisley and Harlow Carr. He is now the National Trust's Garden and Countryside Manager at Polesden Lacey, Surrey. 303.

Jon Ardle is Technical Editor at *The Garden*, with a specialis interest in bonsai and orchids. 151

Stephen Barstow, an oceanographer, gardens in Norway, where he has developed an extensive collection of unusual edible plants. He is author of *Around the World in 80 Plants* (2014). 208.

William Bateson VMH (1861–1926) was the first person to use the word 'genetics' to mean the study of biological inheritance. He was also the first to popularise Gregor Mendel's theories on inheritance in Britain. He became Director of the John Innes Institute in 1910. 231–234.

Vanessa Berridge launched and edited *The English Garden* magazine before becoming a freelance writer on gardening and garden history. She has a London and a Gloucestershire garden. 249, 257.

Chris Beardshaw is a garden designer and broadcaster who has also worked in commercial horticulture and teaching. He presented the BBC series *British Gardens in Time*. 212, 227.

Matthew Biggs, plantsman and broadcaster, is the author of gardening books such as the *Complete Book of Vegetables* (2009). He is a regular panellist on BBC Radio 4's *Gardeners' Question Time*. 66, 187, *224*, 247.

Viscountess Byng of Vimy, Evelyn (1870–1949), born in London, lived in India and Canada after her marriage to Lord Byng, a WWI Field Marshal and then Governor General of Canada. *Up the Stream of Time* (1945) is her autobiography. 266, 276

Adrian Bloom VMH, nurseryman, gardener and writer, developed the garden at Foggy Bottom and introduced many popular perennials through Blooms of Bressingham nursery in Norfolk. *161*, 173.

Val Bourne is a garden writer living in Gloucestershire. She is a member of the panel that judges the perennial and dahlia trials at RHS Garden Wisley. *104*, 140.

E A Bowles VMH (1865–1954) is most remembered for the garden he created at Myddleton House, Middlesex. A writer and self-taught botanical artist, he served as RHS Vice-President for 28 years. Many plants bear his name. *11*, *104*, 105, *119*.

Rosie Boycott, former newspaper editor, is Chair of the London Food Board. A writer and broadcaster, she also owns a smallholding in Somerset. 189.

John Brookes, influential garden designer with an international practice, has a career spanning 50 years. He has served as Chairman of the Society of Garden Designers. His own garden, Denmans, is in West Sussex. Among his most famous books are *Room Outside* (1979) and *The Small Garden* (1996). *292*.

Bob Brown is the plantsman-owner of Cotswold Garden Flowers, a Worcestershire nursery specialising in unusual perennials. He writes, lectures and travels widely in search of new plants. *104*, 111.

Jane Brown writes about landscape and garden history. Her many books include studies of Lancelot Brown, Edwin Lutyens and Gertrude Jekyll, as well as the great gardens of the twentieth century. *145*, 147.

Ursula Buchan was for many years a gardening columnist, including for *The Garden*. She now writes books and lectures, particularly on garden history. 7, 19, 22, 29, 43, 53, 70, 176, 179, 220.

Philip Clayton spent two years as a student at RHS Garden Wisley before joining *The Garden*. He is the magazine's Features Editor and a member of Hortax (the horticultural taxonomy group). 125, 217.

Nigel Colborn VMH is a plantsman, writer and broadcaster. He is chair of RHS Trials Advisory Committee and a judge at flower shows, including Chelsea. *104*, 132, *291*, *302*.

Sarah Coles is a garden writer who travels widely. She has served on the committee of the Historic Roses Group of the Royal National Rose Society. 122.

Ian Currie is author and editor of *Weather Eye* magazine and Fellow of the Royal Meteorological Society, 28.

Lila Das Gupta, former journalist, is a media trainer and communications specialist who also runs a 'meetup' group called Perfume Lovers London. 298.

Helen Dillon is a gardener, plantswoman and writer living in Dublin, Ireland. Her garden has been open to the public for the last 20 years. She lectures frequently in the United States and New Zealand, as well as in Britain. *212*, *219*.

Nigel Dunnett is Reader in Urban Horticulture at the University of Sheffield. His research interests include sustainable planting design, green roofs and rain gardens. 62, 76, *81*, 95.

Geoffrey Dutton (1924–2010) was a scientist, author and poet. He created a wild garden on 3.6ha (9 acres) of marginal farmland in Perthshire, described in *Harvesting the Edge* (1994) and *Some Branch Against the Sky* (1997). 15, 17, 23, 29, 256.

Brent Elliott was appointed RHS Historian in 2007, having previously served as the Society's librarian and archivist. He is the author of many books, including *Victorian Gardens* (1986). *33*, 46, 198, *298*.

Ambra Edwards, author of *Gardening in a Changing Climate* (2011), is a gardening writer and regular contributor to magazines and national newspapers. *34*, 37.

George Forrest VMH (1873–1932), born in Falkirk, Scotland, was a plant collector who travelled in northwest China and Tibet. Hundreds of the plants he introduced, including many rhododendrons, are still in cultivation today. *265*, *270*, *272*.

Mike Grant, formerly Senior Botanist at RHS Garden Wisley, is Editor of *The Plantsman*. *232*, *239*.

Spence Gunn writes about commercial horticulture, in partnership with Claire Shaddick. In the past he edited *Horticulture Week* and later *Kew* magazine. 241.

Sarah Jane Gurr is Professor of Molecular Plant Pathology at the University of Oxford, President of the British Society for Plant Pathology and (in association with Oxford Botanic Garden) has taken part in the Chelsea Flower Show. 243.

Andrew Halstead, a Fellow of the Royal Entomological Society, was until his retirement in 2013 the RHS expert on garden pest problems. 72, *254.*

Susie Holmes is an independent soil science and growing-media consultant who specialises in peat alternatives. *81,* 91.

Richard Hutson studied meteorology during his service as a navigation officer in the Royal and Merchant navies. 19.

Gertrude Jekyll vmh (1843–1932) was a nurserywoman and prolific garden designer whose ideas on the use of colour have been highly influential. She lived at Munstead Wood, Surrey, in a house designed by Edwin Lutyens. *147, 161, 164, 169,* 172, *173, 292.*

Geoffrey Jellicoe (1900–1996) was one of England's foremost landscape architects. He designed gardens at Shute House, Dorset, and Sutton Place, Surrey. *161,* 163, *181.*

Hugh Johnson, an expert on wine and trees, gardened at Saling Hall, Essex, for 40 years. He wrote a monthly column, Tradescant's Diary, for *The Garden* from 1975 to 2008. *11, 34, 52, 82,* 83, *215, 255, 261, 290.*

Mary Keen is a garden designer, writer and lecturer who regularly contributes to *The Garden* magazine. She gardens in the stony Cotswolds, describing this as her favourite project. *129,* 177, *232, 238.*

Wesley Kerr, broadcaster and writer, has a lifelong interest in London's heritage. He is a member of the RHS Chelsea Show Gardens Panel and was appointed to the Royal Parks Board in 2013. 295.

Tony Kirkham has worked with trees all his life. He has been Head of the Arboretum at the Royal Botanic Gardens, Kew since 2001, and is a trustee of the *Tree Register. 104,* 120.

Stephen Lacey is a well-travelled garden writer, lecturer and broadcaster, with a particular interest in planting design. He has a garden in north Wales. 34, *104,* 108, *266, 284.*

Tom La Dell is a landscape architect, ecologist and environmentalist. He is trustee of Brogdale Farm in Kent, where the National Fruit Collection is held. 195.

Lucinda Lambton is a photographer, television presenter and writer whose work focuses on architectural history and British heritage. She is a past president of the Garden History Society. *33, 35.*

Roy Lancaster vmh was the first curator of the Hillier Arboretum, Hampshire. A notable plantsman, author and broadcaster, he has travelled widely to see gardens and plant habitats in different parts of the world. *11, 34, 56, 104,* 107, *146,* 149, 267.

Joy Larkcom is an influential and highly-respected writer on vegetable-growing. She lives in west Ireland. *184,* 192, 201.

Lia Leendertz is a freelance garden writer living in Bristol, with a particular interest in allotments. She contributes an opinion column to *The Garden.* 208.

Stuart Logan, an amateur gardener for two decades, works designing orchards and pruning fruit trees, and has gained the RHS Master of Horticulture. *253.*

Lynne Maxwell is a freelance garden writer and editorial consultant living in Peterborough. *81,* 89.

Kevin McCloud, design guru, is a writer and presenter of the popular Channel 4 series *Grand Designs.* In 2006 he formed Hab Housing, which undertakes sustainable housing projects. *62,* 77.

Joan Morgan, apple expert and fruit historian, is Chairman of the RHS Fruit Trials Sub-Committee and co-author of *The New Book of Apples* (2002). She runs the fruit identification service at Brogdale Collections, Kent. *185.*

Niall Moore is Head of the Non-native Species Secretariat for Great Britain, the government body responsible for fighting invasive species, based in York. 85.

Toby Musgrave is a garden historian living in Denmark. His books include *Heritage Fruits and Vegetables* (2012) and *The Plant Hunters* (1998). *82, 86, 271.*

Alice Oswald is an award-winning poet with interests in gardening, ecology and music. She lives in Devon. *Memorial* (2011) is her sixth book of poetry. *146, 158.*

Anna Pavord is gardening correspondent for the *Independent* and author of the best-selling *The Tulip* (1999). *11, 104,* 115.

Josephine Peach is an organic chemist and has spent most of her working life at the University of Oxford. She opens her Gloucestershire garden under the National Gardens Scheme. *243.*

David Pearman is a former President of the Botanical Society of the British Isles and co-editor of the *New Atlas of the British and Irish Flora* (2002). 84, *85.*

Matthew Pottage is Garden Manager for the Hardy Ornamental department at Wisley and a committee member of the British Conifer Society. *16, 25.*

Graham Rice, writer and plantsman, is the author of more than 20 books and runs the RHS's *New Plants* blog. He divides his time between Pennsylvania and Northamptonshire. *104, 130, 134.*

Tim Richardson was founding editor of *New Eden* magazine. He writes about gardens, landscape design and history. His books include *The New English Garden* (2013). He is also founder of the Chelsea Fringe. *162,* 181, *297.*

Alan Romans, lives in Scotland, and drew on his experience in the seed potato industry to write *The Potato Book* (2013). *203.*

John Sales vmh joined the National Trust in 1971 and for 25 years was Chief Gardens Advisor, in which role he pioneered the use of systematic historical surveys of parks and gardens. *82, 99, 146, 157.*

John Scrace is a freelance plant pathologist with experience of diagnosing problems both on garden plants and commercial crops. He lectures and gives advice at the main RHS flower shows. *259.*

Claire Shaddick is a freelance journalist specialising in commercial horticulture, who regularly contributes to *Horticulture Week* and *The Vegetable Farmer* magazines. *225.*

Nigel Slater describes himself as a cook who writes. He has been food columnist for

*The Observer* for 20 years. *Tender* (2011) is the story of his London vegetable patch. *183, 206.*

Lalage Snow is a photographer, journalist and film-maker who lived in Kabul for several years and has worked on projects for organisations such as Oxfam and Afghan Aid. *282.*

Nicola Stocken Tomkins is a London-based garden writer and photographer whose work has appeared in many publications. *277.*

Roy Strong, art historian, was director of the Victoria and Albert Museum from 1973 to 1987. He has written extensively on history and garden design. *Remaking a Garden – The Laskett Transformed* (2014) describes developments at his formal garden in Herefordshire. *146, 156.*

Julian Sutton runs Desirable Plants, a Devonshire nursery specalising in choice herbaceous perennials and South African *Iridaceae. 136.*

Elspeth Thompson (1961–2010) was gardening columnist for the *Sunday Telegraph* and the author of many popular books, including *The London Gardener* (2004). *126.*

Ken Thompson is a Senior Research Fellow at the University of Sheffield whose key interests include the ecology of gardens, urban ecology and biological invasions. He is author of *An Ear to the Ground* (2006) and *Where do Camels Belong?* (2014). *11, 62, 63, 65, 86.*

M A H Tincker was a scientist at the Welsh Plant Breeding Station, Aberystwyth, in the 1920s and later Keeper of the Laboratory at RHS Garden Wisley. *216.*

Jean Vernon is a garden writer living in the West Country who contributes to the *Daily Telegraph, The Garden* and the RHS website. *34, 40, 305.*

Keith Wiley was Head Gardener at The Garden House, Buckland Monachorum, from 1978 to 2003 and made his name creating innovative planting schemes inspired by natural landscapes. He now runs Wildside Nursery. *61, 73, 285.*

Matthew Wilson is Managing Director of Clifton Nurseries in West London, having previously held the post of RHS Head of Creative Development. He writes about gardening and design, and is a regular panellist on Radio 4's *Gardeners' Question Time.* 213, 300.

James Wong is an ethnobotanist with an interest in underutilised edible plant species, a TV presenter and author. He was appointed an RHS Ambassador in 2014, with a remit to champion horticultural science. *143.*

Helen Yemm is a writer, broadcaster and gardening coach. She writes a weekly column for the *Telegraph*, is author of *Gardening in Pyjamas* (2013) and has a 'pint-sized' garden in East Sussex. *82, 93, 221.*

Chris Young is Editor of *The Garden*. With a background in landscape architecture, he was Editor of the *Garden Design Journal* and Editor-in-Chief for the *RHS Encyclopedia of Garden Design* (2009). *7, 34, 49.*